The Improv 2 for Windows Handbook

Denise Martineau
Patricia Quinn
L. John Ribar

Osborne **McGraw-Hill**

Berkeley   New York   St. Louis   San Francisco
Auckland   Bogot   Hamburg   London   Madrid
Mexico City   Milan   Montreal   New Delhi   Panama City
Paris   São Paulo   Singapore   Sydney
Tokyo   Toronto

Osborne **McGraw-Hill**
2600 Tenth Street
Berkeley, California 94710
U.S.A.

For information on translations or book distributors outside of the U.S.A., please write to Osborne **McGraw-Hill** at the above address.

The Improv 2 for Windows Handbook

1234567890 DOC 99876543

ISBN 0-07-881974-1

Acquisitions Editor
William Pollock

Associate Editor
Emily Rader

Project Editor
Mark Karmendy

Technical Editor
Robert Kermish

Copy Editor
Carol Henry

Proofreader
Mick Arellano

Indexer
Richard Shrout

Computer Designer
Marcela V. Hancik

Cover Design
Compass Marketing

■ ■ ■ ■ ■ ■ ■ ■ ■

To Albert, whose difficulties with mathematics are far greater than mine, and Bill C., thanks for all those noontime chats.   -DM

To Carol Carmick, whose consummate knowledge of the English language continues to inspire me.   -PQ

To Louis, Jamie, Michael, and Leah, the four best kids I know
(an unbiased assessment, I'm sure!).   -LJR

Contents

Part I
Improv Basics

Part II
Improv in Two Dimensions

8 Using Formulas 111

Part III
Improv in Three Dimensions

Part IV
Presentations with Improv

Part V
More Improv

Part VII
Appendixes

Acknowledgments

This book was truly a group effort. Many thanks to the staff at Osborne/McGraw-Hill, the independent writers and editors who contributed very ably to its final form, and my supportive circle of friends. A special thanks to Bill Pollock, Emily Rader, and Bob Kermish for their expert guidance; Patricia Quinn, Susan Sirrine, Tom Martin, and Lynne Fitzpatrick for their writing contributions; plus Michael Goldsmith, Lisa Grinnell, and Cary Nordsworthy for their friendship.

    -DM

    Thanks also to Carol Henry and Mark Karmendy, whose inspired editing helped bring this book great strides toward its final form; and to Bill Pollock, who continues to trust my judgment and abilities.

    -LJR

Introduction

Spreadsheets have been improving since the first accountant sat down with a pencil and pad of accounting paper. Once Visicalc hit the personal computers, even greater strides have been taken. Now there are many spreadsheet applications available and everyone seems to have a favorite. But the basic functionality has not changed greatly since the early days. Until now.

WHAT IS IMPROV?

Improv is a new class of spreadsheet application. Improv uses the concepts of items, groups, and categories to create dynamic views of data unlike that available with more conventional spreadsheets. New spreadsheet models are created using drag-and-drop techniques, formulas are more English-like and are independent of specific locations, and the naming of data cells is finally understandable. In many ways, therefore, Improv is truly innovative.

WHO WILL USE IMPROV?

Improv is appropriate for both beginners and the more experienced spreadsheet user. Beginners will appreciate the "thought-based" approach, which allows you to think about your problem and its solution, rather than worrying about how rows and columns should be created. This user-friendly approach also has far fewer commands and codes to remember than conventional spreadsheets.

Experienced users will appreciate the ease of creating powerful applications and presentations in minutes, with minimal effort. It may take a little time to start "thinking Improv," but once the change has been made, the results are amazing!

IMPROV FOR USERS OF 1-2-3, EXCEL, AND QUATTRO PRO

This book strives as much as possible to ease the possible pain involved in changing gears for users of other spreadsheets. Since most people trying Improv will already be familiar with one of these other applications, there is a chapter devoted exclusively to users of these programs. In addition, the enclosed command card includes Improv command equivalents for 1-2-3, Excel, and Quattro Pro. With the help of this book, you can discover the power and ease of use that Improv provides with a minimum amount of effort.

HOW THIS BOOK IS ORGANIZED

This book is divided into six sections, each describing a different facet of Improv. The sections, as much as possible, stand alone. Therefore, you can follow each one sequentially, or skip to the section or chapters that are of most interest. The sections are:

- Part 1, "Improv Basics," covers the basics of Improv, including an overview of Improv's capabilities. Chapters in this section cover getting started with Improv and moving around the user interface. Also included is information for new users of Improv who are making the transition from another spreadsheet application.

- Part 2, "Improv in Two Dimensions," describes the basics of mastering worksheets in Improv. Chapters describe using formulas; building and editing your worksheets; working with groups, items, and categories; and saving your work.

- Part 3, "Improv in Three Dimensions," describes how to create multiple models; how to plan an Improv model; how to create multiview models; and how to use items, groups, and categories to get the most out of your models.

- Part 4, "Presentations With Improv," shows how to present your model at its best. Included in the chapters are instructions for creating charts and graphs, building Improv presentations, using data from other Windows applications, and printing your final results.

▰ Part 5, "More Improv," covers more advanced aspects of using Improv. These include importing and exporting data, customizing your copy of Improv, and recording and writing scripts to automate common and repetitive tasks.

▰ Part 6, "Instant Improv: Using the Improv Example Models," describes the sample models that are provided with Improv, but not well documented in the Improv manual. We will show you how to get them up and running instantly and how to get the most use from them. These models show real-life examples of spreadsheet use that can be customized for your own use. The models cover such tasks as managing integrated financial information, creating and printing an expense report, analyzing loans, managing a checkbook register, and handling accounts receivable.

In addition to these six sections, the appendixes contain useful information, including a complete function reference, script command reference, and a listing of Improv defaults. Two command cards provide Improv shortcuts, and a cross-reference between Improv commands and those of 1-2-3, Excel, and Quattro Pro.

WHAT SHOULD YOU DO NEXT?

It is our hope that you will *use* this book! While mastery is always a goal in learning a new skill, you need to have fun along the way. This is especially true with a product as innovative as Improv. If you can't spend time having fun with Improv, trying out the examples, moving and rearranging your own work, creating a few extra presentations, and just doing a little exploring on your own, *just to see what happens,* the learning won't be as profound (or as enjoyable).

CONVENTIONS USED IN THIS BOOK

Throughout this book, certain conventions are followed to make your journey simpler. For instance, any information you are asked to type will appear in **boldface** type. Key presses are indicated with SMALL CAPS; simultaneous keystrokes are separated by a plus (+) symbol, while sequential keystrokes are separated by a comma.

PARTONE

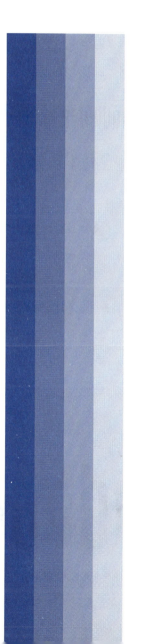

Improv Basics

Improv 2

- New Concepts Embodied in Improv

- Installing Improv

Handbook

CHAPTER 1

Introducing Improv

Improv is not just another spreadsheet program.
Ever since the introduction of Visicalc, new
spreadsheet programs have been trying to better
each other, one feature at a time.

Improv, however, is almost a new class of
application—*almost,* because it is still strongly
based on the concept of the spreadsheet. But it
adds enough of its own new concepts to be considered on its own, rather than just as an up-
grade to the current state of the market in
spreadsheet applications.

This chapter will introduce you to some of
these new concepts. It also outlines the Improv
installation process and tells you how to start Improv once you install the program.

With this knowledge, you'll be ready to try
Improv yourself, and experience what the next
generation is all about.

NEW CONCEPTS EMBODIED IN IMPROV

Improv has many features that set it apart from other spreadsheet applications. Some of the major improvements include the dynamic arrangement of data, the size and flexibility of Improv models, the naming of data, and the extensibility of the Improv program.

Dynamic Data Arrangements

Improv allows you to dynamically rearrange the way data is displayed. This can happen in *seconds,* not in minutes or hours! Each view of your data is created as easily as picking up an item and moving it to a new location. This ability to change data dynamically provides the ability to explore relationships not easily accessible (or even available) in more conventional spreadsheet programs.

In fact, the ability to quickly arrange your data, and to create multiple views of the data, will soon have you thinking in terms of multiple spreadsheets and three dimensions in no time. The two-dimensional, static spreadsheet becomes a piece of an Improv model, and your imagination becomes your only limit.

Improv allows you to easily import and export data in formats that allow simple sharing with other spreadsheet applications. This allows you to quickly move your existing spreadsheets into Improv. Once in Improv, your ability to review the data, and to create dynamic presentations and viewing capabilities, is greatly enhanced.

If your associates have not yet moved to Improv, the import and export capabilities will allow them to share data with you.

Model Size and Flexibility

Improv allows you to create truly multi-dimensional spreadsheet models. You can categorize your data with up to twelve categories active at any time. Each category can have 63,999 items (pieces of data). This means that Improv can probably handle any spreadsheet task you may have in mind.

You are also able to create up to 100 worksheets in a single Improv model, with up to sixteen different views of each worksheet. Think of the possibilities for "in-depth analysis!" Now add the capability to create presentations within each model, using Improv's 20 major chart and graph types, and the ability to import text, data, and graphics from other Windows applications. Improv is truly an innovative solution to your data gathering, analysis, and presentation needs!

Data Naming

One of the welcome changes in Improv is the naming convention. Forget cell names like B12 and GG53. Improv identifies each item (row or column) by name. These are names that you assign! As shown in Figure 1-1, this results in names like February:Insurance, rather than C3.

These names are also used in formulas, such as

Savings = Income − Expenses

rather than the more conventional

B7 = B6 − B5

This type of naming convention makes your formulas self-documenting. Naturally, as you change the names of items, Improv updates the formulas.

You can now start to use a spreadsheet with your own business terms, and not worry about archaic A1, B2 terms clouding your thought process.

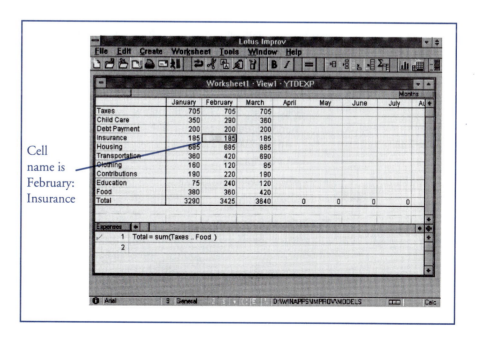

Cell name is February: Insurance

Extending Improv

With all the capabilities Improv presents, you can even add more! Three types of extensions can be used to provide additional abilities for your Improv models.

The first type of addition involves Improv's Script Recorder. This is used to record, and later replay, a sequence of steps that you perform on a regular basis in your models. The recorder allows you to perform the steps once, and then assign them to a keystroke for later recall.

The second type of extension involves the use of the LotusScript language. When you record scripts, Improv actually saves them in the LotusScript language. This language, loosely based on the BASIC language, provides a great deal of power for those of you interested in programming additional capabilities into your models. In addition, with the Lotus Dialog Editor you can create complete dialog boxes that can be accessed from your scripts. In this way, you create new windows that look like they are part of the Improv program itself.

The third type of enhancement that can be added to Improv involves programming in the C language. While not covered in this book, C language routines are used to enhance the LotusScript language, adding functions and features not available in any other way. If the script language is lacking something you need, C language programming can come to the rescue.

INSTALLING IMPROV

Before you install Improv, you need to verify that your system has the configuration necessary to run the program. You'll need the following minimum hardware, software, and memory components:

- *Hardware*: You need, at minimum, an IBM PC, PS/2, or compatible 386SX/20MHz-class computer with 4MB RAM, a VGA monitor, and a Windows-supported mouse. For optimum program performance, a 386DX/33MHz system with 6MB RAM is recommended. If you plan to print Improv documents, you'll also need a Windows-compatible printer.

- *Hard Disk Capacity*: You need at least 7MB of free hard disk space to load the minimum Improv installation. You need 12MB for the full Improv setup.

- *Operating System*: Your system must be running MS-DOS 3.31 or later, and Microsoft Windows 3.1 operating in 386 Enhanced mode. To get the best performance when you use Improv, create a permanent Windows swap file of at least 4096K, but preferably 6144K or more (see your Microsoft Windows User's Manual for more information on creating or modifying a swap file).

Performing the Installation

The Improv Install program makes it easy to copy the program's files onto your hard drive. To install Improv for Windows, follow these steps:

1. Make a backup copy of each disk supplied with your Improv for Windows software. Store the original disks in a safe place, and use your backup copy to install the program.

2. Start Windows as you normally do. Be sure to use 386 Enhanced mode.

3. Place the backup copy of the Install disk in the drive you are using to install the program. This should be the first disk in the Improv set.

4. From the Windows Program Manager, select Run from the File menu.

5. In the Command Line text box, type **A:INSTALL** and click OK. (If you're installing the program with the Install disk in a drive other than A, substitute the letter of that drive in the INSTALL command.) The Install program copies its working files to your hard disk. You then see the Welcome to Install window, which contains copyright information.

6. Click OK to continue the installation. You see the Install Program Main Menu, shown in Figure 1-2.

7. Click the icon that says Install Improv. Next, you'll see the Type of Installation window shown in Figure 1-3. Improv gives you two installation options: Install with Defaults, or Install with Options.

8. If you have at least 12MB of free space on your hard disk, choose Install with Defaults. If you have limited space on your hard disk, select Install with Options.

FIGURE 1-2

Improv Install
program main menu

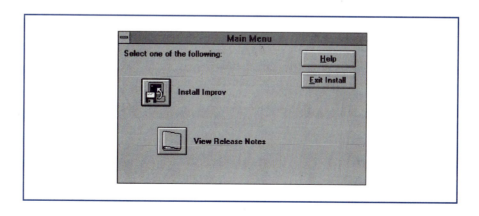

FIGURE 1-3

Options for Improv installation

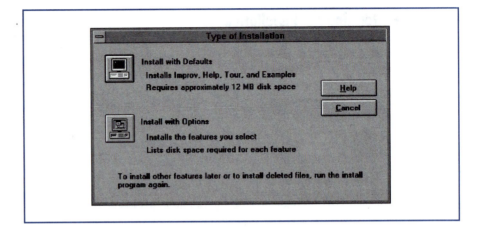

9. Finish the Install procedure using one of the following sets of instructions that correspond to the installation option you selected in Step 8.

Note

If you need assistance at any time during the installation, click the Help button that appears in most of the Install program windows.

Install with Defaults

If you chose Install with Defaults, continue your Improv installation as follows:

1. When the default installation continues, you see the Specifying the Program Directory dialog box. To use the default drive and directory (C:\IMPROV), just press ENTER or click OK. If you want to store the Improv files in a different location, type in that location in the Program Directory box and click OK to continue.

2. Next you'll see the Confirm Directory dialog box. Click Yes to confirm the directory. Then the Transferring Files dialog box appears, which will tell you the progress of the Install program as it copies all the Improv files (Improv, Improv Help, LotusScript Help, Guided Tour, Example Models, and Templates) to your hard disk.

3. When the program prompts you, insert each backup Improv disk one at a time until the Install procedure is finished.

Install with Options

If you chose Install with Options, continue your Improv installation as follows:

1. When the Install with Options installation continues, you see the Specifying Files and Directories dialog box shown in Figure 1-4. Click the check box next to each set of Improv files that you want to install. To exclude an option, leave the check box empty (to remove an X from a check box, click it).

2. When you have selected the files you want to include in your installation, click OK. You see the dialog box shown in Figure 1-5.

3. To install Improv into a Windows program group other than Lotus Applications, click the down arrow button to the right of the Group Name list box. A list of groups will open; click the group you want to use. Then, click the check box next to each Improv icon that you want to display in the Improv group. To exclude an icon, click the check box to remove the X. When your selections in this dialog box are as you want them, click OK. You will then see the Specifying the Program Directory dialog box.

4. To use the default drive and directory (C:\IMPROV), just press ENTER or click OK. If you want to store the Improv files in a different location, type in that location in the Program Directory box and click OK to continue.

5. You'll next see the Confirm Directory dialog box; click Yes to confirm the directory. Then the Transferring Files dialog box appears, which will tell you the progress of the Install program as it copies the files to your hard disk for the Improv options you selected.

FIGURE 1-4

Choosing files for an Improv Install with Options

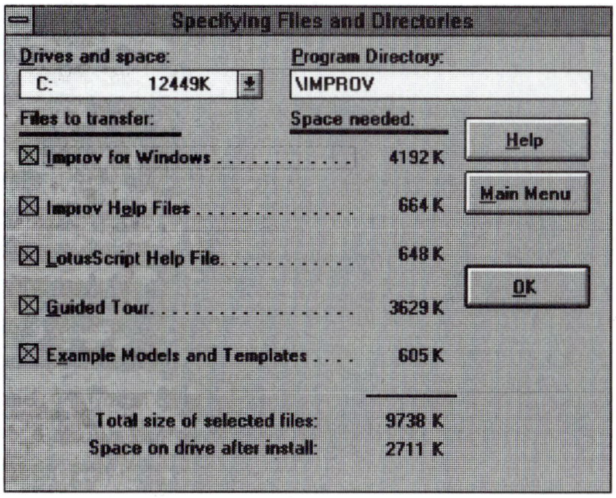

FIGURE 1-5

Improv icons for Lotus
Applications program
group

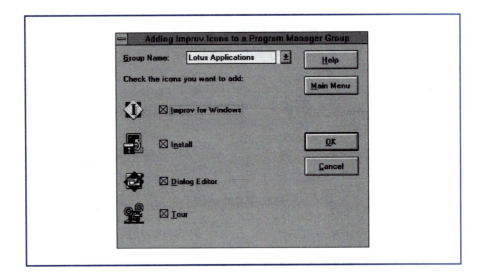

6.   When the program prompts you, insert each backup Improv disk one at a time
until the procedure is finished.

Now you're ready to start the program and use the Guided Tour presentation to
become more familiar with the program.

Starting Improv

Once the installation process is complete, you see the Lotus Applications group window
(or the program group you specified), which contains the four Improv icons, similar to
Figure 1-6. (If you chose Install with Options, the Lotus Applications group window will
contain icons for only the files you chose to install.)

To start Improv, just double-click the Improv for Windows icon that displays in
the Lotus Applications group window. The first time you start Improv, the Improv
Guided Tour, discussed in the next section, will run automatically. The Guided Tour
runs best under a VGA driver.

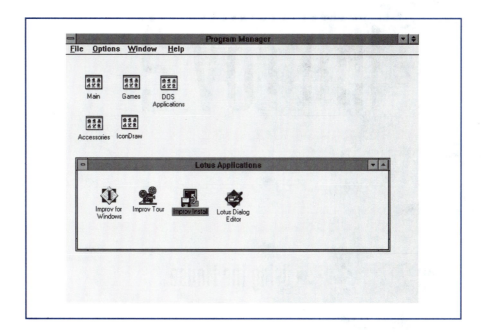

FIGURE 1-6

Lotus Applications
program group
window

Taking the Improv Guided Tour

Before you start the Guided Tour, turn off any screen saver that's running in Windows and use the Windows 3.1 VGA display driver. This ensures the best on-screen viewing of the Guided Tour, which runs automatically the first time you start the program. If you don't have the VGA driver installed, instructions for installing this driver are given in your Windows documentation.

The Guided Tour is an non-interactive animated introduction to Improv. The tour gives you the opportunity to explore basic Improv concepts and features. As stated earlier, if the Guided Tour is installed, it will run automatically the first time you start Improv. If you want to run it again after the first time, just click the Improv Tour icon in the Lotus Applications program group.

When you no longer need the Guided Tour as a reference, you can delete the \TOUR subdirectory from your \IMPROV directory to make that space available on your hard disk. Once you've completed the Guided Tour, use the material in this book to help you explore Improv on your own.

Improv 2

- Using the Mouse

- Using Shortcut Keys to Execute Commands

- Working with Improv Windows

- Traveling in 3-D

Handbook

CHAPTER 2

Moving Around in Improv

In Chapter 4, you will start exploring Improv's user interface, including how to use SmartIcons, the InfoBox, menus, and tools to help you in your work. But first, you should learn how to navigate, or move around in the Improv screens.

This chapter explains the basic look and feel of Improv, including how to use the mouse to navigate in the Improv windows, ways to arrange multiple Improv windows, and how the Browser is used to move among and manage model elements. You'll also find a list of the more common keyboard *command equivalents*—that is, key-combinations and function keys that serve as shortcuts for executing frequently used Improv operations.

USING THE MOUSE

Improv for Windows is designed to be used with a mouse, which lets you move the cursor rapidly around the Improv screen. This section explains how to use the mouse to select menu options and the various worksheet and presentation elements.

Controlling the Cursor

The mouse controls the location of the screen cursor, which takes different shapes based on the operation you are performing. For example, when you are entering a formula, the cursor is a vertical line, and shows where you will enter the text; when you are moving the cursor around a worksheet, it's shaped like an arrow. When you are sizing a row or a column, a double bar cursor is used.

Selecting with the Mouse

Before you can execute an Improv command, usually you must first select the worksheet or presentation element that the command will affect. Often the quickest way to make a selection is to use the mouse.

To select elements with a mouse, use the standard Windows techniques: Click to select; double-click to perform an action; click and drag to select a contiguous area or move an element.

Using the Mouse in Menus

You have learned that Improv is organized around its menus. Figure 2-1 shows the Worksheet menu, for instance. To open a drop-down menu, just click on the menu name in the menu bar. Or, to display a submenu (one whose name is followed with an ellipsis, as in Settings...), click the submenu name in the drop-down menu list. See "Using Improv Menus" in Chapter 4 for a complete description of each menu and its options.

To select an option on a menu, use any of the following techniques:

▪ Point to the menu option and click the mouse. Do the same for submenu options.

▪ Press the ALT key and then the letter key that is underlined in the option name.

FIGURE 2-1

The Worksheet menu

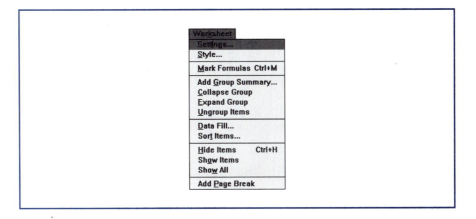

▟ If a shortcut key (a function key or key-combination) is displayed to the right of the menu option, you can press these keys on your keyboard to choose the option.

USING SHORTCUT KEYS TO EXECUTE COMMANDS

Software applications often assign *shortcut keys* (also known as *accelerators*) to commonly used commands, menu options, tasks, and procedures. A shortcut key is a single keystroke (such as ENTER), key-combination (such as CTRL+C), or function key (such as F1). When you press this shortcut key, Improv quickly executes the menu command, option, or series of steps associated with the key. This section lists the shortcut keys that have been assigned to Improv tasks.

Keystroke and Key-Combination Equivalents

Here is a list of Improv commands and procedures with shortcut keys that are on your main keypad:

Command/Option	Shortcut Key
Create Formula	= (equal sign)
Create Item Group	CTRL+G
Create Worksheet	CTRL+W
Edit Add	ENTER
Edit Copy	CTRL+C
Edit Cut	CTRL+X

Command/Option	Shortcut Key
Edit Delete	DEL
Edit Paste	CTRL+V
Edit Select All	CTRL+A
Edit Undo	CTRL+Z
File New	CTRL+N
File Open	CTRL+O
File Print	CTRL+P
File Save	CTRL+S
Worksheet Hide Items	CTRL+H
To manually check formulas	CTRL+K
Worksheet Mark Cells/ Mark Formulas	CTRL+M

Function Keys

Here is a list of Improv tasks and functions that have associated function keys. The function keys are the keys on your keyboard labeled F1 through F12.

Task/Function	Shortcut Key
Close document	CTRL+F4
Compose sequence to enter Improv character set	ALT+F1
Display next document	CTRL+F6
Display Run Script dialog box	ALT+F3
Edit current selection	F2
Execute highlighted script statements in Console	F3
Exit Improv	ALT+F4
Get Help	F1
Recalculate	F9
Switch between data pane and formula pane	F6
Zoom data or formula pane	ALT+F6

WORKING WITH IMPROV WINDOWS

Improv uses multiple windows, all within the main Improv Window, to display portions of your models. This includes your worksheets, presentations, and scripts. The following sections describe more about these windows.

Window Arrangements

Your Improv models will often contain several elements (multiple worksheet views, presentations, and so forth), each contained in its own window. Improv gives you the ability to arrange multiple windows in three ways: overlapping, cascaded, or tiled.

Overlapping Windows

Using overlapping windows allows you to have several files or file components open at the same time, all in view on the screen. This display is the default viewing method for most Windows applications and is similar to a stack of paper on your desk. The window you are currently using is in front, in full view, and the others are all partially visible behind the current window.

There are various ways to bring a different window to the front. You can click inside that window, or select the element's name from the Window menu, or select Browser from the Window menu and click on the element's icon in the Browser. (The Browser is discussed later in this chapter.)

When several overlapping windows are open and you want one to be displayed full screen, click the Control menu box in the upper-left corner of the window to display the Control menu, and click Maximize. Or click the Maximize button in the upper-right corner of the window. The other open elements will remain on the screen, hidden behind the maximized window.

Cascading Windows

The Cascade option arranges all open windows so that only the title bar and left edge of each window are displayed. Select Cascade from the Window menu. Figure 2-2 shows a model with cascaded windows.

The Cascade arrangement is useful when you want to display a large portion of one window but you still want quick access to the other open windows. To bring a different window to the front, click anywhere within that window, including on the title bar.

Tiled Windows

Tiled windows, as shown in Figure 2-3, arrange all open windows side by side, with each window taking up an equal part of the work area. This is useful when you want to view various model elements simultaneously. Although this arrangement usually displays only small portions of a window, you can use the window scroll bars to change the display within each window. You can also resize the windows so that some display more data than others.

FIGURE 2-2

Cascaded windows

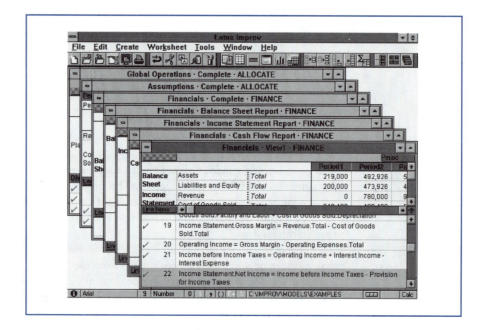

FIGURE 2-3

Tiled windows

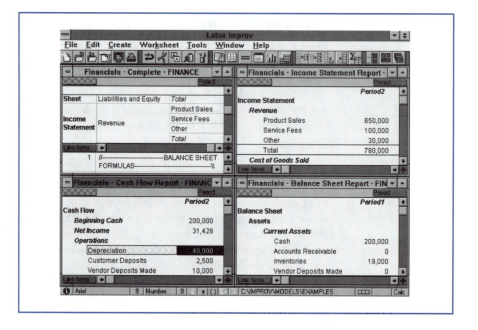

Using the Dynamic Status Bar

The *dynamic status bar*, illustrated just below, displays at the bottom of the Improv screen. You will use this bar frequently in your work with Improv; it contains several information items and buttons that help you quickly see and control common information that is used in your model. The sections of the dynamic status bar are described in the paragraphs that follow.

InfoBox

By clicking the InfoBox icon at the far-left end of the dynamic status bar, you tell Improv to display the InfoBox, which lets you add, change, or delete text, number, line, and fill attributes for worksheet views and presentations. The InfoBox icon is always present on the bar, no matter what element you select. The InfoBox is fully discussed in Chapter 4.

Font, Size, Numeric Format Indicators

To the right of the InfoBox icon are three sections that tell you what typeface (such as Helvetica), point size (such as 10), and numeric format (such as General) are assigned to the selected element in the data pane or presentation. Click on any of these indicators to see a list of other options, from which you can select. When the cursor is in the formula pane, this section of the status bar is blank.

Quick Options Buttons

The center section of the status bar contains a series of buttons that you can click to change the format of a selected item, based on the type of item.

For a numeric item (or a group of numeric items), the following buttons are available:

Button	Function
2	Specifies the number of decimal places in the number.
$	Toggles currency format on and off.
,	Toggles comma separators on and off. In reports, comma separators make larger numbers easier to read.
( )	Toggle; lets you show negative numbers in parentheses, rather than with a minus sign (or vice versa).
E+	Toggles exponential display on and off.
%	Toggles percentage display on and off.

For date/time items, only one button is available. It allows the selection of the date or time format.

For custom formatted items, only one button is available. It lets you choose the format of your number from a list.

Current Path, Selection, Date and Time

To the right of the Quick Options buttons is a section that displays several items of information. When you start Improv, it displays the drive and directory location of the currently active model. Click in the section, and the display changes to the current date and time. Click the section again to display one of the following:

- When a script is selected, the bar displays the line number where the cursor is located.

- When the Browser is selected, the bar shows the name of the element that's currently highlighted.

- When the cursor is in the formula pane, the bar shows the number of the currently selected formula. (When you enter or edit a formula, the status bar changes to the formula bar; see "The Improv Formula Bar" in Chapter 8.)

- When the cursor is in the data pane, the bar displays the name of the currently selected cell or item.

- When a presentation is active, the bar displays the name of the currently selected part of that presentation.

SmartIcon Icon

Click the SmartIcon icon (it looks like three blank buttons in a row) to remove the SmartIcon toolbar from the Improv window. Click again to redisplay the SmartIcons.

Formula Status

If a worksheet formula contains a circular reference, error, or mismatch, this section displays a status indicator. See "The Improv Formula Bar" in Chapter 8 for more information.

Calc

The button at the far right end of the status bar displays the status of worksheet values that Improv calculates from formulas. When the manual calculation setting on the InfoBox Recalc page is selected, you can click this button to recalculate worksheet values. See Chapter 8 for more information about using manual or automatic recalculation.

Using the Browser

The Browser window lists each element in the currently open model, like a table of contents. You can use the Browser to rename model elements, to open or move among the various elements in the model, or to duplicate or delete any element a model contains.

When you use the File New command to create a new model, Improv automatically creates a Browser window that contains the name of the new model's worksheet, but the Browser is not displayed on the screen. Each time you add a new worksheet view, presentation, or script to a model, Improv adds the name to the Browser.

To display a model's contents, select Browser from the Window menu. The following illustration shows the Browser for one of Improv's sample models, the Checkbook.

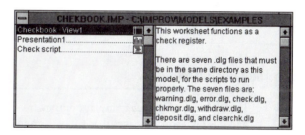

The left side of the Browser displays each element's name, followed by an icon that identifies its type. The first icon in the Browser illustrated above looks like a small blank spreadsheet; this identifies the element as a worksheet view. The second icon looks like a small graph; this is the icon for a chart or presentation. The third icon looks like rows of text; this is for a script. When an element is closed, its icon is dimmed.

When you select an element in the left side of the Browser, a note associated with the selected element appears on the right side of the window.

Note

Browsers for new models have no notes. To add a note, click the Note icon in the lower-right corner of the Browser, and type in a description or other information in the blank note pane that Improv displays. The Note icon only appears if the notes are not shown.

To remove the Browser from the screen, double-click on the Close box in the Browser's upper-left corner.

The following instructions explain how to use the Browser's features to manage the elements in a model:

Rename Elements   To rename any element in a model, double-click the element's name. You will then be able to type the new name into the Browser. Then press ENTER to make the change permanent.

Open Elements   To open any element in a model, double-click on that element's icon in the left side of the Browser.

Copy Elements   To duplicate an element, click the element's name to select it. Select Copy and then Paste from the Edit menu. Improv duplicates the element, assigns it a new name, and adds the name to the Browser. The new element is then opened in the Improv window. You may at this point wish to change the name of the element in the Browser.

Delete Elements   To delete part of a model, click the name of the element you wish to delete in the Browser, and then press the DEL key or select Delete [View/Presentation/Script] from the Edit menu.

Using the Console Window

Improv's *console window* displays output from LotusScript, Improv-specific functions, and custom error messages that you write and use the PRINT statement to display. To display the console window, select Console from the Window menu. Use of the console window for script use is covered in Chapter 17, and in Improv's on-line Script Help.

TRAVELING IN 3-D

One of Improv's important features is that a model can contain several worksheet views, scripts, and presentations. This means that all of the information related to one financial area of your business can reside in one file. There's no need to open, close, and reopen a variety of files to view or work with related data—Improv lets you quickly move among the elements of any open model.

How you select an element in a model depends on the element's status. Each element in a model has one status: Open/Active, Open/Inactive, or Closed.

Open/Active   The element that displays at the front of the Improv window is the open and active element. When you open a model, all its elements may be open, but only the one displayed at the front of the Improv window is active.

Open/Inactive   Elements that are open but not at the front of the Improv window are open but inactive. You may be able to see some or none of an open/inactive element, depending on whether the active element's window is maximized.

To activate an open/inactive element, do one of the following:

- Double-click the element's icon in the Browser.

- Select the element's name from the bottom of the Window menu.

- If the windows are cascaded, you can click the title bar of the element's window.

Closed   You close an element by double-clicking in that element's Close box in the upper-left corner of the element window, or by clicking the Close box once and selecting Close from the menu that displays. Closing one element in a model with several elements does not close the entire file. If you close all the elements in a model, the file will be closed.

To activate a closed element, double-click the element's icon in the Browser. Improv doesn't display the names of closed elements on the Window menu.

To close an Improv file without closing all the separate elements, select Close from the File menu. To close one element of an Improv file, double-click the Close box in the upper-left corner of the element window.

To close all open Improv models and exit the program, select Exit from the File menu. If models are open that are new and haven't been named, or if model elements have changed since the last time the model was saved, Improv displays a dialog box where you have the opportunity to save any changes before exiting.

Improv 2

- Thinking Improv

- Working with Improv's Dynamic Views

- Improv for 1-2-3 Users

- Improv for Excel Users

- Improv for Quattro Pro Users

Handbook

CHAPTER

3

Improv for Users of Other Spreadsheets

Improv for Windows is a powerful spreadsheet program that offers a dynamic new approach to creating and working with numerical data. If you've come to Improv from a conventional spreadsheet program, such as 1-2-3, Excel, or Quattro Pro, you'll be surprised at the ease with which you can perform routine tasks. You'll also be excited by Improv features that are unavailable in other spreadsheet programs; for instance, you can quickly rearrange data and view it from different perspectives, and analyze up to 12 separate categories of data within one worksheet.

Most of the time, you won't have to re-create spreadsheets you've already constructed in other spreadsheet applications in order to work on them in Improv. Improv lets you import data in a variety of formats, making it easy to transform 1-2-3 and Excel files into Improv worksheets. However, your "thinking habits" may need to change; Improv can be simple to use, but it requires that you take a somewhat different approach to your spreadsheet data.

The first part of this chapter will help you learn to "think Improv"—that is, how to translate conventional spreadsheet structures and operations into Improv's organization and procedures. The second part of the chapter gives Improv task and command equivalents for 1-2-3, Excel, and Quattro Pro functions, and explains how to convert spreadsheets from each program into Improv format.

In addition to reading this chapter, you'll want to make use of Improv's extensive on-line Help system, which includes special topics that help 1-2-3 and Excel users begin working with the program.

THINKING IMPROV

Improv organizes worksheet data and expresses formulas in ways that are different from other spreadsheet programs. Becoming familiar with some basic Improv concepts will make your early work with the program start out more smoothly. This section explains the fundamental differences between Improv and standard spreadsheet applications, in the areas of worksheet structure, cell references, formula syntax, and dynamic viewing capabilities. Figure 3-1 displays a sample Improv worksheet and identifies some of the important differences between it and other programs' spreadsheets.

Think Items Instead of Cells

Conventional spreadsheet programs divide the work area into a fixed grid, defined by columns with fixed letters (A, B, C, ...) and rows with fixed numbers (1, 2, 3, ...). The area where each column and row intersect defines a *cell*, and cells are identified by their location, or *cell address*. For example, a cell in Column D and Row 8 is cell D8. You may specify labels for the rows and columns, but the labels have no actual data connection to the cells they reference.

Improv worksheets begin with one row and one column, which intersect to form one cell. Each column and row is an Improv *item*, identified by an *item name*. The terms *item* and *category* refer to both rows and columns because both items and categories can change location; that is, Improv lets you rearrange rows as columns and columns as rows to gain different perspectives of your data.

As Figure 3-1 shows, Improv identifies worksheet cells by their name rather than their location. For example, Improv identifies the cell at the intersection of Period1 and Revenue as Period1:Revenue.

FIGURE 3-1

The Improv worksheet
window

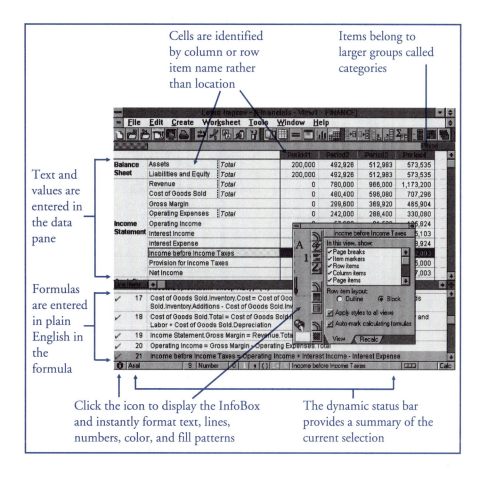

Cells are identified
by column or row
item name rather
than location

Items belong to
larger groups called
categories

Text and
values are
entered in
the data
pane

Formulas
are entered
in plain
English in
the
formula

Click the icon to display the InfoBox
and instantly format text, lines,
numbers, color, and fill patterns

The dynamic status bar
provides a summary of the
current selection

Think of Formulas in Plain English

Conventional spreadsheet programs such as 1-2-3 and Excel perform calculations based
on commands that represent row and column formulas. These formulas can also be based
on *ranges* of cells. Nevertheless, the formulas are, at the lowest level, based on the naming
scheme A1, B2, and so on.

Improv is different: it allows you to enter formulas in plain English. Improv
formulas always use item names, which greatly aids in understanding your worksheets.
In addition, the formulas are stored in a separate part of the worksheet window—the
formula pane, which is discussed in Chapter 5. The every-day formula syntax and the
helpful formula pane give you and other users a better, easier way of locating and
interpreting the calculations.

Figure 3-2 shows a simple Excel spreadsheet that tracks invoices. The formula for cell D7,

=SUM(D2:D6)

calculates the total invoice amount. You can see the Excel formula on the formula bar, but only when the cell containing the formula is selected.

Figure 3-3 shows the same spreadsheet in Improv. The Improv formula that calculates the total invoice amount is much easier to interpret:

Amount:Total=sum(Amount:Invoice1..Amount:Invoice5)

Although both the Excel formula and the Improv formula perform the same calculation, Improv's formula is expressed in plain language that you use every day, referencing actual item names instead of using codes that represent cells or cell locations. And the formula is easy to locate in Improv's formula pane, which lets you view all formulas for the current worksheet, no matter what data you select.

Select First, Then Execute

When you work with data in Improv, you first select the item with which you want to work, and then select the command you want to execute. The commands that are available

FIGURE 3-2

An Excel worksheet

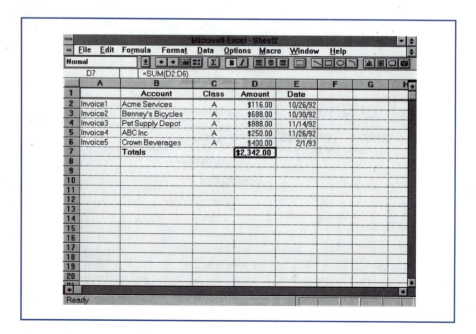

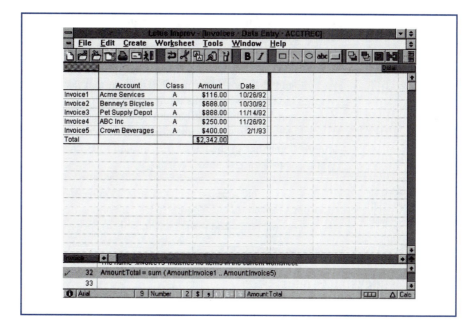

will depend on what you select. If you select a formula, for instance, the available commands are different from those available when you select an item name.

To add a new item, you first select the row above or the column to the left of where you want the new item to be positioned, then you open the Create menu and select the Add Item command. When you want to change the font used for a text item, you first select the item, and then select the font from the dynamic status bar or from the InfoBox's Style panel.

WORKING WITH IMPROV'S DYNAMIC VIEWS

Improv organizes data in a hierarchy of classifications: categories, groups, and items. Each classification is subordinate to the one above it; that is, each item can be part of a group, and all items and groups are part of one or more categories. You classify related items within a category as item groups. Improv lets you dynamically manipulate these classifications to hide and display items, to collapse and expand groups, and to rearrange categories.

Hiding Items

Improv is not the only spreadsheet application to enable the hiding of data, but this capability is an important feature for enhancing flexibility in your formulas and presentations of data. Suppose you want to share information from a worksheet with someone else, but you don't want them to see *all* of the data in the worksheet. In Improv, you can hide the data, rather than deleting it from the spreadsheet, so that it can still be used in calculations.

Figure 3-4 shows an Improv worksheet that performs loan analyses. Let's say you want to hide the Assumptions column; just click on the Assumptions item name to select the column, open the Worksheet menu, and select the Hide Items command.

Figure 3-5 shows the same worksheet with the Assumptions column hidden. Notice the small gray bar to the left of the Amount1 item name; this is the marker uses to tell you there are hidden items. To redisplay the hidden items, double-click the marker.

Note

Hiding items only affects the worksheet's current view. The worksheet's structure and data don't change. You can't hide all of the items within a category. If you try to, Improv will reset the worksheet so that all of the items are showing.

Collapsing Groups

You have learned that Improv lets you arrange related items that are in the same category into a group and create a summary for that group. The summary might be the total, average, minimum or maximum, count, or standard deviation of the values in the group.

FIGURE 3-4

Improv worksheet before hiding items

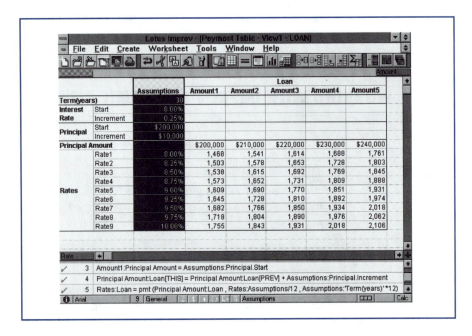

FIGURE 3-5

Improv worksheet
after hiding items

Hidden
columns
marker

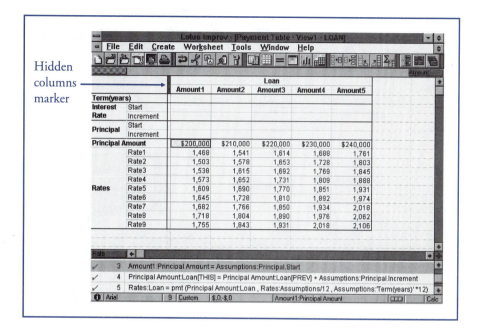

You can display each item in the group, or only the summary value. This is useful when you have a large worksheet with several item groups; you can collapse all of the groups to only display the summaries.

Figure 3-6 shows a worksheet in which the items to the right of "Other Monthly Payments" are grouped. To display just the summary total for this group, you click the group name (Other Monthly Payments) to select that group, open the Worksheet menu, and select the Collapse Group command.

Figure 3-7 shows the same worksheet with the Other Monthly Payments group collapsed. Notice the dotted line to the right of "Other Monthly Payments." This marker tells you that this group is collapsed. To redisplay items in a collapsed group, click the item group name, open the Worksheet menu, and select the Expand Group command.

The example worksheet used in Figures 3-6 and 3-7 is taken from the Loan model (LOAN.IMP) provided with Improv, which is described in Chapter 20. In our examples here, the group summary has been added.

Note

Improv won't let you collapse a group unless the items have a summary group total.

Rearranging Categories

One of the most dynamic features in Improv is the ability to rearrange categories to gain a different perspective on your data. As stated earlier, all worksheet items belong to a larger classification known as a category. When you create a new worksheet, Improv provides two default categories, and you can add up to ten more for a total of twelve.

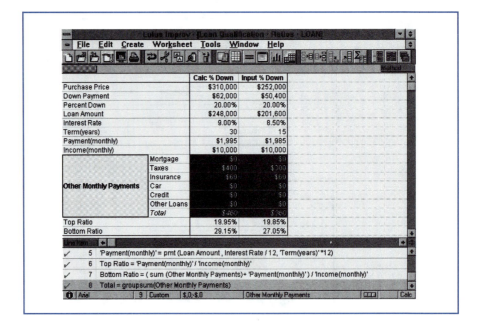

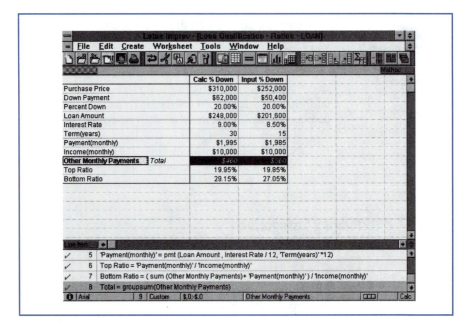

Category names are located on the category tiles located in the data pane. The category tile at the top-right represents columns; the tile at the bottom-left represents rows; and the tile at the top-left represents pages. Pages are used to view item groups one at a time, like pages in a book; each page is another element in the category.

To rearrange worksheet categories and get a different perspective of your data, click on a category tile and drag it to one of the other category tile locations. Let's look at an example of this process. Figure 3-8 shows part of an Improv worksheet that analyzes the allocation of company resources in four categories: by company division (plastics, electronics, aerospace, etc.), by item, by period, and by type (planned and actual). The row items contain the percentage allocations within each division. The column items show the actual and planned allocation for each period. Notice that because of the way the categories are arranged, the screen only displays allocations for one division. In this situation it might be useful to look at the same information from a different perspective.

In Figure 3-9, the Division category has been relocated to the column tile, and the Period category has been moved to the page tile. With this arrangement, you can see the allocations for all divisions, one period at a time. To see the next period's allocations, you can click on the Page Forward button located just to the right of the page category tile.

Figure 3-10 shows another possible arrangement of the categories. The Division category has been moved back to the row tile, the Line Item category has been moved to the column tile, and the Period category has also been moved to the column tile. This arrangement emphasizes the planned and actual allocations of each line item for each division.

FIGURE 3-8

Improv worksheet before rearranging categories

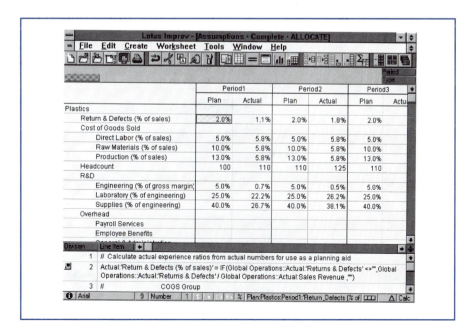

FIGURE 3-9

Improv worksheet
after first
rearrangement

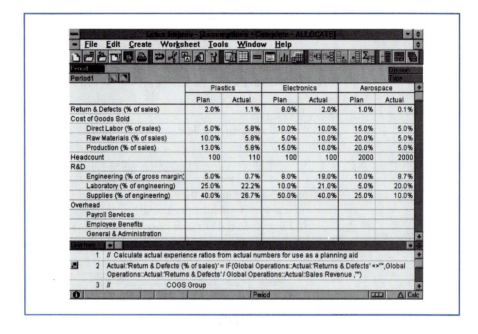

The foregoing examples illustrate how easy Improv makes it to dynamically rearrange worksheet data and add an entire new dimension to spreadsheet analysis.

FIGURE 3-10

Improv worksheet
after second
rearrangement

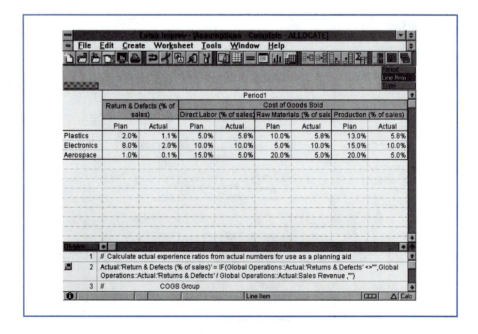

IMPROV FOR 1-2-3 USERS

Improv has made it easy for 1-2-3 users to become familiar with Lotus's dynamic new spreadsheet program. Although Improv has many capabilities not found in 1-2-3, various user interface features will be familiar to you. For example, several of Improv's SmartIcons and several options on the File, Edit, Worksheet, and Tools menus are the same or similar as those found in 1-2-3 for Windows.

Here in this section you'll find the specific information you need to make the move from 1-2-3 to Improv, including how to import spreadsheets you've already created in 1-2-3. We've provided helpful tables listing the Improv equivalents for common 1-2-3 terms, tasks, and commands.

Converting 1-2-3 Spreadsheets

Improv makes it easy to import 1-2-3 spreadsheets and convert them to the Improv format. This means you don't have to reenter your data or re-create an entire spreadsheet. Improv imports 1-2-3 data files with the following formats:

- 1-2-3 for Windows, Version 1 (.WK1 files)
- 1-2-3 for Macintosh, Version 1 (.WK1 files)
- 1-2-3 for DOS, Versions 2 and 3 (.WK1 and .WK3 files)
- 1-2-3 for Windows, Version 4 (.WK4 files)

Importing a 1-2-3 file into Improv involves three steps, which are described in the following paragraphs. See Chapter 15 for detailed instructions on preparing 1-2-3 files, running the import procedure, and customizing the new worksheet.

1. Preparing the File   Before you import a 1-2-3 file, you need to format it. This preparation helps you achieve the best results when Improv converts the file. Formatting the spreadsheet involves the following activities: showing hidden data; removing overlapping ranges; assigning range names to cell ranges that you want Improv to import as separate worksheets; rewriting formulas to reference only the cells that you want to import; and deleting macros, which Improv doesn't use (Improv introduces a Script language to replace macros; see Chapter 17).

2. Importing the File   Once you have prepared a 1-2-3 file to ensure that the data imports correctly, you open the File menu and select the Open command, and then specify a 1-2-3 file to open. Improv will automatically begin a translation, or import, procedure. When the procedure finishes, you are returned to the Improv window, where the imported data displays in one or more worksheet windows, depending on how you chose to import the data.

3. Customizing the File   When Improv imports data from 1-2-3, it only formats the column width. Also, the 1-2-3 formatting, such as special typefaces and borders, is excluded. You'll need to modify the new Improv worksheets to display data in a format that fits your needs. Rename, add, or delete items and categories; group related items; resize rows and columns; rename the worksheet; rewrite repetitive formulas; edit unequal formulas; and rewrite commented formulas. Once you customize the new worksheets, you can use Improv's dynamic display capabilities to rearrange categories and take advantage of the powerful formatting and display features.

Improv Equivalents

Remember

In Improv you select the items first, and then select the menu option.

This section contains tables that list the Improv equivalents for 1-2-3 terms or components, tasks, and commands. If Improv doesn't use a particular 1-2-3 term, task, or command, it's followed by "n/a" in the table.

Equivalent Terms

One of the fundamental differences between Improv and other spreadsheet applications lies in the terminology used by the program. For instance, 1-2-3 refers to spreadsheet row and column headings as *labels*, but Improv refers to them as *item names*. Table 3-1 lists the Improv term or component that is equivalent or similar to those commonly used in 1-2-3.

TABLE 3-1

1-2-3 Terms and Their Improv Equivalents

1-2-3	Improv
Address	n/a
Cell	Cell
Columns, rows	Items
Edit line	n/a
Formula bar	Formula pane
Format line	Dynamic status bar (similar)
Labels	Item names
Macros	Scripts (similar)
Multiple sheets	Model
Range	Range
SmartIcons	SmartIcons
Status line	Dynamic status bar (similar)
Worksheet	Worksheet or view

Equivalent Tasks

Table 3-2 lists common 1-2-3 spreadsheet tasks and gives the action you need to take in Improv to complete the same task and where to look for more information.

TABLE 3-2

1-2-3 Tasks and Their
Improv Equivalents

1-2-3	Improv
Add a new worksheet	Use the Worksheet option on the Create menu. See Chapter 6 and Chapter 10.
Delete a worksheet	Use the Browser. See Chapter 2.
Rename a worksheet	Use the Browser. See Chapter 2.
Enter a label	Use the Items option on the Create menu. See Chapter 7.
Change label appearance	Use the Style option on the Worksheet menu or click the InfoBox icon on the dynamic status bar. See Chapter 7.
Enter a number	Click the cell and type the number. See Chapter 6.
Assign numeric format	Use the Style option on the Worksheet menu or click the InfoBox icon on the dynamic status bar. See Chapter 7.
Add a formula	Type directly in formula pane. See Chapter 8.
Copy a formula	You don't need to copy formulas in Improv. See Chapter 8.
Insert row or column	Create a new item. See Chapter 7.
Change column width or row height	Click and drag the border line around the row or column. See Chapter 6.
Hide or display a column	Use Hide Items on the Worksheet menu. See Chapter 9.
Delete a row or column	Delete the item. See Chapter 7.
Transpose rows and columns	Move category tiles. See Chapter 3 and Chapter 5.
Create a named range	Add items, categories, or item groups. See Chapter 7.
Move data	Use Cut or Copy and then Paste from the Edit menu. See Chapter 7.
Sort data	Use the Sort Items option on the Worksheet menu. See Chapter 4.
Create a macro	Improv doesn't use macros, but does use scripts, which perform a similar but greatly expanded function. See Chapter 17 and Appendix B.
Create a graph	Use the Chart option on the Create menu. See Chapter 12.

Equivalent Commands

Table 3-3 lists commonly used 1-2-3 commands and the equivalent commands in Improv.

IMPROV FOR EXCEL USERS

This section provides the specific information you need to make the move from Excel to Improv, including how to translate your Excel worksheets. You'll also find tables of the Improv equivalents for common Excel terms, tasks, and commands.

TABLE 3-3		
1-2-3 Commands and Their Improv Equivalents	**1-2-3**	**Improv**
	/DATA FILL	Worksheet Data Fill
	/DATA QUERY	(Select functions)
	/DATA SORT	Worksheet Sort Items
	/FILE COMBINE	Edit Cut, Edit Paste, File Open
	/FILE IMPORT	File Open
	/FILE LIST	Window Browser
	/FILE SAVE	File Save
	/FILE XTRACT	Edit Cut, File Close
	/GRAPH	Create Chart
	/PRINT	File Print
	/QUIT	File Exit
	/RANGE LABEL	Worksheet Style
	/RANGE NAME	(Name item or category)
	/RANGE TRANSPOSE	(Rearrange categories)
	/RANGE ERASE	Edit Delete Item, Edit Delete Category
	/WORKSHEET COLUMN	(Click and drag column line)
	/WORKSHEET DELETE	Window Browser, Edit Delete View
	/WORKSHEET GLOBAL	Tools User Setup
	/WORKSHEET HIDE	Worksheet Hide Items
	/WORKSHEET INSERT	Edit Add Item, Create Worksheet
	/WORKSHEET STATUS	Tools User Setup
	/PRINT PRINTER OPTIONS SETUP	File Print Setup
	/FILE ERASE	File Close, No

Converting Excel Spreadsheets

Improv makes it easy to import worksheets created in Excel and convert them to the Improv format, which means you don't have to reenter your data. Improv imports Excel for Windows (Version 4.0) files that have the extension .XLS.

Importing an Excel file into Improv involves three steps, which are described in the following paragraphs. See Chapter 15 for detailed instructions on preparing Excel files, running the import procedure, and customizing the new worksheet.

1. Preparing the File   Before you import an Excel file, you need to format the file. This preparation helps you achieve the best results when Improv converts the file. Formatting the spreadsheet involves the following activities: showing hidden data; removing overlapping ranges; assigning range names to cell ranges that you want Improv to import as separate worksheets; rewriting formulas to reference only the cells that you want to import; and deleting macros, which Improv doesn't use (Improv uses scripts, as discussed in Chapter 17).

2. Importing the File   Once you have prepared an Excel file to ensure that the data imports correctly, open the File menu and select the Open command, and then specify the Excel file you want to import. Improv automatically starts the translation, or import, procedure. When the procedure has finished, you are returned to the Improv window, where the imported data displays in one or more worksheet windows, depending on how you chose to import the data.

3. Customizing the File   When Improv imports data from Excel, it only formats the column width. Also, Excel formatting, such as special typefaces and borders, is excluded. You'll need to modify the new worksheets to display data in a format that fits your needs. Rename, add, or delete items and categories; group related items; resize rows and columns; rename the worksheet; rewrite repetitive formulas; edit unequal formulas; and rewrite commented formulas. Once you customize the new worksheets, you can use Improv's dynamic display capabilities to rearrange the categories and take advantage of the powerful formatting and display features.

Improv Equivalents

This section contains tables that list the Improv equivalents for Excel terms or components, tasks, and commands. If Improv doesn't use a particular term, task, or command, it's followed by "n/a" in the table.

Equivalent Terms

One of the fundamental differences between Improv and other spreadsheet applications lied in the terminology used by the program. For instance, Excel refers to worksheet row and column headings as *labels*, but Improv refers to them as *item names*. Table 3-4 lists the Improv terms or components that are equivalent or similar to those commonly used in Excel.

Equivalent Tasks

Table 3-5 lists common Excel spreadsheet tasks and gives the action you need to take in Improv to complete the same task, and where to look for more information.

Equivalent Commands

Table 3-6 lists commonly used Excel commands and the commands you should use in Improv for the same action.

IMPROV FOR QUATTRO PRO USERS

This section provides the specific information you need to make the move from Quattro Pro to Improv, including how to transfer your Quattro Pro worksheets. You'll find tables of Improv equivalents for routine Quattro Pro terms, tasks, and commands.

TABLE 3-4

Excel Terms and Their Improv Equivalents

Excel	Improv
Worksheet	Worksheet or view
Multiple sheets	Model
Cell	Cell
Columns, rows	Items
Labels	Item names
Address	n/a
Range	Range
Tool Bar	SmartIcons
Formula Bar	Formula pane

TABLE 3-5

Excel Tasks and Their
Improv Equivalents

Excel	Improv
Add a new worksheet	Use the Worksheet option on the Create menu. See Chapter 6 and Chapter 10.
Add a workbook	Use the Create menu options to add worksheets, views, and presentations to the current model. See Chapter 10.
Delete a worksheet	Use the Browser. See Chapter 2.
Rename a worksheet	Use the Browser. See Chapter 2.
Enter a label	Use the Items option on the Create menu. See Chapter 7.
Change label appearance	Use the Style option on the Worksheet menu or click the InfoBox icon on the dynamic status bar. See Chapter 7.
Enter a number	Click the cell and type the number. See Chapter 6.
Assign numeric format	Use the Style option on the Worksheet menu or click the InfoBox icon on the dynamic status bar. See Chapter 7.
Add a formula	Type directly into Improv's formula pane. See Chapter 8.
Copy a formula	You don't need to copy formulas in Improv. See Chapter 8.
Insert a row or column	Create a new item. See Chapter 7.
Change column width or row height	Click and drag the border line around the row or column. See Chapter 6.
Hide or display a column	Use Hide Items on the Worksheet menu. See Chapter 9.
Delete a row or column	Delete the item. See Chapter 7.
Transpose rows and columns	Move category tiles. See Chapter 3 and Chapter 5.
Create a named range	Add items, categories, or item groups. See Chapter 7.
Move data	Use Cut/Copy and Paste from the Edit menu. See Chapter 7.
Sort data	Use the Sort Items option on the Worksheet menu. See Chapter 4.
Create a macro	Improv doesn't use macros, but does use scripts, which have a similar purpose and provide much more power. See Chapter 17 and Appendix B.
Create a graph	Use the Chart option on the Create menu. See Chapter 12.

TABLE 3-6

Excel Commands and
Their Improv
Equivalents

Excel	Improv
Data Series	Worksheet Data Fill
Data Find	(Select function)
Data Sort	Worksheet Sort Items
Edit Clear, Formulas	Edit Clear Cell
Edit Copy, Paste	Edit Copy, Paste
Edit Copy, Paste Special, Transpose	(Rearrange categories)
Edit Delete, Entire Row or Column	Edit Delete Item
File Close	File Close
File Exit	File Exit
File Open, Text	File Open
File Page Setup, Printer Setup	File Print Setup
File Print	File Print
File Save	File Save
Format Column Width	(Click and drag column line)
Format Column Width	Worksheet Hide Items
Format Font	Worksheet Style
Format Style (select style name), Define Number (select format)	Tools User Setup
Formula Define Name	(Name item or category)
Formula Select Special Edit	Select Item Names or Select Cells Only
Graph New	Create Chart
Options Add-ins, Add...	File Open...open ADDINS20.DLL open ADDINFNS.XLA

Converting Quattro Pro Spreadsheets

Improv can't read Quattro Pro files, but you can import a Quattro Pro file as ASCII text that Improv *can* read. When you import a text file, Improv reads the file as a series of records separated by carriage returns. Each record contains several text fields separated by *delimiters* (symbols such as a tab, space, or comma) that mark the beginning or end of a unit of data; for example, a tab usually marks the beginning of a string of text.

For each line in the text file, Improv creates a row in the resulting worksheet. For every text field separated by a delimiter in the longest line of the file, Improv creates a column. Improv displays the contents of each delimited text string in a separate cell.

Importing a Quattro Pro worksheet as a text file involves three steps, which are described in the following paragraphs. See Chapter 15 for detailed instructions on preparing Quattro Pro worksheets to import as ASCII text files, running the import procedure, and customizing the new worksheet.

1. Preparing the File. Before you import a text file into Improv, you must format the file to ensure that the text you import appears correctly. This preparation helps you to achieve the best result when Improv converts the file to a worksheet. Formatting a Quattro Pro file includes inserting carriage returns to separate lines of text for rows, removing comma separators from numbers that you want to appear within one cell, and placing delimiters (such as tabs, spaces, or commas) around text for cells. If the file will occupy more than 256 columns or 8,192 rows, you'll have to break it up into smaller files and import them separately.

2. Importing the File   Once you have prepared a Quattro Pro file to ensure that the data imports correctly as a text file, open the File menu and select the Open command, and then specify the file you wish to convert. Improv will run the import procedure. When the procedure has finished, you are returned to the Improv window, where the imported text displays in one or more worksheet windows, depending on how you chose to import the data.

3. Customizing the File   When you import a text file, Improv excludes formatting, such as special typefaces, that was supplied by the source program. You'll need to modify the imported text file to display the data in a format that fits your needs. Rename items and categories, rearrange data, resize rows and columns, and format numbers.

Improv Equivalents

This section contains tables that list the Improv equivalents for Quattro Pro terms or components, tasks, and command. If Improv doesn't use a particular term, task, or command, it's followed by "n/a."

Equivalent Terms

One of the fundamental differences between Improv and other spreadsheet applications lies in the terminology used by the program. For instance, Quattro Pro refers to spreadsheet row and column headings as *labels*, but Improv refers to them as *item names*. Table 3-7 lists the Improv terms or components that are equivalent or similar to those commonly used in Quattro Pro.

TABLE 3-7

Quattro Pro Terms and Their Improv Equivalents

Quattro Pro	Improv
Worksheet	Worksheet or view
Workspace, file	Model
Cell	Cell
Columns, rows	Items
Labels	Item names
Coordinates	n/a
Block	Range
SpeedBar	SmartIcons
Edit/input line	Date pane, formula pane

Equivalent Tasks

Table 3-8 lists routine Quattro Pro worksheet tasks and gives the action you need to take in Improv to complete the same procedure, and where to look for more information.

TABLE 3-8

Quattro Pro Tasks and Their Improv Equivalents

Quattro Pro	Improv
Add new worksheet	Use the Worksheet option on the Create menu. See Chapter 6 and Chapter 10.
Delete worksheet	Use the Browser. See Chapter 2.
Link worksheets	Use the Create menu options to add worksheets, views, and presentations to the current model. See Chapter 10.
Rename a worksheet	Use the Browser. See Chapter 2.
Enter a label	Use the Items option on the Create menu. See Chapter 7.
Change label appearance	Use the Style option on the Worksheet menu or click the InfoBox icon on the dynamic status bar. See Chapter 7.
Enter a number	Click the cell and type the number. See Chapter 6.
Assign numeric format	Use the Style option on the Worksheet menu or click the InfoBox icon on the dynamic status bar. See Chapter 7.
Add a formula	Type directly in formula pane. See Chapter 8.
Audit formulas	Use the formula status indicators on the dynamic status bar and the Settings option on the Worksheet menu. See Chapter 8.
Copy a formula	You don't need to copy formulas in Improv. See Chapter 8.
Insert a row or column	Create a new item. See Chapter 7.
Change column width or row height	Click and drag the border line around the row or column. See Chapter 6.
Shrink or enlarge worksheet view (zoom)	Use the Hide/Show Items options or the Collapse/Expand Groups options on Worksheet menu. See Chapter 7.
Delete a row or column	Delete the item. See Chapter 7.
Create block names	Add items, categories, or item groups. See Chapter 7.
Move a block	Use Cut/Copy and Paste from the Edit menu. See Chapter 7.
Sort data	Use the Sort Items option on the Worksheet menu. See Chapter 4.
Create a macro	Improv doesn't use macros, but does use scripts, which have a similar purpose. See Chapter 17 and Appendix B.
Create a graph	Use the Chart option on the Create menu. See Chapter 12.

TABLE 3-9

Quattro Pro
Commands and Their
Improv Equivalents

Quattro Pro	Improv
/Database|Sort	Worksheet Sort Items
/Edit|Copy Special	Edit Copy, Edit Paste
/Edit|Erase Block	Edit Clear Cell
/Edit|Fill	Worksheet Data Fill
/Edit|Insert	Edit Add Item, Create Worksheet
/Edit|Name|Create	(Name item or category)
/Edit|Name|Labels	Worksheet Style
/Edit|Transpose	(Rearrange categories)
/File|Erase	File Close
/File|Exit	File Exit
/File|Open	File Open, Window Browser
/File|Save	File Save
/Graph|Overall	Create Chart
/Options|File List	Window Browser
/Options|Formats	Tools User Setup
/Print	File Print
/Style|Block Size|Setup	(Click and drag column line)
/Style|Define Style| Create	Worksheet Style
/Style|Font	Worksheet Style
/Style|Hide Column|Hide	Worksheet Hide Items
/Tools|Extract	Edit Cut, File Close
/Tools|Library| Load (.OLL file)	File Open... open ADDINS20.DLL
/Tools|Import	File Open (identify file to import)

Equivalent Commands

Table 3-9 lists the Improv terms or components that are equivalent or similar to those commonly used in Quattro Pro.

Improv 2

- Improv User Interface

- Using Improv Menus

- Improv Tools

Handbook

CHAPTER

4

Getting Started with Improv

This chapter provides the general information
that you need to begin using Improv for
Windows. It first introduces you to Improv's
user interface: all the visual elements that make
up the Improv screen. It then discusses other
Lotus applications that come with Improv, and
some additional Improv features to help you get
the most out of using the program.

IMPROV USER INTERFACE

Figure 4-1 illustrates the Improv screen and points out the various elements that make up the program's visual interface; these are the parts of the screen that let you interact with the Improv program. Several elements are common to most Windows applications, for example, the title bar, the Minimize and Maximize buttons, and the horizontal and vertical scroll bars. This section describes each element in the Improv screen user interface.

Working with Windows

Initially, the Improv screen contains two windows: the outer window is the *Improv* (or *application*) *window*. The inner window is the *worksheet window*. Once you begin using Improv, you'll see that the inner area can display several windows at one time.

The Improv window and the worksheet window have several interface elements in common.

FIGURE 4-1

Elements of the
Improv user interface

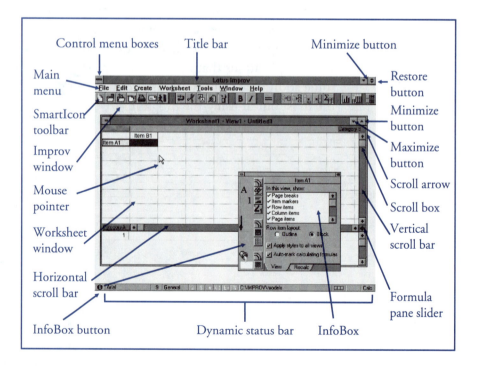

Title Bar Across the top of each window is the *title bar*, which displays the name of the window. In Figure 4-1, the outer window's name is "Lotus Improv" and the inner window's name is "Worksheet1 - View1 - Untitled1." If you saved Worksheet1 under the filename Budget, Improv would replace "Untitled1" with "Budget."

Control Menu Button At the left end of the title bar is a box with a bar; you can double-click this box to display the Control menu. Most windows with a title bar have this *Control menu button*. The options on the Control menu allow you to resize, reposition, and close the window. There are also options that let you switch to or run another application without quitting the program you're in.

Minimize, Restore, and Maximize Buttons At the right end of the title bar are two boxes with arrows. The box with an up-arrow is the Maximize button, which lets you enlarge the window to its maximum size. For the main Improv window, Maximize will let Improv fill your entire screen. For a window within Improv, Maximize allows the window to fill the entire Improv window.

The box with the down-arrow is the Minimize button, which lets you reduce the window to an icon at the bottom of the screen. Double-click the icon to redisplay a minimized window.

In any maximized window you'll see a button at the right (where the Maximize button used to be) with both an up- and a down-arrow (see Figure 4-1). This is the Restore button. Double-click the Restore button to return the window to its pre-maximized size.

Some of the elements shown in Figure 4-1 are specific to either the outer or inner Improv window.

Main Menu Bar Under the title bar of the Improv window is the *main menu bar* that displays the program's menu options.

Scroll Bars, Scroll Boxes, and the Formula Pane Slider An Improv worksheet window has two parts: the data pane on top and the formula pane on the bottom. The right side of both worksheet panes contains a *vertical scroll bar*. The window also has a *horizontal scroll bar* that separates the data and formula panes. As in other Windows applications, scroll bars let you move through a worksheet when all the information doesn't fit in one window. To scroll through a worksheet or presentation, click one of the arrows at either end of the scroll bar, or click and drag the *scroll box* along the scroll bar.

Between the vertical scroll bars for the data and formula panes is a box with two horizontal lines and two arrows (one up, one down), called the *formula pane slider*. Click and drag this box up or down to change the portion of the worksheet window occupied by the data and formula panes.

Using SmartIcons

A SmartIcon is a small picture that provides a shortcut to performing a frequently used Improv task. When you click a SmartIcon, Improv performs the associated task. Figure 4-1 shows the default set of SmartIcons that display in the *SmartIcon toolbar* when you're in a worksheet window. When you're in a presentation (for example, after you've created a chart), Improv displays a different set of SmartIcons that correspond to presentation tasks. You can customize the SmartIcon sets or create new sets of your own, by using the SmartIcons option from the Tools menu. You can also change the position on the screen where the SmartIcon is displayed. See Chapter 16 for complete instructions on customizing SmartIcons. Also, pictures and descriptions of all the Improv icons are shown on the inside front and back covers of this book.

Using the InfoBox

The Improv InfoBox is a powerful formatting tool that lets you control the style and settings of worksheet views and presentations. Figure 4-2 illustrates the InfoBox as it appears when you're in a worksheet window. The left side of the InfoBox is the Style panel, which lets you control worksheet text, line, and fill attributes. The right side of the InfoBox is the Settings panel, which lets you control the worksheet layout.

The options available on the Style or Settings panel vary depending on whether the element you've selected in the window is part of a worksheet view or a presentation.

FIGURE 4-2

Improv InfoBox
(for a worksheet)

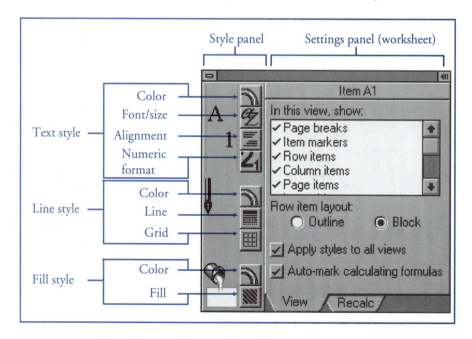

Most elements that you select will result in a multiple-page Settings panel with "tabs" at the bottom of the panel that resemble upside-down file folder tabs. To display a different page of settings, click one of the tabs. Figure 4-3 shows how the Settings panel looks when you are modifying a chart.

To bring up the InfoBox, click the InfoBox icon at the far left end of the dynamic status bar at the bottom of the Improv screen. You can select Settings from the Worksheet or Presentation menu (the Worksheet menu changes to the Presentation menu when you're in a presentation window). You can display just the InfoBox Style panel by selecting Style from the Worksheet or Presentation menu. The InfoBox remains on the screen until you click the Close box in its upper-left corner or you exit Improv.

Changing Text Styles

To change the attributes of the text in your worksheet (in the data pane) or presentation, first select the text you want to format, and then click one of the text style boxes in the Style panel. Depending on the style element you select, you can change the following:

- The color of the text display

- The font and point size of the text, and whether it will be displayed with bold, underline, or italic attributes

- Left, right, or center alignment, and whether the text is justified

- The display format for numbers—for example, the number of decimal places, whether to include comma separators or currency notation, and so on

FIGURE 4-3

Improv InfoBox (for a presentation)

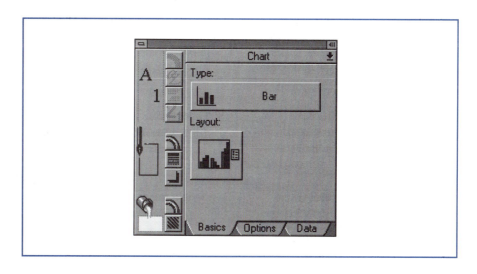

Changing Line Styles

To change the attributes of lines in a worksheet or presentation, first click the line that you want to format, and then click one of the line style boxes in the Style panel. You can change the following:

- The display color of the worksheet grid lines, or other lines in the worksheet or presentation

- The line width and style (solid, dashed, and so on)

- How and where worksheet grid lines display

- Whether presentation frames are displayed with a shadow

Changing Fill Styles

To change the fill attributes of elements in a worksheet or presentation, first select the range of worksheet cells or the presentation element that you want to fill, and then click one of the fill style boxes in the Style panel. You can then change the background color and pattern of your selection.

Changing Worksheet Settings

As Figure 4-2 shows, the first page of the worksheet settings is for the worksheet view (notice that the tab at the bottom of the Settings panel says "View"). The top of the worksheet Settings panel lists the elements that make up the worksheet, such as the row and column items. If you want an element to remain visible in the worksheet, click the element's name in the list to place a check mark in front of the name. If you want to remove an element from the worksheet display, click its name again to remove the check mark. Use the scroll bar on the right of the list box to move through the list. The default layout is to show every element listed.

Below the box of worksheet elements are two radio buttons for row item layout: Outline and Block. The Outline layout indents the row item and group names and may use less worksheet space. The Block layout (the default) places each item and group name in a separate block to the left of worksheet data cells. Click the button of the layout style you want to use.

Next in the panel are are two check box options that you can turn on or off. When you select Apply Styles to All Views, the changes that you make in the InfoBox will affect all worksheet views in the current model. When you select Auto-Mark Calculating Formulas, Improv automatically shades any cell that Improv calculates from a formula.

Finally, beneath the View page is the Recalc page. Click the Recalc tab, and you will see settings that change how Improv recalculates worksheet values. Normally, Improv automatically recalculates values whenever data is changed. However, you can change this to speed up data entry, for instance, and cause Improv to calculate values only when you click the Calc button on the dynamic status bar.

Changing Presentation Settings

Figure 4-3 shows the Settings panel for presentations; there are three pages: Basics, Options, and Data. The Basics page lets you select a chart style; the Options page lets you choose settings for the selected chart type; and the Data page lets you specify whether to plot values by row or column.

Click the title bar at the top of the presentation Settings panel to select a presentation component (such as Chart, as shown in Figure 4-3). Based on your selection, additional or different settings pages will be available, depending on the selected chart type, and so on. See Chapter 12 and Chapter 13 for more information on using the InfoBox to format charts and presentations.

USING IMPROV MENUS

You have learned that Improv is organized around its menus. Once you start the program, you see the main menu bar across the top of the screen, as shown here:

File	Edit	Create	Worksheet	Tools	Window	Help

Each option on the main menu bar represents a type of Improv activity. In this section you'll find a brief summary of each Improv main menu option and its associated commands and options. Most of the summaries also include references to additional information.

You may notice that some menu items end with the ellipses (...). This means that the item will call up a dialog box that requires your input. Also, many of the menu items have shortcut keys listed. These shortcut keys can be used to perform the menu command with which it is listed, without having to call up the menus at all! A list of these shortcut keys is shown on the Command Cards included with this book.

File Menu

The Improv File menu is shown below. As described in the paragraphs that follow, the commands on this menu let you create and work with Improv files, control page and printer settings, exit the program, and more.

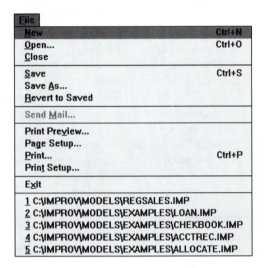

New   Select New to create a new Improv model.

Open...   Use this command to open an existing Improv model or script library file. Open also lets you import files from other Windows applications (such as 1-2-3 and Excel), into Improv, as discussed in Chapter 15.

Close   Use this command to close an Improv model that you currently have open.

Save/Save As...   The Save commands allow you to save your current work as an Improv model or library script file, under a new or existing filename. These commands also let you save your work in a non-Improv format (1-2-3, Excel, ASCII text, or Improv NeXT), which enables you to export the file into other Windows applications (discussed further in Chapter 15).

Revert to Saved   Select this command to close the model that is currently open, and reopen the last saved version of the same model.

Using Revert to Save causes all changes to the model that have been made since the last save to be lost!

Send Mail...   This command allows you to send messages and Improv files to other users through Lotus Notes or cc:Mail. This option will only be available if one of these two programs is installed on your system.

Print Preview...   Use this command to view the final look of your output on the screen before you print it.

Page Setup...   Use this command to enter or change the format options for printed pages—margins, orientation, headers and footers, and so on.

Print...   Use this command to print your Improv document (worksheet view, chart, script, or presentation).

Print Setup...   Use this command to add or change your printer's settings.

Exit   Select Exit to end the current Improv work session. If you have not saved any changes, you will be prompted to save your work before Improv exits.

Last 5 Files   At the bottom of the File menu, Improv lists the last five files that were edited. This enables you to quickly resume work where you last stopped.

Edit Menu

As described in the paragraphs that follow, the commands on the Edit menu let you undo your last action, and select, add, delete, or move various worksheet elements. See Chapter 7 for detailed instructions on using this menu's commands.

Undo   Select Undo to reverse the last action that you performed. If the Undo option is dimmed, the last action you performed cannot be reversed. Undo is followed on the menu by the type of action that will be reversed, such as Undo Clear Cell, or Undo Format.

Cut   Select the Cut command when you want to *remove* a selected element from a worksheet or presentation and place it on the Windows Clipboard, to be pasted elsewhere. The selected element will no longer be available in the file from which it was cut.

Copy   Select the Copy option when you want to *copy* a selected element from a worksheet or presentation to the Windows Clipboard, to be pasted elsewhere. In contrast to the Cut operation, with Copy the original element will still be available in the file from which it was copied.

Paste   Select the Paste command to take a worksheet or presentation element that you've cut or copied to the Windows Clipboard and paste it into your current worksheet or presentation.

Clear Cell   This command erases data from the selected cells. You can erase everything related to the selection (data, formulas, and formatting), erase only the data (leaving the format and formula), or erase only the format (leaving the contents).

Paste Special...   Paste Special has two roles. The command lets you control how worksheet elements are pasted into cells (for example, you can paste an element with or without its format). It is also used to paste text or graphics from another Windows application into an Improv presentation.

Add   Select this command to add an item, category, or formula to the currently selected worksheet. Add is followed on the menu by the type of element that will be added.

Delete   Select this command to delete the currently selected element from a worksheet or presentation. Delete is followed on the menu by the type of element that will be deleted.

Select All   To select the entire worksheet, click anywhere on the worksheet and choose the Select All command.

Select Item Names   Click, or click and drag to select a worksheet range, and then choose Select Item Names to select only the item names within that range; Improv excludes the data cells from the selection.

Select Cells Only   Click, or click and drag to select a worksheet range, and then choose Select Cells Only to select only the data cells within that range; Improv excludes the item names from the selection.

Create Menu

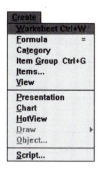

As described in the following paragraphs, the Create menu commands help you add various elements to your current model.

Worksheet   Select Worksheet to add a new blank worksheet to the current model. See Chapter 7 for more details.

Formula   Select Formula to add a new formula for the currently selected item. See Chapter 8 for more information.

Category   Select Category to add a new category to the current worksheet. See Chapter 9 for more information.

Item Group   The Item Group command allows you to create another level of worksheet detail by grouping related items in the same category. See Chapter 9 for more information.

Items...   Select Items to add a new worksheet item. See Chapter 9 for more information.

View   The View command lets you copy the currently selected worksheet to a new worksheet window, where you can rearrange the data to see it from another perspective. Views of a worksheet share the same worksheet data, but not the same display. See Chapter 11 for more information.

Presentation   Select Presentation to display a new, blank presentation window. See Chapter 13 for more information.

Chart   Select Chart to have Improv create a chart that plots the currently selected data. See Chapter 12 for more information.

HotView   The HotView command is available only when you're working in a presentation window. Select Hotview to copy selected worksheet data to a presentation. The data appears as text, not as a chart. See Chapter 13 for more information.

Draw   The Draw command is available only when you're in a presentation window. You can draw a line, rectangle, oval, or button in a presentation. See Chapter 13 for more information.

Object   The Object command is available only when you're in a presentation window. Select this command to add data or graphics from other Windows applications. See Chapter 13 for more information.

Script   Use the Script command when you want to create an Improv script. See Chapter 17 for more information.

Worksheet Menu

The commands on the Worksheet menu, described in the paragraphs that follow, let you control worksheet settings and style, and manipulate items and item groups. The Worksheet menu is replaced by the Presentation menu when you create or open a presentation window (discussed in Chapter 13), and by the Script menu when you are working in a Script window (discussed in Chapter 17).

Settings...   The Settings command brings up both panels (Style and Settings) of the InfoBox. For more information, see "Using the InfoBox" earlier in this chapter.

Style...   Select the Style command to display the InfoBox Style panel. For more information, see "Using the InfoBox" earlier in this chapter.

Mark Cells/Formulas   This command lets you quickly see the relationships between formulas and the cells they calculate. Use Mark Cells to highlight the cells that a selected formula calculates. Use Mark Formula to highlight the formula(s) used to calculate the selected cells.

Add Group Summary...   This command lets you add a group summary item, which performs a calculation for all items in the selected group. See Chapter 9 for more information.

Collapse Group   This command lets you hide individual items in the selected group. In order for you to collapse group, it must have a group summary. See Chapter 9 for more information.

Expand Group   This command lets you redisplay individual group items that you've excluded using the Collapse Group command. See Chapter 9 for more information.

Ungroup Items   Select this option to remove, or disassemble an item group. The individual items remain, but Improv no longer classifies them as a group. See Chapter 9 for more information.

Data Fill...   Select this command to display the Data Fill dialog box, which allows you to fill a selected range of cells or item names with a specified value.

Sort Items...   This command lets you organize worksheet data by cell values or by item names.

Hide Items   Select this command to hide items or item groups from the current worksheet view. A gray bar displays in the location where the items were hidden. See Chapter 9 for more information.

Show Items   Select this command to redisplay items or item groups that you've hidden using the Hide Items command. The gray bar, which had been visible in place of the hidden items, is no longer shown. See Chapter 9 for more information.

Show All   Select this command to redisplay all hidden items or item groups in the current worksheet view.

Add Page Break   This command lets you add a page break after the selected item, or clear a manually-set page break in the current worksheet view.

Presentation Menu

The commands on the Improv Presentation menu, described in the following paragraphs, let you control presentation settings and style, and manipulate presentation objects. The Presentation menu changes to the Worksheet menu when you create or select a worksheet view.

Settings...   The Settings command brings up both panels (Style and Settings) of the InfoBox. For more information, see "Using the InfoBox" earlier in this chapter.

Style...   Select the Style command to display the InfoBox Style panel. For more information, see "Using the InfoBox" earlier in this chapter.

Bring to Front   This command lets you control the order in which objects are arranged in the presentation window. Bring to Front moves the selected objects in front of other presentation objects.

Send to Back   This option lets you control the order in which objects are arranged in the presentation window. Send to Back moves the selected objects behind all of the other presentation objects.

Group Use this command to classify selected objects as a group, which you can format, resize, move, copy, or delete as one object.

Ungroup Select Ungroup when you want to separate presentation objects that you've classified as a group.

Tools Menu

As described in the following paragraphs, the Tools menu commands help you customize SmartIcons, customize your working Improv environment, and work with Improv scripts.

SmartIcons... Select this command to display the SmartIcons dialog box, which lets you create, modify, or delete SmartIcon sets, and specify the location of the SmartIcon toolbar on the Improv screen. See "Customizing SmartIcons" in Chapter 16.

User Setup... Select this command to display the User Setup dialog box. Here you can set the default font and point size for your Improv screens. You can also control the automatic creation of group summary items, how Improv displays formula overlap information, and the unit of measurement used by the program.

Run Script... Select this command to edit a script and then run it to see if the changes are correct. See Chapter 17 for more information.

Attach Script... Select this command to control where in the current model you attach the current script. See Chapter 17 for more information.

Window Menu

The commands on the Window menu, described below, let you display or hide certain Improv screen elements, and control the arrangement of multiple windows in the Improv window.

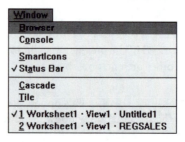

Browser   Select this command to bring up the Improv Browser window that lists each element in the currently open model, like a table of contents. See "Using the Browser" in Chapter 2.

Console   Select this command to bring up Improv's console window, which lets you display output from LotusScript and Improv-specific functions. See Chapter 17 and Improv's on-line Script Help for more information.

SmartIcons   When a check mark appears to the left of this option, the SmartIcons toolbar is displayed in the Improv window. If you click this command and remove the check mark, you remove the toolbar from the screen.

Status Bar   When a check mark displays to the left of this option, the dynamic status bar is displayed at the bottom of the Improv window. If you click this command and remove the check mark, you remove the status bar from the screen.

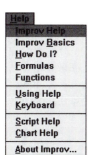

Cascade   Select Cascade to arrange all open windows (within Improv) so that their title bars and left edges are visible. When you want to bring a different window to the front, click that window's title bar.

Tile   Select Tile to arrange all open windows (within Improv) side by side, with each window occupying an equal part of the Improv work area.

List of Window Titles   At the bottom of the Window menu are listed the names of all open Improv windows. To bring a particular window to the front of the current model, double-click the window title in this list.

Help Menu

Improv's extensive on-line Help lets you quickly look up information about program features, procedures, and commands. To access the general Help system, select Help from the Improv main menu. The Help menu lists several categories of topics from which you can select, and is discussed more fully in Chapter 5.

To access context-sensitive help (that is, help on a specific procedure that you're performing or an Improv element that you've selected) press F1 when you're performing the activity or after you've selected an element.

Using the Dynamic Status Bar

As shown earlier in Figure 4-1, the dynamic status bar displays across the bottom of the Improv screen. It contains the InfoBox icon, attributes of the selected item, numeric format options, current selection/path/date and time indicators, the SmartIcons icon, the formula status indicator, and the Calc button.

The dynamic status bar displays additional or different items depending on the Improv element that you select. Style, format, and selection information appears on the bar when you select a presentation object or a data pane element. If you're entering or editing a formula, the formula bar appears, containing mathematical symbols, keywords, and the Functions button. See "Using the Dynamic Status Bar" in Chapter 2 for more information.

IMPROV TOOLS

Improv comes with several other Lotus applications that let you create graphic representations of your data, or use advanced programming features. These applications are Lotus Chart, LotusScript, and the Lotus Dialog Editor. You can access Lotus Chart and LotusScript from within the Improv application. The Lotus Dialog Editor is a separate application with its own icon in the Lotus Applications program group window. There is also a feature that enables you to communicate with other users (Mail) and a feature to help you become more familiar with the program (Model Examples and Templates).

Lotus Chart

With Improv's Lotus Chart application you can easily create and display numeric data in a graphic representation. To create a default chart in Improv, you select worksheet data and then select Chart from the Create menu. Once you create a chart, you can click the InfoBox button on the left end of the dynamic status bar (or select Style or Settings from the Presentation menu) to bring up the InfoBox, which has options for enhancing the chart.

See Chapter 12 for detailed instructions on working with charts.

LotusScript

Improv contains a powerful programming language called LotusScript. You can use LotusScript to automate simple tasks (similar to creating macros in other applications), and to access information from the custom dialog boxes created with the Lotus Dialog Editor.

See Chapter 17 or Improv's on-line Script Help for detailed instructions.

Lotus Dialog Editor

The Lotus Dialog Editor is a separate application that lets you create dialog boxes that LotusScript programs can use. Click the Dialog Editor icon in the Lotus Applications group window to use this program.

See Chapter 17 or the Dialog Editor's online Help for more information.

Mail

The Send Mail option on the Improv File menu lets you use an electronic mail (e-mail) system to type a message and send it to another user. This option is only available if you have cc:Mail for Windows (Release 1.1 or later) or Lotus Notes (Release 2.1 or later) installed on your system.

When the Send Mail option is available, you can type a message, attach an Improv model if you want, and then send the message to another user. For example, you might send preliminary financial statements along with a short message to the company's Controller for review.

If you have the above-referenced e-mail or work group communications software installed, follow these steps to use Improv Mail:

1. If you want to attach an Improv model to your message, open the model.

2. Select Send Mail from the File menu. You see the Send Mail dialog box.

3. If you are attaching a model to your message, click the Save and Attach check box to enable this option, and then click OK. If you don't want to attach a model, leave Save and Attach unchecked and just click OK.

4. If cc:Mail or Lotus Notes is password-protected, enter your password in the dialog box that appears, and click OK.

5. When the cc:Mail or Lotus Notes dialog box appears, type the recipient's name, the subject, and your message.

6. Click Send to send the mail.

> **Note**
> See your cc:Mail or Lotus Notes documentation for more detailed instructions on using electronic mail.

Improv's Example Models

Example models are special models, included with your copy of Improv, that illustrate the real-life use of worksheets. Each model illustrates specific Improv features. For instance, two of the example models are a check register model and a loan analysis model.

If you chose the default Improv installation, the example models were placed in the directory C:\IMPROV\MODELS\EXAMPLES. If you chose to install Improv with custom options, the example files will be in this directory only if you chose to transfer the files for Example Models and Templates. If Improv's example files aren't in the \EXAMPLES directory, you can use the Install program to install them.

You may want to explore these examples to better understand their design; in the process, you will also learn more about the various features of Improv. If the sample models are similar to models that you might need, you can adapt them to meet your own business and personal situations. See Chapters 18 through 22 for detailed information on using Improv's example models.

Improv Templates

A template is a special type of Improv model that you can use as a pattern for other similar models. If you chose the default Improv installation, several templates were placed in the directory C:\IMPROV\MODELS\TEMPLATE. If you chose to install Improv with custom options, the template files will exist in that directory only if you chose to transfer the files for Example Models and Templates. If Improv's template files aren't in the \TEMPLATE directory, you can use the Instal program to install them.

See "Using Templates" in Chapter 16 for complete instructions on working with Improv templates.

Improv 2

- Thinking Improv

- Working with Improv's Dynamic Views

- Using Improv's On-line Help

Handbook

CHAPTER 5

Improv for New Users

Improv for Windows is a powerful spreadsheet program that offers a dynamic new approach to creating and working with financial data. If you've never used an electronic spreadsheet program before, you'll be surprised at the ease with which you can perform routine tasks, because Improv's intuitive user interface makes it easy to learn and use the program. You'll also be excited by Improv features that are unavailable in other spreadsheet programs, including the ability to quickly rearrange data and view it from different perspectives, and the ability to analyze up to 12 separate categories of data within one worksheet.

The first part of this chapter helps you to "think Improv;" it will teach you the important Improv terminology you need, and translate the Improv worksheet structure, operations, and procedures for you. The second part of the chapter describes Improv's dynamic viewing capabilities that let you rearrange your data to see it from different perspectives—without having to create new worksheets. Finally, you'll find a thorough description of Improv's extensive on-line Help system, with detailed directions on how to find exactly the information you need.

In addition to reading this chapter, you'll want to start using Improv's extensive on-line Help right away. Lotus 1-2-3 and Excel users will find special topics to help them begin working with the Improv program.

THINKING IMPROV

Improv organizes worksheet data and expresses formulas differently from other spreadsheet programs. This section explains some basic Improv concepts to help you become familiar with the program: Improv terminology, worksheet structure, cell references, and formula syntax.

Improv Terminology

Before you learn about Improv basic concepts, it may be helpful to familiarize yourself with some of the terms Improv uses. The definitions that follow also tell you where to look in the Improv manual for more information. Figure 5-1 illustrates an Improv screen, with references to many of the terms defined in this section.

Browser   The *Browser* is a window that overlays the Improv screen and lists each element in an Improv model, similar to a table of contents. You can use it to rename elements, to open or move between different elements in the model, and to add, copy, and delete any element a model contains. You can also add notes about each element listed in the Browser. You'll find complete information on using the Browser window in Chapter 2.

Category   A *category* is the largest classification of information in an Improv worksheet. Each item in the worksheet is part of a larger category classification. Categories handle general levels of information such as years, periods, departments, and so on. Category names appear on *category tiles*, located in the data pane (explained later in this section). The category tile at the top-right of the data pane represents columns; the tile at the bottom-left represents rows; and the tile at the top-left represents the page area. Pages are used to view item groups one at a time, like pages in a book; each page is another element in the category.

Improv lets you rearrange the category tiles to view data from a different perspective, as explained in "Rearranging Categories" later in this chapter. For more about categories, see Chapter 9.

FIGURE 5-1

The Improv worksheet
window

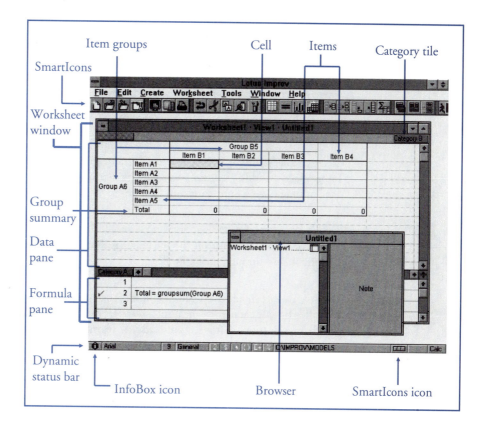

Cell   Each row and column of the worksheet intersect to form one *cell.* Cells contain text or numeric values. Numeric values may be entered by you or calculated by Improv from a corresponding formula in the formula pane (explained later in this section). You can read more about cells in Chapter 6.

Chart   A *chart* is a graphical representation of numeric data. See Chapter 12 for complete information about building and using charts.

Data Pane   The *data pane* is the top portion of the worksheet; this is where you build a structure to hold your worksheet text and values. Each individual piece of data is stored and displayed in a cell. See Chapter 6 for details.

Dynamic Status Bar   The *dynamic status bar* appears across the bottom of the Improv screen. It contains the InfoBox icon, the selected item's attributes and numeric format, quick option buttons, indicators of the current selection/path/date and time, the SmartIcons icon, the formula status indicator, and the Calc button. The status bar will update based on the Improv element that's selected—the data pane, the formula pane, a script, or a presentation (explained later in this section). For complete information, see "Using the Dynamic Status Bar" in Chapter 2, and "Improv User Interface" in Chapter 4.

Formula Pane   The bottom portion of the worksheet is the *formula pane*. This is where you enter the formulas from which Improv calculates values that appear in the data pane. Improv formulas are written in plain English, which makes them easy to interpret. See Chapter 6 and Chapter 8.

Group Summary   When you create item groups (defined later in this section), Improv lets you add a *group summary*, which calculates a subtotal for all items in the group. See "Adding Group Summaries" in Chapter 9.

InfoBox   The *InfoBox* is an important and flexible tool that lets you control the styles and settings for the items on the screen. It is discussed in "Improv User Interface" in Chapter 4, and throughout Part 6.

Item   *Items* provide the details within each category. Each column and row is an item, identified by an item name. The term *item* refers to both rows and columns because items can change location; that is, Improv lets you rearrange rows as columns and columns as rows to display data from a different perspective. See Chapter 9 for details.

Item Group   If you want your worksheet to have more than one level of detail, Improv lets you create *item groups* for related items that are in the same category. See Chapter 9.

Model   An Improv *model* is a set of related worksheets, graphic representations of worksheet data, and scripts; scripts are explained later in this section. All these elements of the model are saved in one file with an .IMP extension. See Chapter 10 for details on working with models.

Presentation   A *presentation* is part of an Improv document that can incorporate both graphics and text from Improv worksheets. Presentations can also use information from other applications. See Chapter 13.

Script   A *script* is a series of instructions that automates a procedure; it is similar to a *macro* in other applications. You create scripts using the LotusScript programming language in Improv to record or enter a series of commands. See Chapter 17 for details on creating scripts.

Settings   In the right-hand side of the InfoBox, you control worksheet and presentation *settings*; these are worksheet components, calculation options, chart types, chart components, and so forth. The settings that are available in the InfoBox depend on whether the selected element is part of a worksheet or presentation. You'll find details in "Improv User Interface" in Chapter 4.

SmartIcon Improv's *SmartIcons* are small pictures that provide a shortcut to performing a frequently used Improv task. Improv displays a particular set of SmartIcons on the *SmartIcon toolbar*, which appears by default across the top of the Improv window (you can reposition it). When you click a SmartIcon with the mouse, Improv performs the associated task. The inside front and back cover of this book contain pictures and descriptions of all Improv SmartIcons. You'll learn more about these icons in "Improv User Interface" in Chapter 4, and "Customizing Improv's SmartIcons" in Chapter 16.

Style The *Style panel* makes up the left side of the Improv InfoBox. From here, you can add, change, or delete the text, line, or fill attributes for a worksheet or presentation. See "Improv User Interface" in Chapter 4.

Template A *template* is a special type of Improv model that you can use as a pattern for other similar models. Templates don't contain any specific values, but they do contain some or all of the following to help you create a worksheet: items, item groups, categories, and formulas. See "Using Templates" in Chapter 16.

Worksheet The *worksheet* is the fundamental structure of items, item groups, categories, and formulas that define a collection of data (text, values, calculations). You'll see worksheets extensively throughout this book, and learn how to create them in Chapter 6 and Chapter 7.

Views When you create a worksheet, you create one *view*, or representation of the data. Improv lets you create more than one view of a worksheet; the views share the same data but display it differently. This feature allows you to see the same data represented differently without having to create a new worksheet. See Chapter 11.

Improv Worksheets

Improv worksheet windows appear in the Improv main window and have two parts: the data pane and the formula pane. This section briefly describes both panes of the worksheet and explains how you execute worksheet commands. You'll learn more as you work through this book.

Data Pane

When you create a new Improv worksheet, it begins with one default row and one column, which intersect to form one cell. Each column and row are Improv items, identified by item names. The term *item* refers to both rows and columns because items can change location; that is, Improv lets you rearrange rows as columns and columns as rows to display data from a different perspective.

Each cell in the data pane is used to hold data. This can be numeric values, text, or answers to formula calculations.

Formula Pane

Improv lets you enter formulas in plain English and store them in the bottom part of the worksheet in the formula pane. This special location for the formulas allows you and other users to easily reference and interpret the worksheet's calculations. You can view all formulas for the current worksheet, no matter what data you select.

Notice the formula pane in Figure 5-2, which shows a simple Improv worksheet that functions as a check register. The Improv formula for the worksheet's beginning Balance is Formula 1:

Balance:Information=Deposit:Information

FIGURE 5-2

Improve Check
Register worksheet

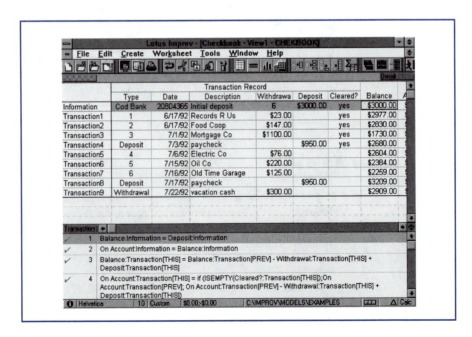

This formula translates as follows: "The cell at the intersection of Balance and Information equals the value in the cell at the intersection of Deposit and Information." Improv expresses formulas in plain language, similar to what you use every day, and references actual item names instead of using codes that represent cells or cell locations.

Executing Worksheet Commands

When you work in an Improv worksheet, you first select the item with which you want to work, and then select the menu command you want to execute. Different commands may display depending on what item you select. For example, if you select a formula, the commands available are different from the ones that are available when you select an item name. When you add a new item, you select the row or column that is positioned above or to the left of where you want the new item to be, and then select the Item command option from the Create menu. To change the font used for a text item, you select the item and then choose the font from the dynamic status bar or from the InfoBox's Style panel. This is described in more detail in Chapters 4 and 6.

WORKING WITH IMPROV'S DYNAMIC VIEWS

Improv organizes data in a hierarchy of classifications: items, item groups, and categories. Each classification is subordinate to the one above it. Each item is part of a larger category, and you classify related items within a category as item groups. Improv lets you dynamically manipulate these classifications to hide and display items, to collapse and expand groups, and to rearrange categories. These manipulations each create a different view of your information, even though the information does not change.

Hiding Items

Figure 5-3 shows an Improv worksheet that tracks a company's assets, liabilities, and equity for several time periods.

Let's say that you want to present the company's data at a fourth-quarter management meeting, and you don't want to include the data for the first, second, and third periods tracked in the worksheet. Improv lets you hide the data for these first three periods before you display or print your worksheet. Click the mouse on the Period1 item name, and then drag the cursor to the right until your highlighted selection includes the columns for Periods 1, 2, and 3. Then display the Worksheet menu and select the Hide Items command. Figure 5-4 shows the same worksheet with the three hidden columns.

Notice the small gray bar to the left of the Period1 item name. This is a marker that Improv uses to let you know there are hidden items. To redisplay hidden items,

FIGURE 5-3

Improv Balance Sheet
worksheet

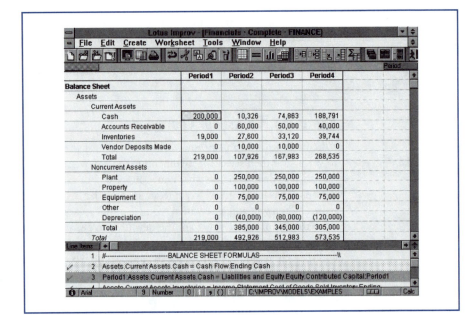

double-click the marker. When you hide items, you only affect the worksheet's current view. The worksheet's fundamental structure and data don't change.

FIGURE 5-4

Improv Balance Sheet
worksheet with
hidden items

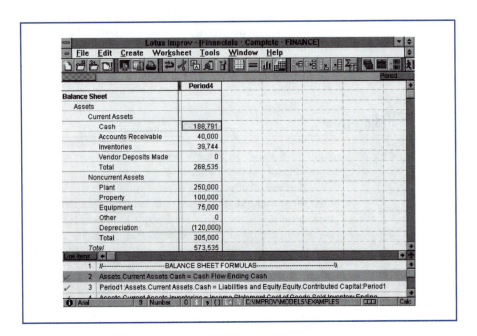

Collapsing Groups

Note

Improv won't let you
collapse a group
unless the group
has a summary
group total.

You have learned that Improv lets you organize related items that are in the same category into an item group and create a summary total for that group. You can display each item in the group or only the summary total. This is useful when you have a large worksheet with several item groups. If the data doesn't all fit in the window, you can collapse all of the groups to display just the summary totals.

Figure 5-5 shows a worksheet on which the items to the right of "Other Monthly Payments" (Mortgage, Taxes, Insurance, and so on) are grouped. To display only the summary total for this group, you click the group name to select that group. Then you open the Worksheet menu and select the Collapse Group command. Figure 5-6 shows the same worksheet after the Other Monthly Payments group has been collapsed.

Notice the dotted line (in Figure 5-6) that appears to the right of "Other Monthly." This is the marker Improv uses to tell you that this group is collapsed. To redisplay the items in a collapsed group, click the item group name, open the Worksheet menu, and select the Expand Group command; or double-click the marker.

Rearranging Categories

One of the most dynamic features that Improv provides is the ability to rearrange categories to gain a different perspective on your data. As stated earlier, all items belong

FIGURE 5-5

A worksheet with
grouped items

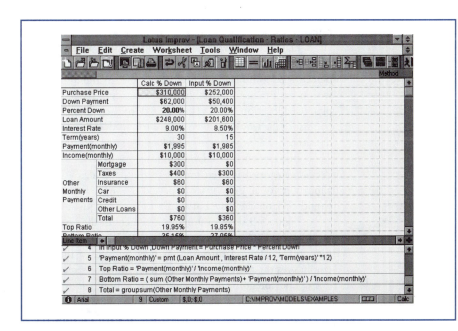

FIGURE 5-6

A worksheet with
collapsed group

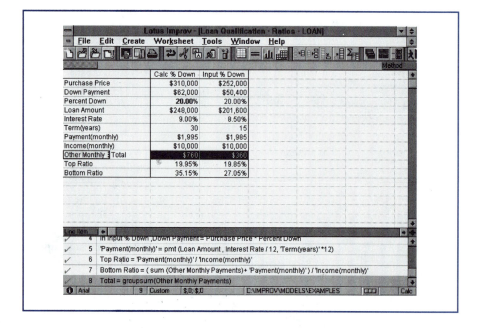

to a larger classification known as a category. When you create a new worksheet, Improv provides you with two default categories, and you can add up to ten more for a total of twelve. Category names are located on the category tiles located in the data pane. The category tile at the top-right represents columns; the tile at the bottom-left represents rows; and the tile at the top-left represents the page area. To rearrange worksheet categories, just click on a category tile and drag it to one of the other category tile locations.

Figure 5-7 shows a portion of an Improv worksheet that analyzes the allocation of company resources by company division, by item, by period, and by planned and actual percentage amounts. The row items contain the allocations (the Line Item category) within each division (the Division category). The column items show the actual and planned allocation (the Type category) for each period (the Period category). Notice that because of the way the categories are arranged, the screen only displays allocations for one division. It might be useful to look at the same information from a different perspective.

In Figure 5-8, the Division category has been moved to the column tile, and the Period category has been moved to the page tile. With this arrangement, you see the allocations for all divisions, one period at a time. To see the next period's allocations, you would click on the Page Forward button that is just to the right of the page tile.

Figure 5-9 shows a third arrangement of the categories. The Division category has been moved back to the row tile, the Line Item category has been moved to the column tile, and the Period category has been moved to the column tile. This arrangement emphasizes the planned and actual allocation for each line item for each division.

The foregoing examples illustrate how easy Improv makes it to dynamically rearrange worksheet data and add an entire new dimension to spreadsheet analysis.

FIGURE 5-7

Allocation Worksheet with four categories

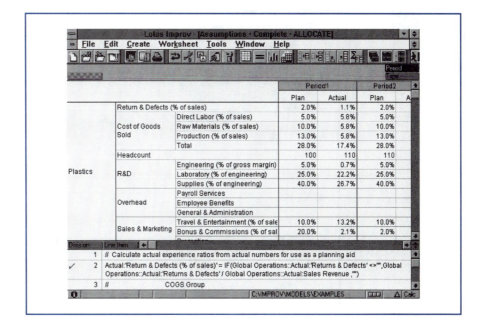

FIGURE 5-8

A second arrangement of the Allocation Worksheet

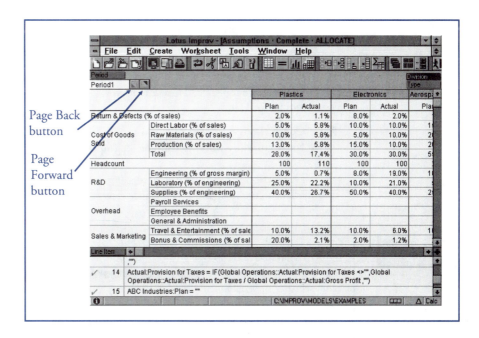

FIGURE 5-9

A third arrangement
of the Allocation
Worksheet

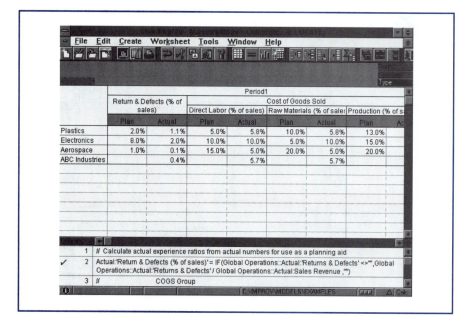

USING IMPROV'S ON-LINE HELP

Improv includes extensive *on-line Help*, built around the Windows Help system. On-line Help allows you to quickly access information or instructions that help you understand and use the Improv program. Improv offers two types of Help: general and context-sensitive.

☑ General Help provides information about a variety of Improv subjects, from the general to the specific. There are three categories: Improv Help, Chart Help, and Script Help.

☑ Context-sensitive Help gives you specific information about the procedure you're currently working with, or the Improv element you've selected.

This section explains how to access Improv's on-line Help, describes the type of information it contains, and gives instructions for moving around and using the Help system.

Note

In addition to help for Improv functions and procedures, the Help system also provides information on Windows operations that are applicable to all Windows applications. For example, you can access Help on using the Windows Print Manager, which controls the printing operations for all Windows applications. See your Microsoft Windows User's Guide for information on Windows-specific Help topics.

Using the Help Menu

To access the General Help system, select Help from the Improv main menu bar. You will see the following Help menu, containing the topics and options listed just below.

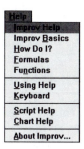

■ Improv Help: Select this to see a list of subtopics that provide definitions or descriptions of Improv concepts, commands, and procedures.

■ Improv Basics: Select this to see information on getting started with Improv and completing basic tasks.

■ How Do I?: This option lets you choose from a list of Improv procedures for which the Help system contains instructions.

■ Formulas: Select this option to get help with formula terminology and basic formula concepts.

■ Functions: Select this option to see a quick reference of Improv functions.

■ Using Help: Here you'll find instructions on using the Help system itself.

■ Keyboard: Select this option to see a quick reference of the keyboard shortcuts assigned to Improv commands and functions.

■ Script Help: Select this option to get specific help on working with scripts. This is not part of the main Improv help file, but is accessible from the Help menu.

■ Chart Help: Select this option to get specific help on working with charts. This is not part of the main Improv help file, but is accessible from the Help menu.

■ About Improv: This option displays a window that tells you the Improv release number, Lotus's copyright information, the program's registered owner, and the memory available on your system.

Getting Context-Sensitive Help

To get help on a specific procedure that you're performing or an Improv element that you've selected, press F1 after you've made a selection. For example, if you selected the Item Group command from the Create menu and then pressed F1, you would see the Help screen displayed in Figure 5-10.

Moving Around the Help System

Whether you bring up the Help window by selecting a topic from the Improv Help menu or by pressing F1, the structure of the Help window is always the same. As an example, let's examine the Help window for the Improv Help topic, shown in Figure 5-11.

You can move, resize, maximize, or minimize the Help window just as you can any other window under the Windows environment.

Using the Menus in the Help Windows

Improv's Help windows have a menu bar below the window's title bar (as do the help windows throughout Windows applications). When you click the commands on the

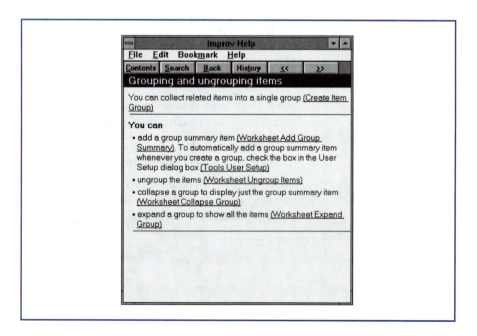

FIGURE 5-10

Context-sensitive Help about item groups

FIGURE 5-11

Improv on-line Help
window

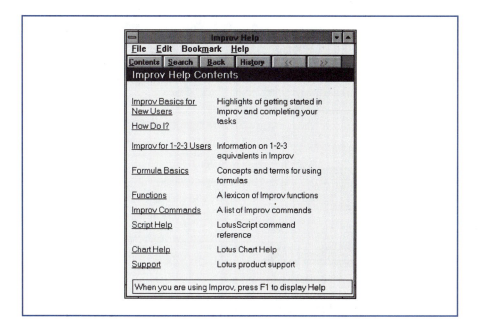

menu bar, you see a list of options that allow you to perform tasks within the Help system. These options are described in the following paragraphs.

File   The File options allow you to open other Help files (Help files have names that end with the .HLP filename extension). For example, you might select File in order to open the Script Help file. There is also a File option that lets you print the currently displayed Help topic, an option that displays the Print Setup dialog box, and an Exit option that lets you leave the Help system.

Edit   The Edit options include Copy, which lets you copy the currently displayed Help text to the Windows Clipboard, and then paste it into another Windows application, such as Ami Pro for Windows.

The Annotate option lets you add a note to any Help topic. When you select Annotate, you see this Annotate dialog box:

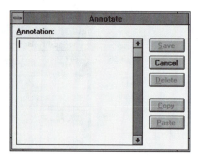

Where the text cursor appears in the Annotation box, just type the information you want to add to the Help topic, and then click the Save button. Improv places a paper-clip icon to the left of the topic title to indicate that the topic contains a note. Figure 5-12 shows an annotated Help topic.

To see the note attached to the Help topic, click the paper-clip icon. The Annotate dialog box appears, containing the note that was entered. Whenever a Help topic note is displayed, you can Delete it by clicking the Delete button, and Improv will remove the paper-clip icon from the topic window. Or, using the Copy and Paste buttons, you can copy the note to a different topic.

When you're done viewing the note, click the Cancel button or double-click the Close box in the upper-left corner to remove the Annotate dialog box from the screen.

FIGURE 5-12

An annotated Help topic

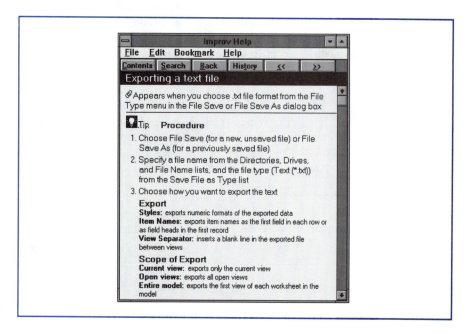

Bookmark   A *bookmark* lets you "mark" a topic that you refer to frequently, so that you can quickly bring it up without searching for it or using the Help menu. To place a bookmark on the current topic, click Bookmark on the Help menu bar and then select the Define command. You see the following Bookmark Define dialog box:

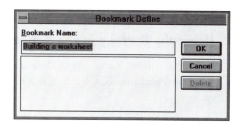

The currently selected Help topic appears in the Bookmark Name text box. To mark the topic, just click the OK command button.

If other topics have already been marked, those topic names appear in the box below the name of the current topic. To remove the mark from a topic, click the topic's name in the list and then click the Delete button.

Once you've marked one or more topics, when you click Bookmark on the Help menu bar a list of the marked topics appears below the Define option in the Bookmark menu, as shown in Figure 5-13. Click any topic on the list to display it in the Help window. If you've marked more than nine topics, the word *More* appears at the bottom of the list. Click More to display the entire list of marked topics.

FIGURE 5-13

List of topics that have bookmarks

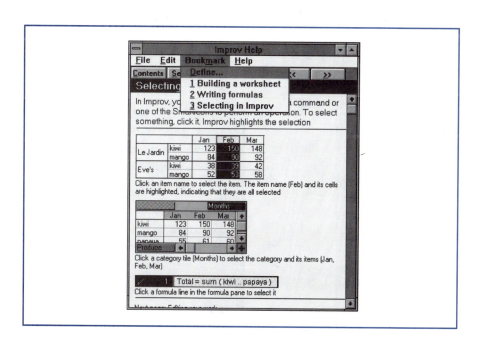

Help   This menu contains options that let you get help on the Help system itself; tell Improv to always display the Help window on top of other Improv windows; and display the Help system's version number, the copyright information, the licensee's name, and the memory available on your system.

Using the Buttons in the Help Window

In addition to the menu bar options, the Improv Help window also contains a row of command buttons—just below the menu bar—that let you navigate through the Help system.

■   The Contents Button: Click this button to see the Help system's table of contents.

■   Search: Click this button to search for information when you don't know which topic contains the information you need. You'll see the Search dialog box shown in Figure 5-14. In the text box, type any word that you associate with the information you want, or use the scroll bar at the right of the list box to find your subject in the list box. After you type in a word or click on a subject in the list box, click the Show Topics button, and a list of related topics appears in the topics list box at the bottom of the screen. Click the topic you want to see, and then click the Go To button. The topic you selected displays in the Help window.

■   Back: Click this button to display the last topic you viewed.

FIGURE 5-14

Help system Search dialog box

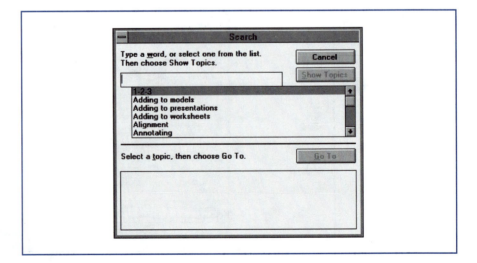

◪   << and >>: Click the << button to display the previous topic in a series of
related topics. When you reach the first topic in the series, the << button is
dimmed. Click the >> button to display the next topic in a series of related
topics. When you reach the last topic in the series, the >> button is dimmed.

Printing On-line Help

It's often very helpful to print out a copy of an on-line Help topic. This is another way
to quickly reference topics that you use frequently. Just select the topic as you normally
would, select File on the Help menu bar, and then select Print Topic.

PART TWO

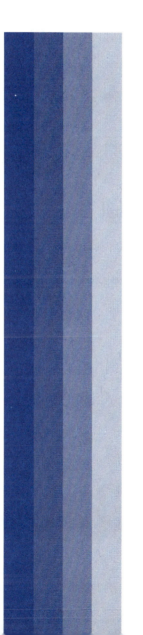

Improv in Two Dimensions

Improv 2

- Worksheet Basics

- Creating a Worksheet

- Saving the Worksheet

Handbook

CHAPTER

6

Building Your Worksheet

The main component of an Improv model is the worksheet. When you create a new Improv model, you start by building a worksheet to hold your data. As you work with the worksheet, you can create other views and rearrange the same data to gain a different perspective on the information. You can add graphic representations of the data by creating charts. You can even combine worksheet data, charts, graphics, and text to create complete reports or on-screen presentations.

This chapter explains how to build and edit a simple worksheet. Once you're familiar with this procedure, use the information in Chapter 8 and Chapter 9 to create worksheets with a more complex structure. Also, use the information in Chapter 11 to create other views of the same data, and the instructions in Chapter 12 and Chapter 13 to plot worksheet data in a chart or include it in a report presentation.

WORKSHEET BASICS

The previous chapters of this book explained the differences between Improv and traditional spreadsheet programs, basic Improv concepts and features, the user interface, and how to move around in the program. Now that you're more familiar with Improv, you're ready to build a worksheet. Before we continue, let's review some basic worksheet concepts.

What Is a Worksheet?

An Improv *worksheet* (sometimes referred to as a *spreadsheet* in other programs) is a table of text and/or numbers arranged in rows and columns. Most often, you'll use Improv worksheets to perform business calculations; for example, to compare planned and actual budget amounts or to track revenue and expenses. You can also use Improv worksheets as a database; for example, to store personnel records or customer information.

Worksheet Elements and Terms

Improv worksheets contain several elements—items, item groups, categories, and formulas—to define a collection of data (text, values, calculations). Figure 6-1 shows the default worksheet that Improv brings up in the Improv application window when you start the program.

The worksheet window has two sections: a data pane and a formula pane. The data pane, where you enter row and column data, displays in the top two-thirds of the worksheet window. The worksheet in Figure 6-1 contains one default row and column, which intersect to form one cell. Each column and row is an Improv item, identified by an item name. Improv uses the term *item* for both rows and columns because you can rearrange rows as columns and columns as rows to display data from a different perspective. See Chapter 11 for complete instructions on rearranging data.

The bottom third of the screen displays the formula pane. This is where you enter the formulas that Improv uses to calculate the data pane values. You write Improv formulas in plain English, which makes them easy for you to enter and interpret (see Chapter 8).

Improv organizes row and column data by category. Each row item is part of a category, which represents a larger classification of data. Categories handle general levels of information such as years, periods, departments, etc. Category names display on "category tiles," located at the top left, top right, and bottom left of the data pane. The category tile at the top right represents the data in each column; the tile at the bottom left represents the data in each row. The tile at the top left, which is empty in Figure 6-1,

FIGURE 6-1

Improv default new
worksheet

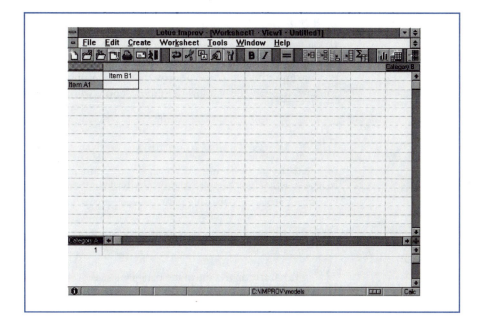

represents the page area; like a book, pages are used to look at different category values, one page at a time (see Chapter 9 for more information).

CREATING A WORKSHEET

When you create an Improv worksheet, the first thing you do is create and name items to represent your information. Item names appear on the worksheet as row and column headings, instead of the numbers and letters or labels that traditional spreadsheet programs use. Each row item corresponds to all the cells in that row, and each column item corresponds to all the cells in that column. When you've set up the items, you enter data (text or values) into the corresponding item cells and add formulas to perform calculations.

This section takes you through the steps of creating a simple worksheet.

Building a New Worksheet

Use the instructions in this section to build a simple Improv worksheet that tracks quarterly sales for four different branches of a company. When you finish, use the remaining sections in the chapter to save and edit your work.

Starting the Program

If you're not running Improv, click the Improv icon in the Lotus Applications group window to start it now. You see the default Improv worksheet shown in Figure 6-1. Click the maximize button (the up arrow box in the upper-right corner of the worksheet window) to resize the window to fit in the entire worksheet area.

Editing the Worksheet Defaults

As stated earlier, the default worksheet already contains two items: Item A1 and Item B1. Item A1 belongs to Category A and Item B1 belongs to Category B. Before we add new items, let's replace the existing item and category names.

1. Click Category A (to the left of the horizontal scroll bar), type **Branch**, then press ENTER.

2. Click Category B (above the data pane's vertical scroll bar), type **Quarter**, then press ENTER.

3. Click Item A1 in the data pane, type **Berkeley**, then press ENTER.

4. Click Item B1, type **Quarter 1**, then press ENTER.

   Your worksheet should now look like Figure 6-2.

Adding and Naming Items

Now you can add the column items that represent the other quarters and the row items that represent the other branches. We'll use one method of adding items to add the additional columns and another method to add the other rows. However, both methods can be used for additional column or row additions.

Adding by Dragging　Move the mouse pointer to the right of the Quarter 1 column. Hold down the mouse button and drag the pointer to the right until you see the names of three more columns in light gray as shown below, then release the mouse button.

FIGURE 6-2

Renaming worksheet
defaults

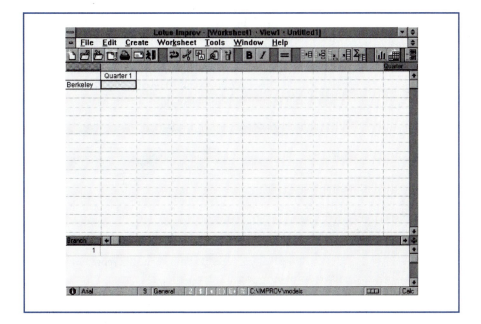

Only use this method when you're adding new items after the last existing column or row.

Notice that Improv based the new item names on the item name that you entered. Because Improv recognizes Quarter 1 as part of an item series, it increases the series sequentially for each new column item after the first. See "Adding Several Items" in Chapter 9 for a list of names that Improv recognizes as item series.

Adding by Menu   If you only want to add one row or column, select Add Item from the Edit menu. Otherwise, click Berkeley, then select Items from the Create menu. You will see the Create Items dialog box shown here.

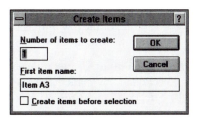

Type **3** for the number of items that you want to create, then press TAB to move to the next field. Type Oakland as the first item name, then click OK. Improv adds three new row items. The first new row has the name "Oakland." The second and third new rows use the default names Item A2 and Item A3. If you had entered a name in the Create Items dialog box that Improv recognizes as an item series, the program would have continued the item names sequentially as it did for the columns.

Click Item A2 and type **Alameda**, then click Item A3 and type **Hayward**. The worksheet should now look like this:

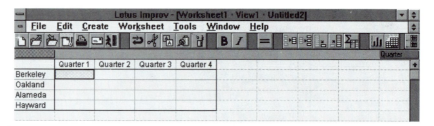

Now that you've added the items that represent your data, enter the corresponding sales values.

Entering Data

You enter data (values and text) directly into the cells that Improv created when you added new row and column items. Before you enter the sales values, keep in mind the following rules:

▰ Don't enter formulas into cells. You enter formulas in the worksheet formula pane. Entering formulas is discussed later in this chapter.

▰ If the data is too wide to fit in a cell, move the cursor to the grid line on the column's right side. The cursor changes to a double-headed arrow. Click the mouse and drag the column line out until the column is the width that you want. To increase a row's height, move the cursor over the grid line on the bottom of the row until you see the double-headed arrow. Click the mouse and drag the row line down until the row is the height that you want.

▰ If you want to enter numbers in a cell and have Improv treat them as text, enter a quotation mark before the number. Improv recognizes as text anything that follows a quotation mark.

Here is the sample worksheet including the sales values:

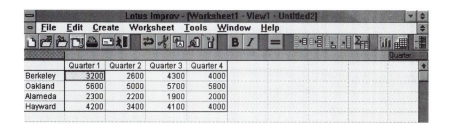

You want your worksheet to look the same, so use the following steps to enter the data:

1. Click a cell where you want to enter a value.

2. Type the number, then press ENTER to confirm your entry.

3. Repeat steps 1 and 2 for each cell that should contain a number.

Tip

When you type a number or text in a cell, you can also press TAB or an arrow key to confirm your entry and move to the adjoining cell.

As the final procedure in building the worksheet, let's add a new row item for sales totals. This gives you the chance to see how easy it is to enter a general Improv formula that calculates all the cell values in the Totals row.

Entering a Formula

Improv formulas contain two sides separated by an equal sign (=). For example, the formula you want to enter for the sales totals will read "Totals=sum(Berkeley..Hayward)." On the left side of the formula (before the equal sign), you name the cells that you want Improv to calculate, in this case, Totals. On the right side of the formula (after the equal sign), you describe the calculation that you want Improv to perform. In our worksheet, that means "Sum the items Berkeley through Hayward for each column."

Use the following steps to add the formula for total quarterly sales.

1. Click the Hayward row item, then select Add Item from the Edit menu.

2. After Improv adds the new row, click the default name and type **Totals** and press ENTER.

3. If it's not already selected, click Totals to select that item, then select Formula from the Create menu. Improv moves the cursor to the first line in the formula pane and inserts the text "Totals=" to start the formula. When you're adding or editing a formula and you point to an item, group, or category name, Improv

inserts that name in the selected formula line. You can also type the information in manually.

4. At the vertical line cursor on the formula line, type the word **sum**, then click the parentheses symbol on the formula status bar below the formula pane.

5. Use the LEFT ARROW key to move the cursor between the parenthesis marks.

6. Click Berkeley and drag down until you highlight all four rows. Improv inserts the item range that you pointed to in the formula line.

7. Press ENTER when you are finished.

Figure 6-3 shows the completed worksheet.

See Chapter 8 and Chapter 9 for more information on using formulas with data pane values.

SAVING THE WORKSHEET

Once you've created a worksheet, you'll want to save the information as a new model. An Improv model is a file that you save with an .IMP extension. A model can contain

FIGURE 6-3

The completed worksheet

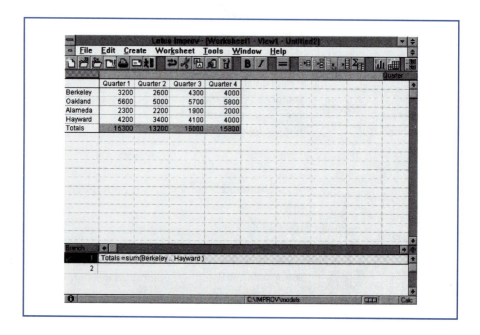

one worksheet or a set of related worksheets and presentations that you save in one file with an .IMP extension. Follow these steps to save the new worksheet.

1. Select Save As from the File menu. You see the Save As dialog box shown below:

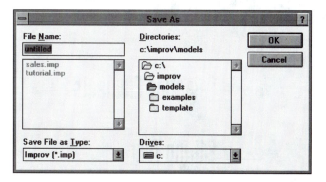

2. In the File Name text box, type **Sales**, then click OK to accept the default Save options (drive C:, the \MODELS directory, and an Improv .IMP file type). You can also use the dialog box to save a previously saved file under a different name, to save files in other locations, and to save a worksheet as a different file type. See Chapter 15 for more information.

    The File menu has two additional options you can use to save Improv models:

File Save   Use this option to save changes to a previously created file, or one which has already been saved with the correct name.

File Close   Use this option to close a file. Improv prompts you to save the file.

When you create a model with multiple worksheets or worksheet views, Improv automatically saves all the documents in the model when you select Save or Save As from the File menu.

Reverting to the Last Saved Version

If you want to experiment with a model but don't want to save your modifications, select Revert to Saved from the File menu. Improv closes the model without saving any changes made since the last time you saved the file, and opens the last saved version.

See Chapter 7 for detailed instructions on making additions, changes, or deletions to Improv models.

Improv 2

- Selecting Elements

- Editing Text

- Using the Cut, Copy, and Paste Options

- Making Additions

- Making Deletions

- Reversing and Reverting

Handbook

CHAPTER 7

Editing Your Worksheet

As a normal part of working with Improv models, you'll need to edit various elements of a worksheet. For example, you may need to move a row item to a different location, correct typographical errors, or delete superfluous information.

Improv provides several options that let you modify worksheet elements if a worksheet doesn't turn out the way you want. Of course, if things are really bad, you can also discard your entries and start over with a new worksheet, a new view, or an entirely new model.

This chapter explains how to select the worksheet element that you want to work with and the how to proceed with the changes you want to make.

SELECTING ELEMENTS

When you work with Improv, you select the item you want to work with (which makes it "active"), then you perform the desired procedure. For example, to edit a formula, you click the formula with your mouse, then make the change. When you select a worksheet element and make it active, Improv highlights it with a different color or shade and a border. Figure 7-1 shows an Improv worksheet that has a range of cells selected.

While selecting a single element or cell seems straightforward enough, you may want to select large portions of your worksheet at one time. In these cases, you can use one of the following methods to make your selection.

Entire Worksheet   To select everything in the data pane, click anywhere in the data pane, then choose Select All from the Edit menu. Improv highlights the entire worksheet.

There is also a simpler way to select the entire worksheet. Click the cell in the upper-left corner of the worksheet. This is the cell where the item names from rows and columns come together (above the row titles and to the left of the column titles). This cell is always blank in Improv. Clicking there will select the entire worksheet.

All Cells   To select only cells and exclude item names, first select the entire worksheet, as descibed above. Then, choose Select Cells Only from the Edit menu. Improv narrows

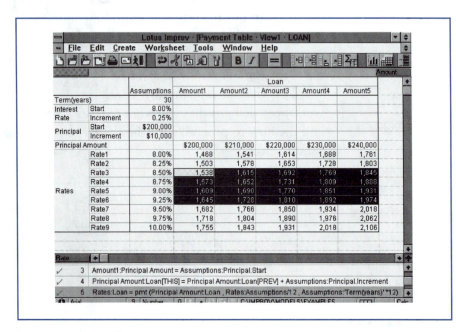

FIGURE 7-1

Selected cell range

the selection to include only cells that contain values.

All Item Names   To select only item names and exclude cell values, first select the entire worksheet, as descibed above. Then, choose Select Item Names from the Edit menu. Improv narrows the selection to include only item names.

Cell or Item Range   To select cell values or items that are adjacent to each other, click a cell or an item name and hold down the mouse button as you drag the cursor over the other item cells or item names that you want to select.

Entire Rows or Columns   To select an entire row or column, simply click the desired item title. The entire row or column will be highlighted. To select a contiguous group of rows or columns, click the first item name, and drag the mouse to the last item name. Release the mouse button and your rows or columns will be selected.

One Cell, Item, Group, Category, or Formula   Click the cell, item, group, category tile, or formula that you want to select.

EDITING TEXT

Improv makes it easy for you to change an entry if you enter the wrong information in a worksheet, enter the right information but misspell it, or just want to replace existing data. For example, you may misspell an item name, transpose numbers in a cell value, type the wrong punctuation mark in a formula, or just decide to rename an item. If you make a mistake when you type information in a worksheet or you just want to replace information with new data, use either of the following procedures.

- To correct a mistake while you're still typing an entry, press the BACKSPACE key to erase one character or number at a time, or press ESC to erase the entire entry. For example, suppose you add a new item that represents monthly expenditures and you type the name "Expnses." Press the BACKSPACE key to erase "s,e,s,n" then type "enses." Now the item name reads "Expenses."

- To correct a mistake after you've made the entry, (that is, after you've typed the data and pressed ENTER), click the worksheet element that contains the error (item, group, or category name, cell value, formula line, etc.) and type the correct information. You can also double-click the element to position the cursor at the end of the entry and use the BACKSPACE key to erase the error, after which you can retype the data.

USING THE CUT, COPY, AND PASTE OPTIONS

There may be times when you want to rearrange or duplicate a worksheet and move or duplicate data from one worksheet to another. Use the Cut and Copy options on the Edit menu to copy items, cell values, formulas, charts, and presentation objects to the Windows clipboard, then use the Paste option on the Edit menu to paste them in another location.

Before you use the Cut option on the Edit menu, familiarize yourself with the following Improv rules governing this command:

▧   Cut deletes only text that is selected.

▧   You can't cut the last remaining item in a category (use Delete on the Edit menu to remove the category); a category must contain at least one item.

▧   You can't cut just an item name. When you cut the item name, you cut the item and its associated cells.

▧   If you cut items or categories that are linked to other worksheets, cutting severs the link, and the link will not be re-established when you use the Paste option.

▧   You can't cut cell values that a formula calculates. Improv instead copies the actual calculated values. The data is then available for use with the Paste command. Use the Clear Cell option on the Edit menu to overwrite calculated cells.

▧   If you cut all the views of a worksheet, Improv deletes the worksheet from the model.

When you want to use the Cut, Copy, and Paste options, select the worksheet element that you want to move or duplicate, and then select Cut or Copy from the Edit menu. Next, select the location into which the data will be placed. Finally, select Paste from the Edit menu. You may wish to review the instructions in the first section of this chapter, "Selecting Elements," when you select worksheet elements.

MAKING ADDITIONS

When you work with models that you update on a regular basis, you might need to add new elements to a worksheet. For example, if you have a worksheet that tracks your income and expenses, you may need to add a new expense item, or you may decide to create an item group to add another level of detail.

This section explains how to add items, groups, categories, and formulas to an Improv worksheet and how to add new worksheets and views to an Improv model. After you add new elements, use the instructions in the previous section to change the default names that Improv enters for the new elements.

Adding One Item

Improv lets you add one item before, after, or between existing items. To add one item, use the Add Item option on the Edit menu. To add several items, use the instructions in the next section. Use one of the following procedures to insert one new item in a worksheet.

▧   To add an item between or before existing items, click the item after which you want the new item located and press SHIFT+ENTER.

▧   To add an item after the last item, click the item after which you want the new item located and press ENTER. You can also hold down the left mouse button and drag one row down from the selected row or one column to the right of the selected column.

Adding Multiple Items

Improv also lets you add several items at one time. The procedure that you use depends on whether you want to add the items before or between existing rows or columns, or whether you want to add the items after the last row or column on the worksheet.

Before or Between Existing Items

To add several items before or between existing items, click the item name that appears before or after the position where you want the new item located. Select Items from the Create menu. You see the Create Items dialog box shown here:

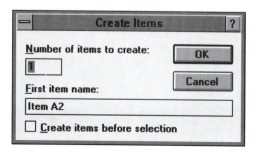

| Note | If the items you're adding aren't part of a series and you're adding them after the last existing column or row, you can simply click and drag beyond the last item to add more items, rather than using the procedure described here. Select the last worksheet item, hold down the left mouse button, then drag down from the row or out to the right of the column until you have as many new items as you want. |

Number of Items to Create   Type the number of items you want to add and press TAB to move to the First Item Name text box.

First Item Name   Type the first item's name. Improv recognizes certain item series and will sequentially increase the series for each item after the first. For example, if you type "Quarter 2," Improv names the second item Quarter 3, the third item Quarter 4, and so on. Improv recognizes the items listed in the following table as series. When you type a name in the First Item Name text box that Improv recognizes as a series, Improv assumes that the items you're adding are part of that series and assigns sequential names.

Series	Entry
Months	January, February, March...
	Jan, Feb, Mar...
Weekdays	Monday, Tuesday, Wednesday...
	Mon, Tue, Wed...
Years	1992, 1993, 1994...
Quarters	Quarter 1, Quarter 2, Quarter 3...
	Q1, Q2, Q3...
Quarters and Years	Q1 1993, Q2 1993, Q3 1993...
	Q1 '93, Q2 '93, Q3 '93...
Integers	1, 2, 3...
Letters	A, B, C...
Text and Integer	Invoice 31, Invoice 32, Invoice 33...
	P103, P104, P105...
	10-A, 11-A, 12-A...

You can also combine series items. For example, the first item in the series could be "Jan 1993." Improv will assign the next name in the series when you add a new item to the right of the last data entry column or below the last data entry row.

Create Items Before Selection   To insert the items before the selected row or column, click the check box to mark it with an X. Click again to remove the X. When your entries are correct, click OK to have Improv create the items.

Adding Several Rows and Columns At Once

Improv also lets you add several rows and columns to the worksheet at the same time. Position the cursor anywhere on the worksheet outside the last row and column. Hold down the left mouse button and drag out diagonally. When you have as many new rows and columns as you want, release the mouse button. Click the new item names and type in your own information.

Adding Formulas

When you add new items, item groups, or categories to a worksheet, you may also want to add a new formula. Remember that in Improv you need to select the data for which you want to create a formula, then create the formula.

To add a formula, click the cell, item, group, category, or range upon which you want Improv to perform the calculation, and select Formula from the Create menu. Improv activates the first blank formula line and inserts a reference to the selected worksheet data followed by an equal sign.

Note

Once you have selected the data, you can press the equal sign (=) to start a formula. This performs the same function as selecting Formula from the Create menu.

See Chapter 8 for specific instructions on entering formulas and working with formula types, calculation types, formula rules, functions, and the formula bar.

Adding Categories

When you start with Improv's default worksheet, there are two existing categories (Catagory A and Category B). Improv models can have a maximum of twelve categories: four row categories, four column categories, and four page categories.

If you have a worksheet that tracks company expenses by two categories, city and month, and you want to add a third category (Category C) to track total company expenses, as shown in Figure 7-2, follow these steps:

1. Click a category tile to select the category that you want to use as a marker (the new category will appear in the same row, column, or page area as the selected category).

2. Choose Add Category from the Edit menu or press ENTER. Improv adds a new category tile with a default name.

To change the default category name, click the category tile and type the name you want to use.

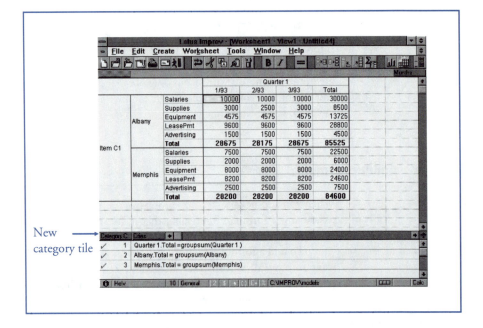

FIGURE 7-2

Worksheet with added
category

Adding Views

When you create a worksheet, you create one *view* or representation of the data. Improv lets you create other views (copies) of the same worksheet, and rearrange the data. This allows you to see the information represented differently without having to create a new worksheet. The views share the same data, but display it differently.

To add a new worksheet view, open the worksheet that you want to copy, then choose View from the Create menu. Improv opens the new view, which is now the active worksheet. Once you create a new view, you can hide items, collapse groups, and move categories to rearrange the way the data displays. See Chapter 11 for more information on working with views.

Adding Worksheets

In addition to allowing different views of the same worksheet, Improv also lets you maintain completely different worksheets in the same model. For example, you could have an accounts payable worksheet and an accounts receivable worksheet in the same model. To create a new worksheet in the currently open model, select Worksheet from the Create menu. Improv opens a new default worksheet and displays it at the front of the Improv screen.

MAKING DELETIONS

Occasionally, you may want to remove unnecessary data from a worksheet. Improv makes it easy to delete entire columns and rows, item groups, categories, and formulas. You can also delete any worksheet, view, presentation, or script that a model contains. This section provides the instructions that you need to delete worksheet elements in Improv.

Deleting Worksheet Elements

Improv's Delete option lets you quickly remove an item, item group, category, or formula from a worksheet. You can also use this option to remove a range of elements.

Before you make deletions, familiarize yourself with the following rules:

- When you delete a category, first delete every item in the category but one (Improv won't let you delete the last remaining item in a category). When one item remains, use the Delete option to remove the category.

- To delete an item group's name without deleting the items in the group, select the group name and choose Ungroup Items from the Worksheet menu.

- To delete an entire group, including all the items in the group, select the group name and use the Delete option on the Edit menu.

- When a group contains only one item, deleting the item also deletes the group.

- To delete a cell value without deleting the formula used to calculate the value, use the Clear Cell option on the Edit menu. You can clear only the cell value (leaving the formula and style), clear only the formula (leaving the value), or erase the value, formula, and format for a cell or cell range.

- When you delete a formula, Improv also erases all worksheet values that the formula calculates.

Keeping Improv's rules for deletion in mind, use the following steps to delete an item, item group, category, or formula from a worksheet.

1.   Select the worksheet element that you want to delete. Use the instructions in the first section of this chapter, "Selecting Elements," for reference.

2.   Select Delete from the Edit menu or press DEL on your keyboard. Improv removes the selected element from the worksheet.

Caution

When you delete a worksheet element, you may see a dialog box with the message "Deleting the selected items will break some formulas in the model." This means that there are formulas in the model that reference (directly or indirectly) some of the elements that you selected for deletion. If you click OK, those formulas will no longer calculate cell values.

Deleting Worksheets, Views, Presentations, or Scripts

Use Improv's Delete option and the Browser window to delete a worksheet, worksheet view, presentation, or script from an Improv model. The following procedure uses one of Improv's model examples to illustrate how to delete a worksheet from a model. Follow the steps to become familiar with the process, then use the information for reference when you want to make your own deletions.

1. Open the Improv model from which you want to delete a worksheet, worksheet view, presentation, or script. For this example, open the LOAN.IMP model located in the \MODELS\EXAMPLES directory.

2. If the Improv Browser window isn't displayed at the front of the screen, select Browser from the Window menu and the LOAN.IMP Browser will appear, as shown here:

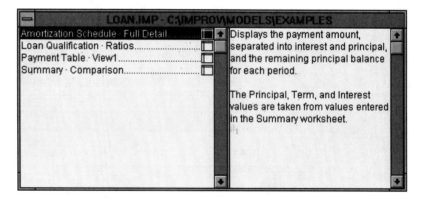

3. Click Payment Table - View1 to select that worksheet view.

4. Select Delete View from the Edit menu or press DEL. Improv removes the worksheet view from the model and the view's name from the Browser.

Use the same instructions to delete any worksheet element that appears on the Browser's list. To retrieve the worksheet view that you just deleted, select Undo Delete View from the Edit menu. In order to reverse a deletion, you must select the Undo option immediately after you delete a worksheet element; that is, before you execute another command or perform another procedure.

REVERSING AND REVERTING

If a worksheet doesn't turn out the way you want, you can always discard your entries and start over. The following procedures describe how to remove different elements.

- To abandon any changes you've made to a worksheet that you've saved at least once, select "Revert to Saved" from the File menu. Improv discards any changes made since the last save.

- To start again with a new worksheet, select New from the File menu. Improv asks if you want to save the changes to the current model—answer no to abandon your work and start over again.

- If you execute a command by mistake, select Undo from the Edit menu. If the option is dimmed, the command or procedure can't be reversed. Select Redo from the Edit menu to cancel the last Redo command.

Note

For information on editing Improv charts and presentations, see Chapter 12 and Chapter 13, respectively. For information on editing scripts, see Chapter 17. For information on changing a worksheet's text, line, and background attributes, see "Using the InfoBox" in Chapter 4.

Improv 2

- What's Different About Improv Formulas?

- The Improv Formula Bar

- Using Dynamic Data Exchange (DDE)

- Formula Basics

- Building Formulas

- Correcting Formula Errors

Handbook

CHAPTER 8

Using Formulas

Formulas are statements, entered in the formula pane of an Improv worksheet, that perform calculations on the items, groups, and categories in the worksheet data pane. Formulas contain various components, which can include data references, text, numeric values, punctuation, math symbols, and predefined functions. Because Improv's innovative formula syntax lets you express formulas in plain English, you'll be surprised at how easy it is to build your worksheet's formulas, whether they're simple (summing a column of figures) or complex (calculating the hyperbolic tangent of an angle).

This chapter provides the information you need to begin entering formulas. It begins by explaining how Improv formulas differ from those in conventional spreadsheet programs. You'll learn about the formula bar, which makes it easy to enter mathematic operators and predefined functions; it explains the Dynamic Data Exchange (DDE) feature, which lets you link data in other applications or other Improv models; and it explains the basic concepts that you need to understand before you start to build worksheet formulas. Finally, the chapter provides complete instructions for entering formulas and tells you what to do if you come across a problem.

WHAT'S DIFFERENT ABOUT IMPROV FORMULAS?

Formulas in traditional spreadsheets (such as 1-2-3, Excel, and Quattro Pro) reference specific spreadsheet cells using coded cell addresses. Formulas are stored in the same cells where the results of the calculations are placed. In these spreadsheets, you can you view the formula (usually on a formula bar at the top of the screen) only when you select the cell where the formula resides.

Improv uses a dramatic new approach to deal with formulas: you enter formulas in plain English, and Improv stores the formulas in a separate part of the worksheet window, the *formula pane*. This approach allows you and other users to easily view and interpret the calculations in a worksheet.

Figure 8-1 shows a simple Excel spreadsheet that tracks regional sales over a period of three months. The formula for cell B6 calculates total sales. The Excel formula, =SUM(B2:B4), is shown near the top of the window under the line of icons. B2 and B4

FIGURE 8-1

An Excel worksheet calculating sales

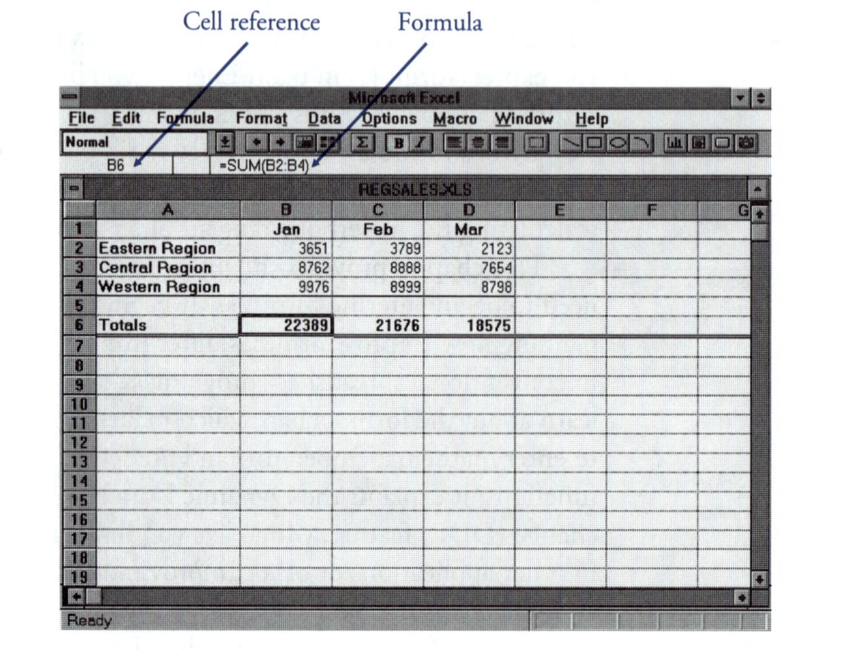

reference the cells at the intersections of column B and rows 2 and 4. It's not easy to determine just from looking at the formula what data is being referenced, and you can only see the formula when you select the cell in which the calculation is performed.

Figure 8-2 shows the same spreadsheet in Improv. Here the formula is clearly displayed in the formula pane. You can view all formulas for the current worksheet at any time, no matter what worksheet data you select.

The Improv formula shown in Figure 8-2 calculates total regional sales for the months of January, February, and March. The formula is expressed as

Totals=Sum(Eastern Region..Western Region)

Because Improv identifies columns and rows by item names rather than letters and numbers, a formula can use the item names instead of cell addresses to reference data. In the Improv formula, "Eastern Region" references the Eastern Region row item on the worksheet; the Excel spreadsheet uses "B2" to reference the same data. Excel and Improv perform the same calculations, but Improv expresses the formula in plain English.

Remember

Improv lets you view an entire worksheet's formulas at any time, all together in the formula pane. And Improv's formula syntax uses the same item names that are in the worksheet, making it easy to see what data a formula references.

FIGURE 8-2

The sales worksheet in Improv

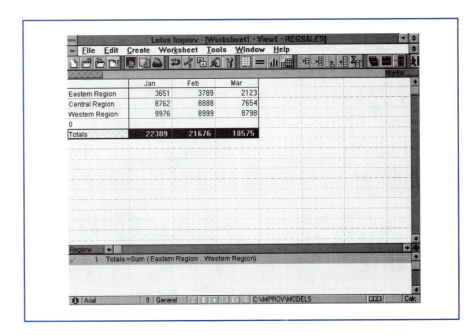

THE IMPROV FORMULA BAR

Note

Throughout this book, you will also see the formula bar referred to as the dynamic status bar, because this bar plays different roles. The formula bar is just one of these roles. When you enter or edit data in a worksheet, Improv normally displays the dynamic status bar at the bottom of the Improv window. When you enter or edit a formula, or select a formula line by double-clicking, the formula bar replaces the dynamic status bar.

Here is Improv's formula bar:

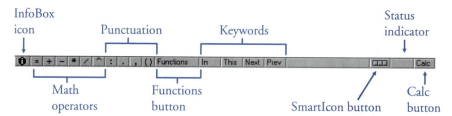

The formula bar has several components: the InfoBox icon, math operator buttons, punctuation buttons, the Functions button, keyword buttons, the SmartIcon button, the status indicator, and the Calc button. These are all explained in the paragraphs that follow.

Using the InfoBox for Formulas

Click the InfoBox icon at the left end of the formula bar to bring up the InfoBox shown below. You can display the same settings by selecting Settings from the Worksheet menu.

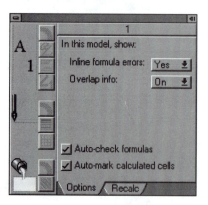

To view the InfoBox settings that are specific to the formula pane, click a line in the formula pane, and then click the InfoBox icon on the formula bar. Because you can't change a formula's text, line, or fill styles, Improv dims the Style panel on the left side of the InfoBox. On the right of the InfoBox, the top line reflects the number of the formula you selected, and two settings pages are offered: Options and Recalc.

InfoBox Formula Options Page

The Options page on the right side of the InfoBox lets you control several formula pane options:

Inline Formula Errors
When you set this option to Yes (the default), Improv displays formula error messages in the formula pane. Set the option to No to have Improv suppress these messages. To change this setting, click the box to the right of the setting, then click the alternate setting.

Overlap Info
When formulas *overlap*, it means that two formulas are competing to calculate the same cell value. To the left of each formula in the formula pane is a system-assigned, sequential priority number. When Improv encounters a formula overlap, it uses the formula with the highest priority number to calculate the overlapping cell values. To change this setting, click the box to the right of the setting and click the option you want to select from the list that appears.

The Overlap Info option has three settings: On (the default), Audit, and Off. These settings determine Improv's actions when an overlap occurs in a formula that you enter, as follows:

- *On:* Improv displays the message "Overlaps formula [formula priority number]" beneath the currently selected formula line.

- *Audit:* Improv displays detailed information about the overlap below the current formula line. If the calculation overlaps more than one other formula, each overlap message appears on a separate formula line.

- *Off:* Improv excludes overlap information from the formula pane.

Note | The section "Correcting Formula Errors" at the end of the chapter explains how to resolve overlapping formulas.

Auto-Check Formulas
When this option is enabled (checked), Improv automatically examines a formula for errors after you enter or modify it. If an error is present, Improv places a status indicator to the left of the formula in question. If you choose not to enable this option, you can press CTRL-K or click the small blank box that's positioned before the formula's priority number to have Improv check a formula.

Auto-Mark Calculated Cells
When this option is enabled (checked), Improv highlights the data pane cells that the selected formula calculates. Keep in mind that

Improv's performance may be slower when you use this option, but it is very useful when you are first building your worksheet.

The Recalc Page

When the formula pane is active (that is, you've selected any formula line), the InfoBox also contains a Recalc page. Click the Recalc tab at the bottom of the InfoBox to display the Recalc page shown here:

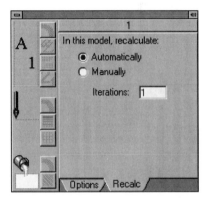

Select Automatically to have Improv recalculate the worksheet whenever you change a value. Improv's performance may be slower when you automatically recalculate values for large worksheets.

Select Manually to have Improv recalculate worksheet values only when you click the Calc button at the far-right end of the formula bar or dynamic status bar.

After you select a recalculation method, in the Iterations box type the number of iterations you want Improv to perform when it is resolving circular references. For further instructions on resolving circular references, see "Correcting Formula Errors" at the end of this chapter.

Inserting Math Operators

The following table lists each math operator button that appears on the formula bar and describes the mathematical function that the symbol represents. To insert one of these operators while entering or editing a formula, click the appropriate button on the formula bar, or press the correct keys on the keyboard. Improv inserts the operator at the current cursor location in the formula.

Operator	Function
=	Equal
+	Addition
–	Subtraction
*	Multiplication
/	Division
^	Exponentiation

Inserting Formula Punctuation

Improv uses certain punctuation marks to separate the parts of a formula. Some of these punctuation marks appear on buttons in the formula bar and some don't.

Using Punctuation Buttons

First we'll examine the punctuation buttons on the formula bar. To use these punctuation marks, just click the button. Improv inserts it in the formula at the point where you've positioned the vertical bar cursor. You can also enter the punctuation marks directly from the keyboard.

Colon (:)   Use a colon in a cell name to separate the row item name from the column item name—for example,

Jan:Totals

references the cell where the Jan column item and the Totals row item intersect. When you enter a formula that references another worksheet (known as an *intersheet formula*), use a double-colon mark (::) to separate the worksheet name from the item name. For example,

Invoices::Over 90 Days:Open

references the Invoices worksheet and the cell where the Over 90 Days column item intersects with the Open row item. To insert the double-colon in a formula, click the colon button in the formula bar twice.

Period (.)   Use a period to separate a group name from an item name that's part of the group, for example:

Monthly Payments.Auto

To enter a range of items in a formula, use two periods (..) to separate the first and last item in the range, for example:

Period1..Period4

To insert a double-period in a formula, click twice on the period button in the formula bar, or press the period key twice.

Parentheses ()   Use parentheses to override the order in which Improv performs a formula's calculations (called *precedence*). Improv calculates each operation in a formula in a certain order; that is, certain operations take precedence over and come before other operations. When you want Improv to calculate a formula's operation with no regard to established precedence, enclose the operation in parentheses. For example, to calculate the total bonus based on the salaries of two employees, at a rate of 10 percent, use this formula:

Bonus = (Joe + Mary)*.10

rather than this formula:

Bonus = Joe + Mary*.10

Enclosing the addition calculation in parentheses overrides the normal precedence that Improv uses (multiplication precedes addition). The discussion "Formula Precedence" later in the chapter explains the order in which Improv calculates mathematical functions.

Comma (,)   Use a comma to separate worksheet elements or conditions in a logical function. Here are two examples:

Total=Sum(Period1,Period3)

Bonus=IF(Tom>=35000,Tom*.10,IF(Tom>=50000,Tom*.15))

Inserting Other Punctuation

Now we'll examine the formula punctuation marks that don't have buttons on the formula bar. To insert these marks in a formula, position the vertical bar cursor where you want to insert the mark on the formula line, and type the appropriate keyboard key.

Square Brackets ([ ])   Use square brackets to indicate an item's absolute position within a group or category. For example,

Sales:Quarter[1]

refers to sales in the first quarter of the Period category. Square brackets are also used in item range references. For example, in

Region[1]..Region[5]

the word Region is the name of a category or group.

Double Slashes (//)   Use two forward slashes to precede additional information in or on a formula line; that is, information not required to perform the calculation (commonly known as *comments*). Since Improv ignores anything in a formula line that follows a double-slash, you can also place this mark in front of a formula to prevent Improv from calculating a formula. This procedure is known as "commenting out" a formula.

To enter a double-slash in a formula, you have to manually type in the two forward slashes. You cannot enter this mark by clicking the division button in the formula bar twice.

Adding Functions to Formulas

The Functions button on the formula bar lets you access a list of predefined *functions* that perform specific calculations. To insert a function using the formula bar, click the Functions button. You will see the following list box:

```
abs ( number )
acos ( number )
asin ( number )
atan ( number )
atan2 ( x , y )
avg ( list )
cellname ( category_name_string , ... )
char ( ascii_number )
choose ( integer , result0 , result1 , ... , resultn )
code ( string )
cos ( radians )
count ( list )
```

Use the scroll bar to move through the list box and find the function you want to insert; then click the function name.

Improv provides nine types of functions, listed below. See Appendix A for a complete description of each Improv function.

Calendar   These functions calculate date and time values, for example, the number that corresponds to the current system date.

Financial   These functions analyze investments and annuities, and calculate depreciation, loans, and cash flow.

Group   These functions perform statistical calculations on values that are part of item groups or ranges. For example, you can calculate the subtotal for all items in an Assets item group.

Logical   These functions calculate cell values based on a condition that is either true or false. For example, you might calculate a bonus based on whether an employee meets a sales quota.

Mathematical   These functions calculate values using trigonometry, logarithms, or numeric operations—for example, to calculate the positive square root of a value.

Select   These functions are used to perform calculations on a selected group of data, based on criteria supplied in the function call. This could be used to determine the total amount of all invoices due, selecting those that are late more than 60 days.

Special   These functions provide information about the contents of a worksheet, for example, a count of the number of items in a specified item group or category.

Statistical   These functions perform statistical calculations on values, for example, finding the average in a list of values.

String   These functions manipulate text strings (text enclosed in quotation marks). String calculations also let you use an ampersand (&) to combine text from several cells—for example, to display the combined text from the street, city, state, and zip code cells in a worksheet.

Using Formula Keywords

The formula bar displays four keyword buttons:

- The In keyword is used in restricted formulas. It is placed at the beginning of a formula to restrict the calculation to a narrow range, or even a single cell, of your worksheet.

☑ The This, Next, and Prev keywords are used in recurrence formulas, which commonly calculate running totals. Recurrence formulas calculate values based on the relative positions of data, such as the previous value, the next value, and so forth.

☑ The First and Last keywords select the first and last items, respectively.

To insert a keyword in a formula, click the appropriate keyword button on the formula bar. For details on using restricted and recurrence formulas, see "Formula Types" later in this chapter.

Displaying the SmartIcons

This button lets you control whether the SmartIcon toolbar is displayed on the screen. This button toggles; click it to remove the toolbar from the screen and click again to redisplay the toolbar. Chapter 4 and Chapter 16 contain detailed discussions about Improv SmartIcons.

Understanding the Status Indicators

Formula indicators are small symbols that Improv places on the formula bar or next to a specific formula in the formula pane to indicate possible problems. The appearance of a status indicator beside a formula doesn't necessarily mean that the formula contains an error; some indicators only alert you that the formula may not be calculating values the way you want.

Improv uses two types of status indicators: *modelwide* indicators and *individual formula* indicators. Modelwide status indicators, which are discussed in this section, appear on the formula bar. Individual formula indicators, discussed in the section "Correcting Formula Errors" at the end of this chapter, appear at the left end of a formula line.

Circular Reference, Attention, and Calc are the modelwide status indicators that Improv displays on the formula bar to alert you to possible problems in a model's worksheet formulas; these indicators are discussed below.

Circular Reference   This symbol indicates that one or more formulas contain a circular reference. A circular reference occurs when a formula refers to itself. For example, you can't calculate the total for an item group that includes the cell Month:Region and display the answer in the Month:Region cell.

Attention   This symbol indicates that a formula contains an error or mismatch. Mismatched formulas are discussed in the last section of this chapter, "Correcting Formula Errors."

Calc   The word *Calc*, displayed in red or a dark color, tells you that the model contains worksheet values that have changed but haven't been recalculated. Click the Calc button in the formula bar (just to the right of the status indicator) to have Improv recalculate the model's worksheet values.

USING DYNAMIC DATA EXCHANGE (DDE)

Dynamic Data Exchange (DDE) is a Windows feature that allows you to create *link formulas* to share data between different Improv models or between an Improv model and another application that supports DDE.

> **Note**   Don't confuse DDE with the Windows OLE (Object Linking and Embedding) feature discussed in Chapter 13.

> **Note**   Not all Windows programs support DDE. If you're uncertain whether a particular program supports this feature, see that program's user manual or your Microsoft Windows User's Guide for more information.

The Windows DDE feature lets you paste and link data from one application to another. For example, you might use DDE to paste and link spreadsheet data from 1-2-3 for Windows to an Improv worksheet. DDE also lets you paste and link data between different Improv models. When you use DDE, the application that's supplying the data is known as the "server"; the application that's receiving the data is known as the "client." To activate the link, both the server application and the client application must be open in Windows at the same time. When the link is active, you can edit the data in the client application, and DDE will update the linked data in the server application.

In Figure 8-3, Formula 2 is the DDE link formula that links data between two Improv models. The formula's left side (before the first equal sign), references the cells that contain the linked data. The data was copied from the server application, in this case another Improv model, and pasted into the client Improv worksheet. The first section on the right side of the link formula (enclosed in double angle brackets << >>), references the name of the server Improv model from which the original data was copied. If the data had been copied from another Windows application, the formula would reference that application instead of the Improv model. The last part of the formula, MapOrder, references the linked data's location in the client Improv worksheet.

Using DDE to Link Data

Now that you're more familiar with DDE, try using it in your own models. Here are the steps:

1. Start the server application (Improv or another Windows application) and open the file that contains the data with which you want to work.

2. In the file in the server application, select the data that you want to link.

3. In the server application, select Edit Copy to copy the data to the Windows clipboard. Leave the server application (or server Improv model) open.

4. Select the Switch To command on the Control menu, and open the client Improv model and worksheet where you want to place the linked data.

5. In the client worksheet, select the cells where you want the data to appear.

Note

You must first create the items in the client worksheet where you want to copy the data; you can't paste linked data into an undefined worksheet space.

FIGURE 8-3

Improv worksheet with a DDE-linked formula

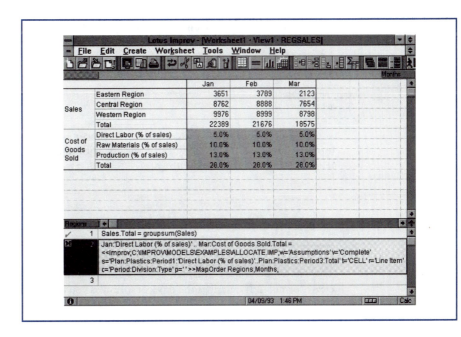

6. In the client application, select Edit Paste Special. You see the Paste Special dialog box shown below. By default, Improv copies the values, as well as the styles of the data, during the link.

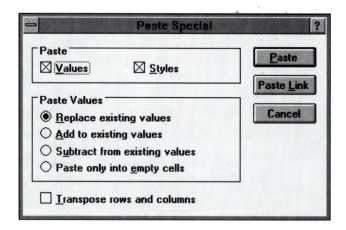

7. In the Paste Special dialog box, click the Paste Link command button to accept the default Improv settings (paste both Values and Styles, and Replace Existing Values in the Paste Values box), or, make changes as necessary for the Paste function you need to perform. Improv pastes the data into the selected cells and creates a link formula in the formula pane. A link indicator then shows next to the formula.

To edit linked data and have Improv automatically update the links when you save the files, you must have both the server application and the client application open at the same time.

To unlink a formula, click the linked status indicator displayed to the left of the formula; Improv replaces the linked indicator with the unlinked indicator and replaces the values in the linked cells with "N/A."

FORMULA BASICS

This section describes fundamental concepts that you should know before you start to create formulas. It describes the types of formulas you can build in Improv and the types of calculations a formula can perform. You'll also learn about the parts of a formula and the order in which you should enter these parts.

Formula Types

The four types of formulas that Improv uses—cell-based, general, intersheet, and linked—are described in the following paragraphs.

Cell-based Formulas

A cell-based formula calculates a value for one cell or a cell range. For example, Formula 1 in Figure 8-4 calculates only the value for the cell where the items Jan and Total intersect.

Because cell-based formulas require that you enter more data, which increases the possibility of errors, use this type of formula only when necessary.

General Formulas

General formulas calculate cell values for all cells contained in an Improv item (row or column). For example, Formula 1 in Figure 8-5 calculates all the cell values for the Total item.

FIGURE 8-4

Cell-based formula

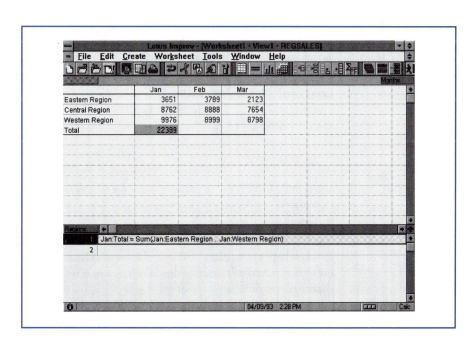

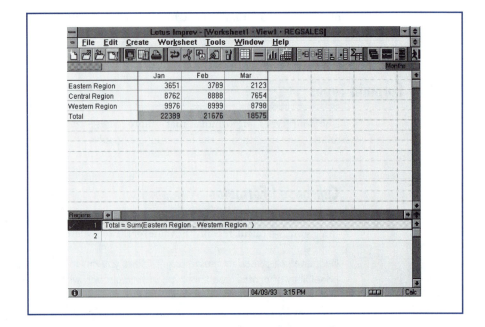

Instead of entering a cell-based formula for each cell that an item contains, you can enter one general formula to calculate all cell values for the entire item. As you can imagine, this saves time because you only enter one formula instead of several. General formulas also reduce the likelihood of data-entry errors—you're less likely to make mistakes when you don't have to enter as much data.

General formulas have three variations: constant value formulas, restricted formulas, and recurrence formulas.

Constant Value Formulas   This variation assigns a specific value to the cells that are referenced by the item name in the left side of the formula. For example, you could enter this constant value formula in a loan worksheet:

Interest=.10

and Improv will display the value of 10% for all cells in the Interest item. Constant value formulas are useful when you want to calculate the same value for several cells in a worksheet.

Restricted Formulas   This variation calculates the value of a specified group of cells that you name in the left side of the formula. A restricted formula essentially narrows the scope (restricts) the calculation of a basic general formula. These formulas use an In clause (which you insert by clicking the In keyword button on the formula bar) to specify the cells to which you want to restrict the calculation.

Formula 3 in Figure 8-6 restricts the general formula calculated in Formula 2. Formula 2 calculates a 10% bonus for all months within the Bonus item, and Formula 3 restricts the formula to calculate a 5% bonus in March only.

Recurrence Formulas   This variation calculates cell values based on the relative location of data, which is useful in calculating running totals. Recurrence formulas use the [NEXT], [THIS], and [PREV] keywords, which appear on keyword buttons in the formula bar, and [FIRST] and [LAST], which don't.

Formula 3 in Figure 8-7 uses a recurrence formula to calculate the new balance by subtracting a withdrawal from and adding a deposit to the previous balance.

Intersheet Formulas

Intersheet formulas use data from other worksheets within the same model to calculate values.

Note   You can use intersheet formulas only to reference data that's in the same Improv model. To share data from other models, use linked formulas.

Intersheet formulas are useful when you want to use a formula from another

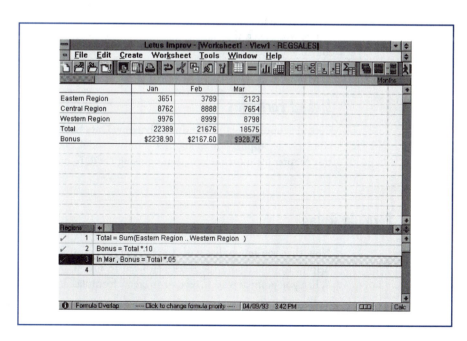

FIGURE 8-6

Restricted formula

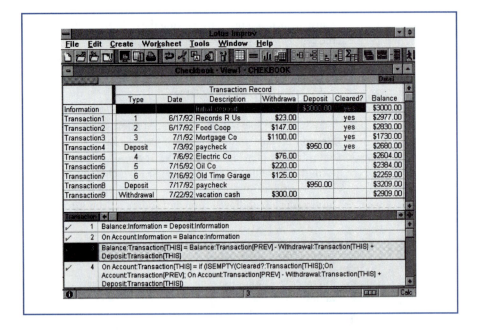

FIGURE 8-7

Recurrence formula

worksheet. Improv lets you reference the other formula, and you don't have to reenter the information in the current worksheet. For example, Formula 1 in Figure 8-8 uses an intersheet formula to calculate the Acct Total amount for each receivable account.

Notice the double-colon mark (::) in the formula. Improv formulas use double-colons to reference intersheet formulas. The name to the left of the colons references the source worksheet; the name to the right of the colons references the specific items in the source worksheet.

Linked Formulas

Linked formulas use the Windows Dynamic Data Exchange (DDE) feature to share data with another application or another Improv model. See the discussion of DDE earlier in this chapter for more information on using DDE to create linked formulas.

Formula Rules

Now that you're familiar with the different types of formulas you can create, it will be helpful to understand the rules you need to follow when you build Improv formulas. When you point at worksheet data to create formulas, Improv provides the correct syntax.

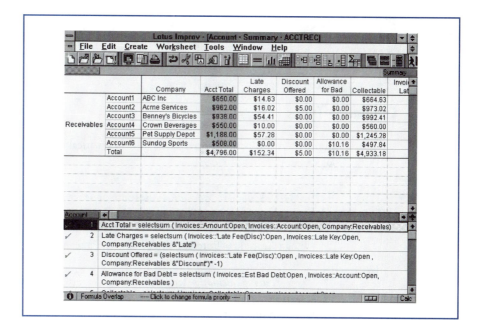

When you type formulas directly into the formula pane, you must adhere to the following rules:

▧ *Item Names:* When you enter item names in formulas, don't include capitalization or extra spaces, which Improv ignores. Use a colon (:) to separate the name of an item from the name of a cell, for example, Expenses:Period1.

▧ *Group Names:* Use a period (.) to separate the name of a group from the name of an item or range of items in the group; type in the group name first. For example, enter the item Auto from the group Expenses as Expenses.Auto, not Auto.Expenses.

▧ *Worksheet Names:* When you type in an intersheet formula, use a double-colon (::) to separate the worksheet name from the item name that you're referencing, for example, Invoices::AcctTotal.

▧ *Numbers:* To use an item, group, or category name in a formula that contains only numbers, enter a colon before the name or surround it with single quotation marks (apostrophes). For example, enter 1993 as :1993 or '1993'.

▧ *Names with Math Operators:* To use an item, group, or category name that contains a math operator (= + * / ^), a period (.), or brackets ([]), enclose the name in single quotation marks (apostrophes). For example, enter the name Cost + 10% as 'Cost + 10%'.

▰ *Names with Punctuation:* To use an item, group, or category name that contains an apostrophe (or single quotation mark), type in an extra apostrophe character when you enter the name. For example, type Ron's Bikes as Ron''s Bikes.

Calculation Types

Improv lets you perform three types of mathematical calculations: numeric, string, and logical, described as follows:

Numeric   A *numeric calculation* uses one or several math operators to calculate cell values, for example:

Loan Amount = Purchase Price – Down Payment.

String   A *string calculation* lets you manipulate text strings (text enclosed in quotation marks), for example, to search and replace certain characters in cells or to change the capitalization of specified text. String calculations also let you use the ampersand (&) to combine text. This is useful when you want to build a final value from the data strings in several cells.

Formula 1 in Figure 8-9 uses a string calculation to combine the text from the Company and Class column items, placing the result in the SelectKey item.

FIGURE 8-9

String calculation

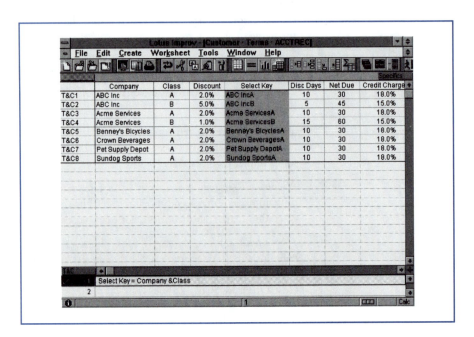

Logical A *logical calculation* lets you review a condition and return the number one (1) if the condition is true, or the number zero (0) if the condition is false. This is useful when you want to check a value to see if it meets a certain condition before you use it in other formulas. Logical calculations use the IF function and the following logical operators:

Logical Operator	Definition
<	Less than
>	Greater than
=	Equal to
<>	Not equal to
>=	Greater than or equal to
<=	Less than or equal to
#NOT#	Logical NOT
#AND#	Logical AND
#OR#	Logical OR

Formula 1 in Figure 8-10 illustrates a logical calculation. The logical calculation translates to "If the daily fee is less than $1000, place the photographer's first name in the priority code field; otherwise (if the daily fee is greater than $1000), enter zero (0) in the priority code field."

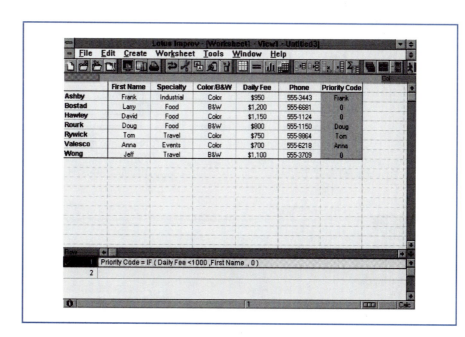

FIGURE 8-10

Logical calculation

Formula Structure and Syntax

Improv formulas contain two "sides"—left and right—separated by an equal sign (=). Consider this formula:

Payment = Principal + Interest

The left side of the formula (before the equal sign) names all of the cells that you want Improv to calculate. The right side of the formula (after the equal sign) describes the calculation that you want Improv to perform on the cells named on the left side.

On the left side of a formula, you can name one cell; a range of cells; one item, group, or category; or a range of items, groups, or categories. When a formula calculates more than one cell, it's called a general formula.

Improv assigns each formula a sequential priority number that displays at the left of the formula in the formula pane. The only time the priority numbers are important is when you have formulas that overlap; that is, when the worksheet contains two different formulas that calculate the value of the same cell or range of cells. When this situation occurs, Improv uses the formula with the highest priority number to calculate the value. See "Correcting Formula Errors" at the end of this chapter for instructions on resolving formulas that overlap.

In conventional spreadsheets, you enter a cell's formula and then copy the formula to other cells. The end result is a worksheet that contains many formulas of which you must keep track. In Improv, however, you don't copy formulas—rather, you enter a formula once and reference all of the cells that you want Improv to calculate. This ensures that Improv updates all cells calculated from the same formula.

Order of Precedence

Improv performs each operation in a formula according to that operation's *order of precedence*; certain operations take precedence over and are calculated before other operations. Use the following list to learn the order in which Improv calculates formula operations. In this list, the lower the precedence number, the earlier Improv performs the calculation. For example, Improv performs multiplication before addition and subtraction. If operations have the same precedence number, Improv performs them sequentially from left to right.

You can use parentheses to force a specific order of calculation, rather than using the default precedence rules.

Precedence Number	Operation	Math Operator
1	Exponentiation	^
2	Multiplication	*
	Division	/
3	Addition	+
	Substraction	−
4	Less than	<
	Greater than	>
	Equal to	=
	Not equal to	<>
5	Less than or equal to	<=
	Greater than or equal to	>=
6	Logical NOT	#NOT#
	Logical AND	#AND#
	Logical OR	#OR#
7	Combine text string	&

Building Formulas

Now that you're familiar with formula types, calculation types, formula rules, functions, and the formula bar, you're ready to start creating formulas. You enter, view, and edit formulas in the formula pane. Improv offers two methods for creating formulas: typing them into the formula pane manually, or building them by pointing with the mouse.

Building formulas by pointing with the mouse is the preferred method. Because Improv enters cell references and correct punctuation when you point to build a formula, your formulas are less likely to contain typing or syntax errors.

Typing Formulas Manually

When you type a formula directly into the formula pane, you type in the cell, item, group, and category names, necessary punctuation, and the math operators that you want the formula to contain. Here are the steps:

1. Double-click a blank formula line. Improv displays a flashing vertical bar, similar to a text cursor, at the beginning of the line you select.

2. To create the left side of the formula, type the name(s) of the cells, range, items, groups, or categories on which you want Improv to perform the calculation that you'll enter on the right side of the formula.

3. Type an equal sign or click the equal sign button on the formula bar.

4. To create the right side of the formula, type the calculation that you want Improv to perform on the cells named in the left side.

5. When you finish typing the formula, press ENTER. Improv then checks the formula for errors, as explained below in "Checking the Formula."

Pointing to Create Formulas

When you point to build a formula, you use your mouse to click and select the formula elements in the data pane or formula bar. Improv inserts the selected cell, item, group, or category names, math operators, functions, and keywords that you want to use in the formula line. Follow these steps to create a formula by pointing:

1. In the data pane, click or click and drag to select the cells, items, groups, categories, or range on which you want Improv to perform the formula calculation.

2. To create the left side of the formula, select Formula from the Create menu. Improv activates the first blank formula line and inserts a reference to the selected worksheet data, followed by an equal sign. A flashing vertical bar cursor appears at the end of the inserted reference.

3. If necessary, click the equal sign button on the formula bar to enter an equal sign after the reference (or press the equal sign key on the keyboard). The flashing vertical bar appears after the equal sign.

4. To create the right side of the formula, click (or click and drag) in the data pane to have Improv place the cell or range references in your formula. Click the appropriate buttons in the status bar to insert the math operators, punctuation, functions, and keywords necessary for your formula. If the element you want to insert isn't represented on the formula bar, manually enter the element from the keyboard.

5. When the formula is complete, press ENTER. Improv checks the formula for errors, as discussed next.

Checking the Formula

When you're done building a formula and you press ENTER, Improv reviews the formula for errors. If none are found, a check mark displays at the far left end of the formula line to indicate that the formula has been checked and is calculating values correctly.

If Improv does detect errors when it reviews the formula, an error status indicator appears at the left end of the formula line. You can click this status indicator to have Improv provide a list of references to the location causing the error. Depending on the formula pane settings that you're using, you may also see an in-line error message below the formula. Descriptions of the error status indicators, as well as instructions for resolving formula errors, are in the last section of this chapter, "Correcting Formula Errors."

Creating Constant Value Formulas

You learned earlier in this chapter that a constant value formula calculates the value of one cell and displays that value in each cell that you name on the left side of the formula. This is useful when you're using the same value in several worksheet cells. For example, if you create a loan payment worksheet (see Chapter 20) that compares five loans with the same principal amounts but at different interest rates, you can use a constant formula (such as Principal = 350000) to enter the principal values. If you want to change the principal amount, you need only change it in one location—in the formula. Then Improv will update every occurrence of the principal item with the new value.

You can also use a constant value formula to calculate the starting value of a recurrence formula. For example, if you create a check register worksheet (see Chapter 18) and use a recurrence formula to keep a running balance, you can use a constant value formula (such as Beginning Balance = 3000) to enter the beginning balance.

Creating a Recurrence Formula

To calculate a running total, start with the current cell and use a recurrence formula to calculate future values. Use the following example, which calculates a running balance for a checking account, as a reference:

Balance:Item[THIS] = Balance:Item[PREV] – Withdrawal:Item[THIS] + Deposit:Transaction[THIS]

Recurrence formulas have a specific format and their own set of rules. When you create a recurrence formula, use the following syntax:

item name:category name[keyword]

or

item name.group name[keyword]

The *keyword* may be [THIS], [PREV], [NEXT], [FIRST], or [LAST], and must be enclosed in square brackets. (If you click a keyword button on the formula status bar to insert a keyword in the formula, it will automatically be enclosed in brackets.)

Following are descriptions of these five keywords:

Keyword	Function
[THIS]	References the cell value in the row or column in which Improv is performing a calculation.
[PREV]	References the cell value in the row or column *before* (to the left of a row or below a column) the value named by [THIS], within the group or category upon which the recurrence formula will act.
[NEXT]	References the cell value in the row or column *after* (to the right of a row or below a column) the value named by [THIS], within the group or category upon which the recurrence formula will act.
[FIRST]	The first cell value in the group or category over which the recurrence formula acts.
[LAST]	The last cell value in the group or category over which the recurrence formula acts.

When you create a recurrence formula, follow these rules:

▨ Use only an item group or category name before the bracketed keyword.

▨ Do not use recurrence keywords in range references.

▨ Do not write a recurrence formula that references both a previous and next cell. For example, this formula

Balance[THIS]=(Balance[PREV]+Balance[NEXT])/2

isn't valid because it references cells that occur both before and after the current cell.

▰   Do not have recurrence keywords modifying references to data in other worksheets.

Since a recurrence formula has to start somewhere, you need to supply the first value (first item in the group). If you don't supply a value to start a recurrence formula, Improv will assume that the value should start at zero.

Creating Restricted Formulas

As stated earlier, restricted formulas restrict or refine the scope of a basic general formula. Suppose you use a general formula to calculate monthly sales bonuses of 5%. You could write a restricted formula that overrides the general formula and calculates bonuses of 8% for December only.

Use the following rules when you create a restricted formula:

▰   Begin the formula with the In keyword (click the In keyword button in the formula bar), followed by the name of a cell, cell range, item, refined item selection, or item group in the current worksheet.

▰   Separate the In clause from the rest of the formula, using a comma (,) or a semicolon (;)—for example:

In Jan,Bonus=5%

▰   Enter only one In clause per formula.

▰   Do not include recurrence keywords in an In clause, as in

In Region1[THIS])..

Rather, use an In clause to modify a recurrence formula, as in

In Region1,Sales:Jan[THIS])...

Creating Intersheet Formulas

Intersheet formulas let you reference the data of one worksheet in the formula of another worksheet, as long as they are both within the same model. For example, suppose you create Worksheet1 to track customer invoices, and then you create Worksheet2 in the same model to age the invoices. Using an intersheet formula, you can reference the Worksheet1 invoices in a Worksheet2 formula. Intersheet formulas save you substantial time because you don't have to enter the same data twice. In addition, this helps reduce the chance of typing errors.

> **Note**
>
> Intersheet formulas can only reference data within the same model. To share data between worksheets in different Improv models, you need to create a linked formula, using the Windows Dynamic Data Exchange (DDE) feature. See "Using Dynamic Data Exchange (DDE)" earlier in this chapter.

When you create intersheet formulas, follow these rules:

- In the left side of the formula, include a reference to the current worksheet.

- In the right side of the formula, enter references to the current worksheet or to another worksheet in the same model.

- Use the pointing method to build intersheet formulas, and let Improv insert the correct punctuation. If you enter intersheet references by typing them in the formula pane, be sure to insert a double-colon mark between the name of the other worksheet and the referenced cells, for example:

    Invoice::Account:Totals

CORRECTING FORMULA ERRORS

When you build formulas, errors can occur; you may misspell cell references, omit operators or punctuation, or leave out function arguments. Before you can fix a formula error, you need to identify the type of error that has occurred. *Formula status indicators* are a valuable tool provided by Improv to help you accomplish this task. These indicators are small symbols that appear at the left of the formula to indicate possible problems. Some of the symbols don't indicate an error, but rather alert you to a situation where the formula may not be calculating values the way you want. If a status indicator appears beside a formula, you can click it to have Improv display a description of the error.

In the earlier section, "The Improv Formula Bar," you learned that Improv uses two types of status indicators: individual formula and modelwide. The modelwide status indicators (Circular Reference, Attention, and Calc) were discussed in that earlier section. Following are descriptions of the individual status indicators.

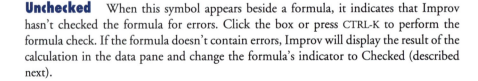

Unchecked   When this symbol appears beside a formula, it indicates that Improv hasn't checked the formula for errors. Click the box or press CTRL-K to perform the formula check. If the formula doesn't contain errors, Improv will display the result of the calculation in the data pane and change the formula's indicator to Checked (described next).

Checked   This symbol tells you the formula has been checked by Improv for errors and confirms that the formula is calculating values correctly.

Error   This symbol means a formula contains one or more errors. You must correct the errors before Improv can perform the calculations in the formula. When a formula has an error, Improv also displays a brief message below the formula; to see the complete error message, click the error symbol.

Mismatch   This symbol tells you that the number or range of cells on the left side of the formula (before the equal sign) isn't equal to the number or range of cells on the right side of the formula (after the equal sign).

Linked   Improv displays this symbol beside a formula that references data shared with another application through Windows's Dynamic Data Exchange (DDE), and tells you that the link is active. See the earlier section, "Using Dynamic Data Exchange (DDE)."

Unlinked   Improv displays this symbol beside a formula that references data shared with another application through Windows's Dynamic Data Exchange (DDE), and tells you that the link is inactive. See the earlier section, "Using Dynamic Data Exchange (DDE)."

Resolving Formula Mismatches

Formula *mismatches* occur when the number or range of cells on the left side of the formula are not equal to the number or range of cells on the right side of the formula. A formula mismatch doesn't necessarily indicate an error; it only means the formula may not be calculating values the way you want it to.

For example, let's say you enter the formula

Eastern Region=Eastern Region:Jan

for the worksheet shown in Figure 8-11. The left side of the formula names all the Eastern Region item cells; there are three of these. The right side of the formula, however, names only the cell where the Eastern Region and Jan items intersect. Thus the left side of the formula names more cells than the right side.

When a formula mismatch occurs, analyze your formula to ensure that it's calculating cell values the way you expect.

Resolving Formula Overlaps

Formula *overlaps* occur when two formulas compete to calculate the same cell value.

Figure 8-12 shows an Improv worksheet with a formula overlap. The overlap details below each formula line are displayed because the Overlap Info option in the InfoBox for Formula settings has been set to Audit. If this option were set to Yes, Improv would only display the message, "Overlaps formulas 1, 2, 3" below Formula 4. If the Overlap Info option were set to Off, Improv wouldn't reference the overlap at all.

You have already learned about the sequential priority number that appears beside each formula. The only time that the priority numbers are important is when you have formulas that overlap, that is, when two different formulas are calculating the value of the same cell or range of cells. When this occurs, Improv uses the formula with the highest priority number to calculate the value.

When the two formulas that overlap calculate the same answer, you can ignore the overlap. However, if the calculations produce different answers, you'll need to change the

FIGURE 8-11

Formula mismatch

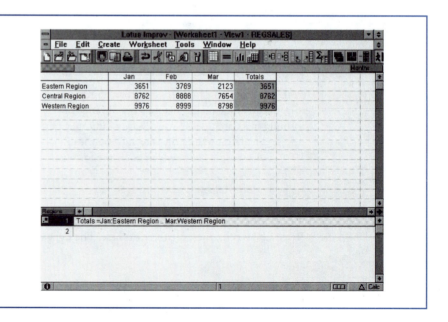

FIGURE 8-12

Overlapping formula

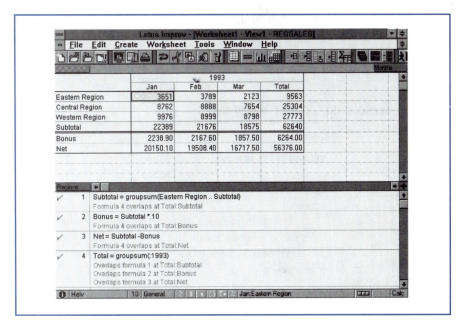

priority numbers of the formulas to resolve the situation. To change an overlapping formula's priority, follow these steps:

1. Click on one of the formulas that overlap. Improv displays the Formula Overlap button on the formula bar.

2. Click the Formula Overlap button to display a list of overlapping formulas, like the one shown just below. The formula with the highest priority number is currently calculating the cell(s) in question.

3. Notice the formula that has two opposing triangular arrows to its left; this is the *formula slider*. Click and drag the formula slider up or down to give the formula a higher or lower priority.

4. Repeat steps 1 through 3, if necessary, until all the formulas have the priorities that you want.

5. Click outside the overlap list or press ESC to remove the list from the screen. The formula pane now displays the formulas with their new priorities and recalculates the worksheet values.

Resolving Circular References

A *circular reference* occurs when a formula somehow refers to itself, either directly or indirectly. For instance, the worksheet in Figure 8-13 calculates the Bonus as a percentage of Net, and calculates Net by subtracting the Bonus from the Subtotal; these two formulas create a circular reference. Improv uses multiple iterations to calculate the correct amounts.

To control iteration, click anywhere on the worksheet data pane and select Settings from the Worksheet menu. In the InfoBox, click the recalculation method you want to use, and then type the number of iterations you want Improv to perform to resolve circular references.

Caution

Don't specify more than 100 iterations for large worksheets; the more iterations that Improv has to perform, the longer it takes to recalculate worksheet values.

FIGURE 8-13

Circular reference

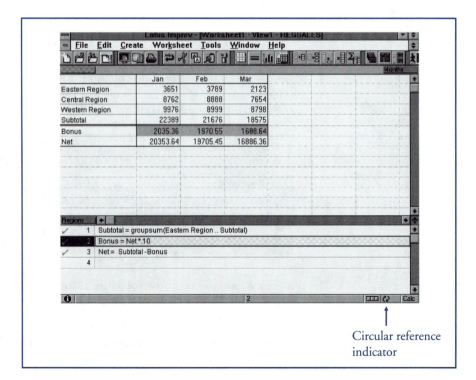

Circular reference indicator

Resolving Other Types of Error

Along with error status indicators, Improv always displays a brief message below the formula, indicating what the error is. Remember that you can click the error symbol to see the complete message; it will help you analyze the formula, locate the cells that are causing the error, and make the necessary corrections to resolve the error.

PARTTHREE

Improv in Three Dimensions

Improv 2

- Working with Items

- Using Item Groups

- Working with Categories

Handbook

CHAPTER 9

Items, Groups, and Categories

You have learned that Improv uses two classifications to structure the data in a worksheet: *items* and *categories*. Every row and column in a worksheet is an item, and each item is part of a larger classification, the category. Categories handle general levels of information such as years, periods, departments, and so forth. Items provide the details within each category. If you want your worksheet to have additional levels of detail, Improv lets you classify related items that are in the same category as *item groups*.

Using the item and category structure, Improv can offer you an important feature: the ability to manipulate data classifications so you can view your data in a variety of ways, using the *category tiles*.

This chapter explains how to work with Improv's data classifications to hide and display items, to collapse and expand groups, and to re-arrange category tiles to see your financial information from a different perspective.

WORKING WITH ITEMS

When you create a new worksheet, Improv automatically provides one row and column, which intersect to form one cell. Columns and rows are items, identified by item names. An item can be either a row or a column because items can change location when you use the category tiles rearrange rows as columns and columns as rows. (You'll read more about rearranging worksheet data later in this chapter.)

Figure 9-1 shows Improv's default new worksheet. Improv names the default row item Item A1. This item belongs to the larger classification, Category A. The default column item has the item name Item B1. This item is part of Category B.

When you build your worksheet, the first thing you do is add more items that represent the spreadsheet's details, as discussed in the following sections.

Adding One Item

When you add a new item (that is, a new column or a new row), Improv lets you add the item before, between, or after existing items.

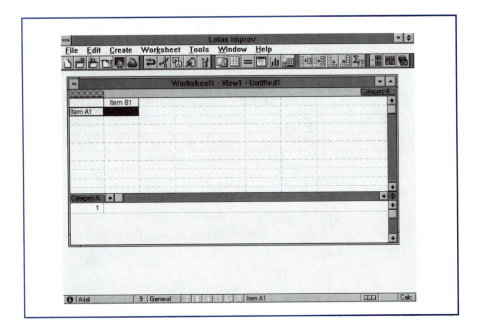

FIGURE 9-1

Improv's default new worksheet

Adding an Item Before or Between Existing Items

Click the name of the row or column item *before which* you want the new item located; that is, the row below or the column to the right of where you want the new item. Then press SHIFT+ENTER. This can be done in any location, including the first row or column.

Adding an Item After the Last Row or Column

Use one of the following methods:

- Click the name of the row or column item *after which* you want the new item located (that is, the row above or the column to the left of where you want the new item), then press ENTER.

- Click the name of the last row or column item. Hold down the left mouse button and drag down from the row or to the right of the column.

Adding Several Items

Improv also lets you add several items at once. The procedure that you use depends on whether you want to add the items before or between existing rows or columns, or whether you want to add the items after the last row or column on the worksheet.

Adding Several Items that Are in a Series

Improv recognizes certain *item series* and will increase the item names sequentially for each item after the first. For example, if you enter Invoice1 as the item name, Improv names the second item Invoice2, the third item Invoice3, and so on. Just type the name of the first item of the series, and Improv will assume that new items you add are in the series and automatically assign sequential names to the new items. For more information on which items Improv recognizes as series, see the "Making Additions" section in Chapter 7.

You can also combine series items. For example, if you enter the first item in the series as Jan 1993, Improv will automatically assign the next name in the series when you add a new item to the right of the last data-entry column or below the last data-entry row.

Adding Items Before or Between Existing Items

To add several items before or between existing items, follow these steps:

1. Click the item name that appears before or after the position where you want the new item.

2. Select Items from the Create menu. You see the Create Items dialog box:

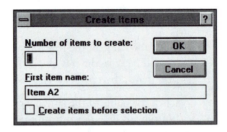

3. In the Number of Items to Create box, type in the number of items you want to add. Then press TAB to move to the First Item Name text box.

4. In the First Item Name text box, type in the first item's name.

As described previously, you can have Improv supply sequential item names.

5. If you want to position the new items *before* the selected row or column, click the Create Items Before Selection check box. To position the new items *after* the selected row or column, leave this check box unmarked.

6. When your entries are correct, click OK, and Improv will create the new items.

Adding Items After the Last Existing Item

To add several items after the last existing row or column in the worksheet, click the name of the last row or column item. Hold down the left mouse button, and drag *down* from the row, or *out to the right* of the column, until you have as many items as you want. If the existing items are part of a series, Improv will use the correct names in the series for the new items.

Improv also allows you to add several rows and columns to the worksheet at the same time. Position the cursor anywhere on the worksheet outside the last row and column. Hold down the left mouse button and drag diagonally outward. When you have as many new rows and columns as you want, release the mouse button. Click the new item names, and type in your own information.

Hiding and Redisplaying Items

Improv lets you hide rows or columns to exclude data from the display. This is useful, for instance, when you want to present worksheet information at a meeting but you want to omit certain items, or when you want to create a chart for data that isn't contiguous. When you hide items on a worksheet, your actions only affect the worksheet's current view; the worksheet's structure and data don't change.

Note   Improv requires that you hide the entire column or row; you cannot hide only part of an item.

Note   You can't hide all the items within a category. If you try to do this, Improv will reset the worksheet so that all worksheet items display.

To hide items, click the item name of the row or column you want to hide, and select Hide Items from the Worksheet menu. You can also click and drag to select several items and hide them all at once.

Look at Figure 9-2. The worksheet in the top half of the screen shows all items. In the worksheet at the bottom, the SelectKey column and the T&C2 and T&C4 rows are hidden. Notice the small vertical gray bar to the right of the Discount column, and the long horizontal gray bars above and below the T&C3 row. These are the item markers Improv uses to tell you there are items hidden on the worksheet. To redisplay the hidden items, double-click the markers.

USING ITEM GROUPS

Improv lets you group related items that are in the same category to add another level of detail to your worksheet. When items belong to a group, you can use the group name in a formula to reference the entire group instead of having to reference each item individually.

Figure 9-3 shows a worksheet with several item groups. Formula 5 uses the group name "Rates" to reference each item in the Rates group, instead of using each item's name (Rate1, Rate2, and so on).

FIGURE 9-2

The worksheet at the bottom has hidden items

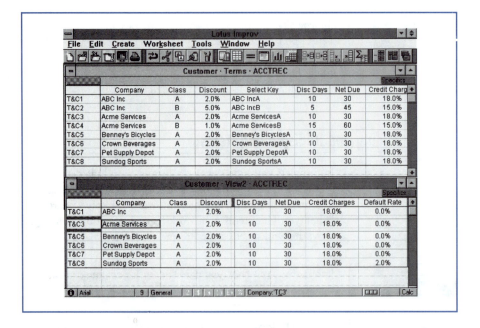

When you use Improv group summaries to create subtotals, you also reduce the likelihood of data-entry errors—the less information you have to enter, the less likely you are to create formula errors. When you add new items to an existing group, Improv automatically updates the formula to include the new item.

When you want to create an item group, first decide which items in the worksheet you want the group to contain: all items or a range of items. Improv provides you with several ways to select items that you want to group:

■ All items in the worksheet: Click on an item, and then choose Select All from the Edit menu. Improv will highlight the entire worksheet.

■ *One item:* Click the left mouse button on the item name or cell you want to select.

■ Range of items: Click on an item name and hold down the mouse button as you drag the cursor over the other item names you want to select.

Once you have selected the items for a group, select Item Group from the Create menu. When you add a row item group, Improv assigns the default name Group A[#], where [#] is a sequential number (beginning with 1). When you add a column item group, Improv assigns the default name Group B[#], where [#] is a sequential number (beginning with 1). If you want to change the default group name, just click the group name and type in your own information. The name of each group is placed to the left of all item names in a row group, or above all items in a column group.

FIGURE 9-3

A worksheet with an
item group

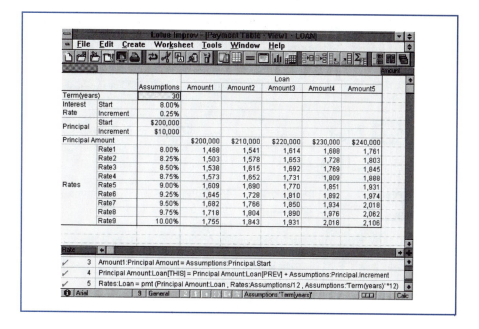

Adding Group Summaries

When you group items, Improv lets you add a *group summary item,* which performs a calculation for all items in the group. This is useful when a worksheet contains several item groups. Later in this section you'll read about collapsing a group to exclude individual group items from displaying on screen. In order to collapse a group, you must have added a group summary.

To create a summary group, click the group name and select Add Group Summary from the Worksheet menu. You see the Add Group Summary dialog box shown below. To select a summary type, just click the appropriate radio button.

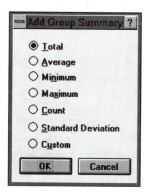

The settings in the Add Group Summary dialog box let you specify the value Improv calculates for the group summary. When you select any setting except Custom, Improv adds a summary item to the group with the default name, such as Total or Average, and then calculates and displays the selected value. Improv also adds a formula to the formula pane using the GROUPSUM function.

Note

The GROUPSUM function prevents Improv from including subtotals in calculations of grand totals. When you include subtotals in grand-total calculations, the grand-total value is incorrectly calculated (that is, the group summary is included in the overall calculation).

Tip

To have Improv automatically add a group summary item when you create an item group, select User Setup from the Tools menu, click the Auto Group Summary list box, click the summary type you want Improv to automatically create, and enable the Auto Group Summary feature.

Following are descriptions of the various types of group summary values you can add to your worksheet.

Total Improv calculates the total value of the items in the group.

Average Improv calculates the average value of the items in the group.

Minimum Improv calculates the smallest value in the group.

Maximum Improv calculates the largest value of the items in the group.

Count Improv calculates the number of items in the group.

Standard Deviation Improv calculates the standard deviation; that is, the square root of the variance, which measures the variance of individual group items from the group mean. A standard deviation of zero indicates that all items in the list are equal.

Custom Choose Custom when you want Improv to calculate any value other than the ones provided in the Add Group Summary dialog box. Improv will add a summary item to the group in the worksheet with the default name Custom, but it doesn't add a formula to the formula pane. You then write a formula that references the item name Custom.

For example, Figure 9-4 shows a worksheet that calculates ratios that lenders use to determine if a borrower qualifies for a loan. Suppose you want to calculate the variance of Calc % Down versus Input % Down in the Loan Qualification-Ratios-LOAN worksheet. Here's how you would do it: Select the items Calc % Down and Input % Down, and then select Item Group from the Create menu. Once Improv creates the

FIGURE 9-4

A worksheet that
needs a group
summary

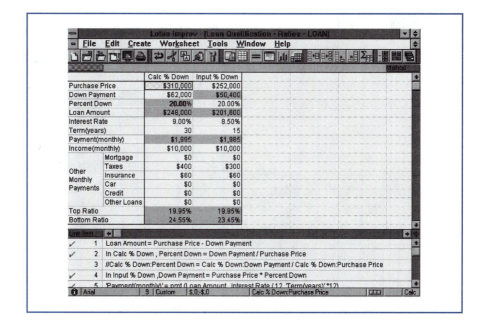

group, change the default group name from GroupB1 to Ratio Variance, to better identify the group. Select the new group, and then select Add Group Summary from the Worksheet menu.

When the Add Group Summary dialog box appears, click the Custom setting. Once Improv creates the group summary item, change its name to Variance, select the new item, and then select Formula from the Create menu. The cursor moves to the formula pane, creates Formula 8, and enters Variance=.

Click the Calc % Down item name, click the minus sign on the formula bar at the bottom of the screen, click Input % Down, and press ENTER. Improv performs the calculation and displays the results in the new Variance column. Figure 9-5 shows the new group, the new summary group item, and the custom summary group formula.

Note   See Chapter 8 for more information on entering Improv formulas.

Collapsing and Expanding Groups

When a group has a summary total, Improv lets you display each item in the group, or just the total. This is useful when you have a large worksheet with several item groups. If the data doesn't all fit in the window, you can collapse the groups to display only the summary totals.

FIGURE 9-5

FIGURE 9-5

Worksheet with a
custom group
summary

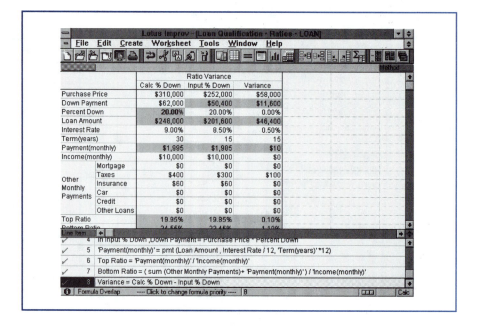

> **Note** Improv won't let you collapse groups unless the items have a summary group total.

Figure 9-6 shows a worksheet that compares the actual and planned allocations of resources for several manufactured items. Notice the item names Cost of Goods Sold, R&D, Overhead, and Sales and Marketing. These are group items, and the items to the right of them are grouped. If you want to see only a summary total for these groups, you click the group name to select that group, and then select Collapse Group from the Worksheet menu. Figure 9-7 shows the same worksheet after the groups have been collapsed.

In Figure 9-7, notice the vertical dotted line to the right of each group name. This is the marker Improv inserts to tell you this group is collapsed. To redisplay items in a collapsed group, double-click the marker or click the item group name and select Expand Group from the Worksheet menu.

WORKING WITH CATEGORIES

As stated earlier, all Improv items belong to at least one category. When you create a new blank worksheet, Improv provides two default categories to which you can add up to ten more categories, for a total of twelve.

Category names display on the category tiles located at the top-left, top-right, and bottom-left of the data pane (see Figure 9-8). The category tile at the top-right represents

FIGURE 9-6

Resources Allocation
worksheet

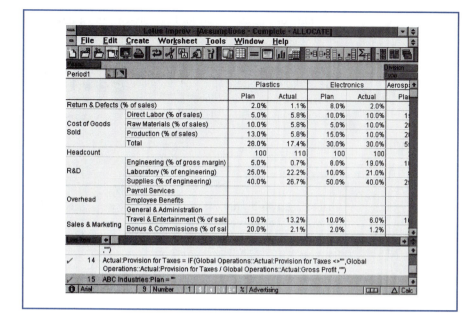

FIGURE 9-7

Resources Allocation
worksheet with
collapsed groups

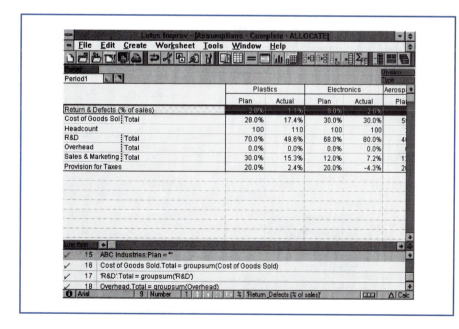

columns; the tile at the bottom-left represents rows; and the tile at the top-left represents the page area, which lets you view item groups one at a time, like pages.

By moving the categories around to different tiles, Improv gives you the opportunity to view the same data in a variety of ways—without your having to reenter the data or re-create the worksheet. For example, you can move the category tile that represents the column data to the tile for the row data, and vice versa. When you move a category tile, Improv automatically rearranges the worksheet data accordingly and updates the calculations.

Adding a Category

When the two default categories on a new worksheet aren't enough, it's easy to create new ones. For example, if your worksheet tracks company sales by month, the month items would be part of one category. You could add another category to also track sales by year.

To add a category, select Category from the Create menu. When Improv adds a new category tile, you can click it and type in the new category's name. Then you can add new items to the category.

Deleting a Category

Before you delete a category, delete all but one of the items in the category. (Improv won't let you delete the last item in a category.) When only one item remains, you can delete the category by clicking the category tile and selecting Delete Category from the Edit menu.

Rearranging Categories

One of Improv's most dynamic features is the ability to rearrange categories to gain a different perspective on your data. To rearrange worksheet categories, simply click a category tile and drag it to one of the other category tile locations.

Figure 9-8 shows an Improv worksheet that analyzes the allocation of company resources in four categories: by company division, by item, by period, and by planned and actual allocation percentage amounts. The row items contain allocations within each division. The column items show the actual and planned allocation for each period. Because of the way that the categories are arranged, the screen only displays allocations for one division. In this situation, it might be useful to look at the same information from a different perspective.

In Figure 9-9, we've relocated the Division category to the column tile and moved the Period category to the page tile. With this arrangement, you see the allocations for all

FIGURE 9-8

Categories can be rearranged to better express your data

Page categories

Column categories

Row categories

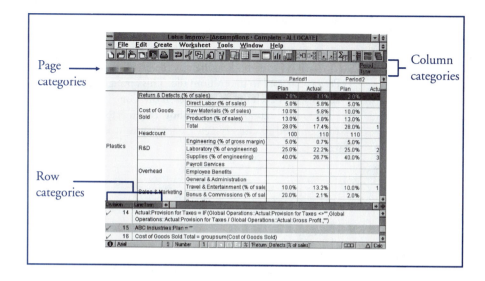

FIGURE 9-9

Another view of the Resources Allocation worksheet

Page Back button

Page Forward button

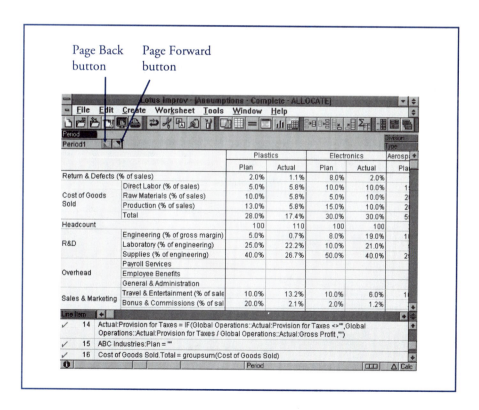

divisions, one period at a time. To see the next period's allocations, you would click on the Page Forward button that appears just to the right of the page tile.

Figure 9-10 shows a third arrangement of the categories. Here we've moved the Division category back to the row tile, the Line Item category to the column tile, and the Period category to the column tile. This arrangement emphasizes the planned and actual allocation of each line item for each division.

These examples illustrate how easy it is for you to dynamically rearrange worksheet data and add an entirely new dimension to spreadsheet analysis.

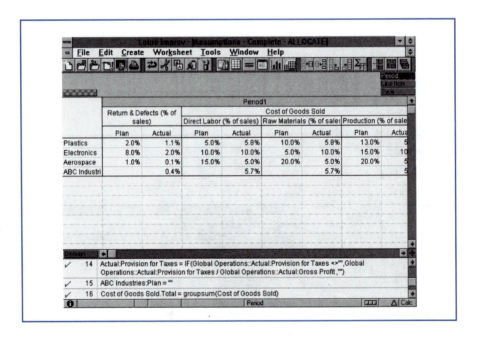

Improv 2

- The Parts of an Improv Model

- How to Plan Your Improv Model

- Linking Worksheets with Formulas

- Linking Worksheets with DDE and OLE

Handbook

CHAPTER 10

Planning an Improv Model

You have already learned that Improv makes significant enhancements to the traditional spreadsheet. One improvement Improv gives to other spreadsheets is in its flexibility. You can easily group and ungroup items, hide or show details items, and rearrange data after you have entered it.

Improv's flexibility is fundamental to the product. One aspect of your ability to successfully analyze your data depends on being able to view it in many different ways. You want to compare data across different time periods so that you can spot trends, you want to try "what-if" projections using the same formula on slightly different data, and you want to use charts and graphs to view or present your data in an easily understood format.

The key to this flexibility is the Improv *model*. A model can contain several worksheets, views, presentations, and scripts all related to the same data. The model is managed using the Improv Browser.

In this chapter you will learn about the parts of an Improv model; planning your model, including using different views and managing your model with the Browser; adding a new worksheet or view; and linking worksheets. In the next chapter you will learn to apply these techniques in your own models, using some of the sample models that came with your copy of Improv as examples.

THE PARTS OF AN IMPROV MODEL

The Improv model can be very simple or very complex. At its simplest, a model contains one worksheet that gives a complete view of your data. At its most complex, a model may contain several worksheets, views for data entry, views for analysis, a presentation including charts and graphs, and scripts to automate routine procedures. All of the parts of the model are listed in the Browser, which acts as a table of contents. The parts of a model are illustrated in Figure 10-1.

HOW TO PLAN YOUR IMPROV MODEL

In order to make the most effective use of Improv's ability to present data in a variety of ways and to adapt data to changing situations, you must plan your model before you begin entering data.

FIGURE 10-1

The parts of an Improv model

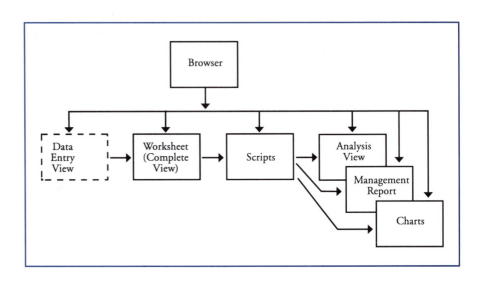

If you aren't able to conceptualize the items, categories, groups, and worksheets of your model, probably the easiest way to clarify your thoughts is to focus on the output and analysis you want from the data. By having your final goal firmly in mind, you can ensure that you enter the initial data in the proper inventory categories, increments, time periods, or whatever. For instance, annual sales totals would be inadequate if you want to track seasonal trends. Or, you might need to track both wholesale-dollars spent and number of units purchased to do adequate "what-if" projections.

Consider any formulas you might use for projections or analysis. Write them out and verify that your input and the formulas will yield the analytical tools you need.

Tip	You can link and use the same formulas across more than one worksheet. This allows data to be manipulated, even if it is not located directly with other related data.

You will want to generate Design reports. If you plan to use your data for presentations, have at least a general idea of the charts and graphs you will need. Don't forget that you can hide the detail items and collapse groups, so you might be able to use the same worksheet for both detailed and summary-level reports.

Some of your planning decisions should be based on the amount of data you have. If your business is large, it might be appropriate to use separate worksheets for different departments or store branches. If your business is small and has a simple structure, you might want to use one worksheet for both income and expenses.

After you've thought through your model as carefully as possible—relax! Improv makes light work of many changes that can be tedious in many conventional spreadsheet programs. For instance, cut and paste of data is powerful: in many situations items can be rearranged simply by dragging to the new location. You can easily create different views of your data, including moving a category of data from the x-axis to the y-axis.

When you installed Improv, the program created a sub-directory called "Examples," which contains several models, each one showing techniques used to build and manage a model. Each of the models focuses on a few techniques and demonstrates those techniques thoroughly: you can use the models as learning tools even if your early models are less complex. We refer to those models in this chapter, and in Chapter 11, use them to illustrate Improv's dynamic viewing capabilities. Each model is analyzed in more detail in Part 6 of this book.

The Complete View Worksheet

Typically, your model will be based on one worksheet that contains your data. The Improv models call this worksheet the *Complete View*. The Complete View worksheet contains the individual data items you want to track and analyze.

In some situations, you might prefer to divide your input data into more than one worksheet. If you are doing budgets for a company, consider a separate worksheet for each department, or for each of the different branches of a store. There are no hard-and-fast rules: the volume of data and how you will be comfortable working with it are the determining factors.

Don't forget that you can cut and paste information among two or more worksheets. This includes formulas as well as data.

Using Items, Categories, and Groups

You already know that the basic building block of your worksheet is the *item*, the cell at the intersection of each row and column. Every item is also organized into a larger classification, called a *category*. A category is used to group information. For instance, a Period category might have items for each month of the year. These become the column or row headings of your worksheet, and help describe the data that is entered as you work.

When you begin to plan your worksheet, you should start with two categories, one running horizontally and the other running vertically. This arrangement gives your data two dimensions.

If, as you plan your analysis, you realize two categories will not yield the divisions or increments you need, add another category. In some situations, you will need to add more categories as you accumulate more data. During your first year of business, it will be adequate to track your sales by month; by the second year of business, you will want to add the category "year." In other situations, you will need to add categories as your analysis becomes more complex: you might need to add sales regions, or new branch offices. Each category adds another dimension to your worksheet.

Tip

Improv can name some sequential items and categories automatically. Improv will enter the names of days and months, years, letters, and numbers in a series. You can do this by either selecting the initial item of the series and dragging the mouse to add the necessary number of items, or by using the Create Items dialog box.

If, on the other hand, you want to show the details of an item, you should use a group rather that a category. The model FINANCE.IMP, included in the examples, uses groups to organize its data.

The data in the Complete Financials worksheet is organized into three groups: Balance Sheet Information, Income Statement Information, and Cash Flow Information. Each of the groups contains detail items; in some of the groups there are three levels of detail. Groups can generally be collapsed to show only the totals for the group.

Deciding Between a Category and a Group

As you plan your worksheet, you may have difficulty deciding whether your data is more appropriately classified into a new category or separated into a new group. Both categories and groups have advantages and disadvantages. Again, there are no hard-and-fast rules, although each can automate calculations or procedures in certain situations.

As a general rule, use categories to handle repeating sets of information, such as months, years, or similar inventory at different locations, or data that you will want to manipulate into many different views or reports.

Tip

You can hide items in one category if you don't want all of the items to show.

- When a category is repeated, all of the items within the category are also repeated. This can save time when you are setting up the worksheet. Remember, however, that the items in each of the duplicated categories will be identical.

- Categories can reduce the number of formulas you need to use to make calculations in your worksheet. Because each item is reproduced in every category, the same formula will apply to every instance of a item name. Thus, one formula will apply to every cell named "Total."

- Categories can also reduce the amount of time you spend applying styles, since the style format will apply to all instances of an item name. However, you can still modify a specific selection if you don't want to apply formatting to every instance of an item name.

- Categories can be easily rearranged. By simply dragging, you move a category and thus reorganize your data, allowing you to look at it from a different perspective.

- Categories cannot be collapsed. If you want to show only the summary information for a category, you must hide all of the individual items that make up the category.

Groups are usually the appropriate choice if the data contained within the groups is not parallel, or if you will not require multiple views.

- Groups can contain items that are unique to that group and not found in other groups.

- Groups can be automatically summarized. Even when you add a new item to a group, it is included in the summary.

- Groups can be collapsed to show only the summary items.

- Groups cannot be easily moved.

Data Entry and Special-Purpose Views

Data entry views can assist you as you enter the data for your worksheet. Typically, they make data entry more intuitive or less prone to error. The Checkbook Register example (CHKBOOK.IMP) uses scripts and dialogue boxes to mimic the paper check-writing system you are used to working with. The Accounts Receivable (ACCTREC.IMP) model has a data entry view that shows only the items that need to be entered and hides items that are derived from formulas and calculations.

Special-purpose views of the worksheet can be developed to query and analyze your data. In the Accounts Receivable model, you can monitor your accounts and display the customer's account status. The Loan Analysis model (LOAN.IMP) has different views to assess your loan qualifications and repayment calculations.

Some special-purpose views can be used for presentations. For example, the Consolidation and Allocation model (ALLOCATE.IMP) includes a bar chart.

Scripts

Improv includes a powerful programming language called LotusScript. You can use it to automate tasks you perform routinely, or to customize your worksheet.

You can create a script either by recording it or by writing it. If you frequently go through the same steps to accomplish a task, you can turn on the Improv recorder, walk through the steps, and then turn off the recorder, saving the sequence of actions. Then, next time you need to do that task, you play the script and Improv performs the same steps for you.

Writing a script is somewhat more complicated and requires an understanding of the script language and the basic concepts of programming. However, writing scripts can give you very powerful results. For more information on script writing, refer to Chapter 17 and Appendix B.

The Browser

Each Improv model is managed with a Browser, which acts as a table of contents for that model. The Browser is a window, displayed when you open a model, with two "panes": on the left side is a list of the names of the worksheets, views, presentations, and scripts in your model. On the right side are your brief descriptive notes about the currently-highlighted element of the model.

 Tip | If the Browser window associated with a model isn't visible, select the Browser option from the Window menu to display the Browser window.

In addition to acting as a table of contents for your model, the Browser can be used to:

- Rename a worksheet, view, presentation, or script.
- Delete elements from a model.

☑ Cut, copy, and paste elements between models.

☑ Bring a particular worksheet, view, presentation, or script to the front and make it the current window.

The Consolidation and Allocation model included with Improv has an extensive Browser, as do most of the examples. You may wish to study these examples to learn more about the capabilities of the Browser.

LINKING WORKSHEETS WITH FORMULAS

If you develop a model with more than one worksheet, you can write formulas in one worksheet that use data from other worksheets in the same model. These formulas are called *intersheet formulas*.

Intersheet formulas follow a fixed syntax:

☑ The left side of the formula contains a reference to the current worksheet.

☑ The right side of the formula references to other relevant worksheets in the current model.

In the Loan Analysis example model, you can study formulas that link worksheets within the model. For instance, Formula 1 of the Amortization Schedule reads

Payment:Period 1 = Summary::"Payment (monthly)"

This formula assigns the value of Payment (monthly) in the Summary work-sheet to the Payment:Period1 item in the Amortization Schedule worksheet, where the formula resides.

LINKING WORKSHEETS WITH DDE AND OLE

You can only link formulas between worksheets in the same model. To share data between two different Improv models, you must use Dynamic Data Exchange (DDE). In addition, Improv supports Object Linking and Embedding (OLE); OLE allows you to display information from another Windows application in your Improv presentation.

You can use DDE to share data between Improv models or between an Improv model and another Windows application. The two models or applications are joined using a *link formula*. The data is dynamic: it can be updated automatically or manually.

You can use Object Linking and Embedding (OLE) to display data from other applications in an Improv presentation. The original data, whether a graphic, text, or part of another document, becomes an object in the Improv presentation. If the object is linked, Improv contains a reference to the data, but the data resides in a separate file. If the object is embedded, it resides in Improv.

Linking data makes better use of system resources than embedding does, because the data is not repeated in two files. Embedding data is useful when you want to control access to the data or to keep all the data in a single Improv file. In both cases, the object is edited using the original application in which it was created. Chapter 13 covers the use of OLE objects in much greater detail.

Improv 2

- Opening an Example Model

- The Multiview Model

- Creating Multiworksheet Models

Handbook

CHAPTER 11

Creating Dynamic Views

In Chapter 10 you learned how to plan an Improv model and all about its different parts. The Improv model gives you an important element of flexibily in working with your data: You only need to enter your data once, and you can then display it in many different ways. Each different display within the model is called a *view*. Views share the same data, but each view of the data is different. These *dynamic views* mimic your real-world tasks: analysis, summarization, presentation, and so on.

Improv comes with several example models that will help you learn how to create your own models. Each of the examples shows some of the components of Improv, and the techniques used to develop each component. In this chapter you will look at some of the components of one of these models—the Financials model (FINANCE.IMP)—and explore different dynamic views of the model.

Later in this book, in Part 6, you will work more extensively with the Financials model, as well as with the other Improv example models.

OPENING AN EXAMPLE MODEL

If you accepted the default Improv installation and installed all its files, the example models will be stored in the Examples directory. To open the Financials model, select Open from the File menu and select the Examples directory. Then open the file named FINANCE.IMP.

Using the Cascade option on the Window menu, you can rearrange the parts of the Financials model so that they are all visible. Your screen should look something like Figure 11-1.

THE MULTIVIEW MODEL

The Financials model has a Browser window, a Complete view (called the integrated Financials worksheet), and three report views.

FIGURE 11-1

The Financials model
(FINANCE.IMP)

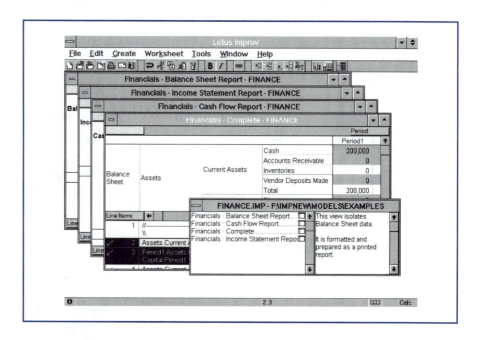

The Browser

In Chapter 2 you learned all about Improv's Browser window. Each Browser acts as a table of contents for the model. When you open one of the example models, its Browser window is also opened. (You can also open a Browser by selecting Browser from the Window menu.) Here is the Browser for the Financials model:

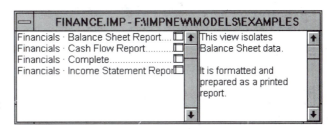

Element list

Element type icons   Note area

If you want to review the complete instructions on using Browser windows, see Chapter 2.

Adding a View to the Browser

Each time you add a worksheet, view, presentation, or script to a model, Improv adds an entry to the Browser. Let's add a new view to the Financials model and see how Improv includes it in the Browser.

In the Browser for the Financials model, highlight the Financials - Complete element. Select View from the Create menu. Improv duplicates this element and adds it to the model, with the default name Financials - View1 - FINANCE. Improv also adds the new view name Financials-View1 on the left side of the Browser. Your Improv window should look like Figure 11-2.

Now change the default view name to one that is more descriptive, such as My Test, using these steps:

1. Double-click Financials - View1 in the Browser window, then press the BACKSPACE key to delete the word View1.

2. Type **My Test** and press ENTER.

Notice that the title bar of the view now reflects the new name. When you change a view name, all instances of the name are updated (in the Browser, intersheet formulas, etc.).

FIGURE 11-2

The Financials model
with an added view

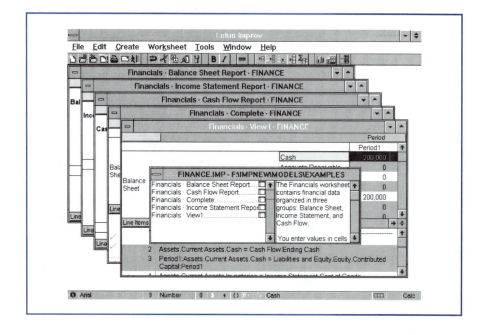

FIGURE 11-2

The Financials model
with an added view

Note

You can also cut/copy, paste, and delete the elements in the left side of the Browser
window. Just select the desired element in the list, and use Cut or Copy, Paste, or
Delete on the Edit menu as needed.

Creating and Editing Browser Notes

After you have renamed the new model element, you can add a note about it on the right
side of the Browser. Just click the Note area in the Browser and begin typing your note.
(Refer to previous illustrations of the Browser for examples of notes.) To edit an existing
note, double-click the Note area and edit the text as desired. To delete text in a note,
double-click and drag to select the text you want to delete, and then press the DEL key.

Your Browser window will now look similar to this one:

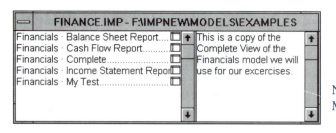

New note for
My Test view

The Complete View Worksheet

One way to organize a model is to enter all of the data in a *complete view worksheet*, and use that as the basis for the other views you create. The individual data items in the complete view worksheet are organized into items and groups, as you learned in Chapter 9. This organization makes it easy to create other views based on the complete view worksheet.

If you start with a well-organized complete view worksheet, you can hide or show information to create new views for analysis or presentations. You have already copied the complete view to a practice worksheet (My Test). A new view of the data can now be created by modifying My Test.

Working with the My Test View

Although the FINANCE model provides a Cash Flow view, you may want to know how such a view was created. Suppose you want to isolate the cash flow information on your worksheet and get an overview of your current situation, including a bar chart of the data. In this situation you will need to hide certain parts of the worksheet and create a summary-level view.

Close the Browser, then click the Maximize button of the window that contains My Test, so there is more room to work. Move the cursor to the bottom of the worksheet. Highlight the six line items that make up the Operations group. Select Hide Items from the Worksheet menu, leaving only the Net item in the group. In Investing and Financing also, hide the detail items and leave the Net items lines showing.

The resulting screen is shown in Figure 11-3. The hidden items are marked by the horizontal grey bars. You should be able to see only the Net line for the Operations, Investing, and Financing groups. The four other groups (Beginning Cash, Net Income, Net Change, and Ending Cash) had only one item per group, so we didn't need to hide any detail. We now have seven summary items in the Cash Flow section of the worksheet.

Hiding the detail line items already gives us a better view of our cash flow, but you might also want to make a bar chart to see a graphic representation of the data (this is covered in greater detail in Chapter 12). Click the Cash Flow group to highlight the group title and its associated data. On the SmartIcon toolbar, click the bar chart icon. Improv creates a presentation, and the summary data is represented there in bar chart form, as shown in Figure 11-4. (If you look at the Browser, you will notice that Presentation 1 has been added to the list.)

If you want to save this chart, the title Presentation 1 in the Browser window can be edited to be more descriptive. Chapter 12 explains how to modify the title and captions and work with the chart more extensively.

Using the integrated Financial worksheet (the complete view), you can also experiment with the effects of collapsing groups. If necessary, review Chapter 9 for complete information on collapsing and expanding groups.

FIGURE 11-3

FIGURE 11-3

The My Test view with hidden items

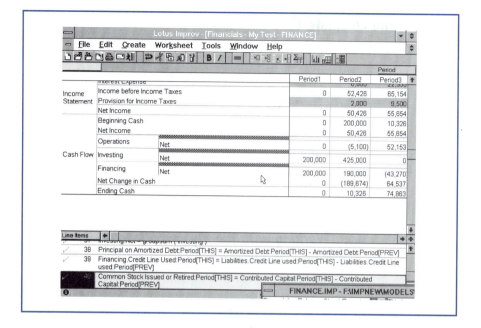

Tip

If you collapse a group, the line items in the group will still show on a chart view of the data. You must hide the items first to get a summary effect in a chart.

FIGURE 11-4

The summarized data shown in bar chart form

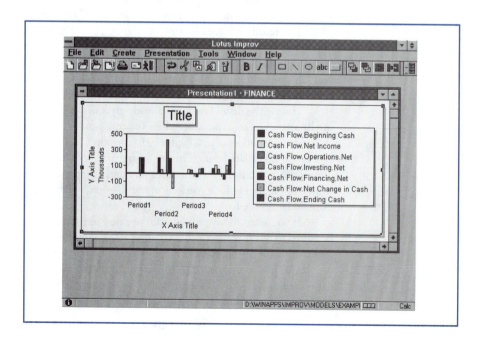

Changing the Display of Elements

In addition to hiding items, and collapsing and expanding groups, you can change the way Improv displays some elements on your screen using the InfoBox. For example, you may want to change the display of markers, grid lines, item names, and text styles in the current view of a worksheet.

Now that you've created new views and added them to an existing model, close the Financials model. Next you'll see at a model with more than one worksheet.

CREATING MULTIWORKSHEET MODELS

In some situations it is appropriate to design a model with more than one worksheet. This decision will be based on the volume and nature of your data, and, to some degree, personal preference. Planning your model was discussed in Chapter 10.

If you decide to include more than one worksheet in your model, you can include formulas in one worksheet that use data from other worksheets in the same model. You learned about these intersheet formulas in Chapter 8.

Linking Worksheets with Intersheet Formulas

In Chapter 20 you will work with another of Improv's example models: the Loans model (LOAN.IMP). This model contains examples of intersheet formulas. For example, the Amortization Schedule worksheet uses values from the Summary worksheet. Formula 3 in the Amortization Schedule is an intersheet formula:

Interest:Period1 = Summary::Principal * (Summary:: ' Interest (annual) ' / 12)

You can practice writing intersheet formulas using the Loan model. Intersheet formulas must include a reference to the worksheet where the data is located. Following are guidelines for creating intersheet formulas; you will also want to review Chapter 8 for additional instructions.

- The left side of the formula contains a reference to the current worksheet.

- The right side of the formula includes references to other worksheets in the current model.

- References to other worksheets are by worksheet name, followed by a double-colon mark and then the name of the cell, range, item, group, or category in the other sheet.

You can copy data from one worksheet to another, rather than retyping it, to prevent possible typing errors.

All intersheet formulas must use data from the same model. If you need to use data from another model, you must access it using Dynamic Data Exchange (DDE), as discussed next.

Linking Worksheet Data with DDE

You can use DDE to share data between two Improv models, or between an Improv model and a worksheet in another Windows application. To link data using DDE, follow the steps detailed in Chapter 8.

Linking Worksheet Data with OLE

You can use Object Linking and Embedding (OLE) to display data from another Windows application in an Improv presentation. The original data, whether a graphic or a part of a spreadsheet, becomes an object in the presentation.

Presentations and the use of OLE are discussed in Chapter 13.

PART FOUR

Presentations with Improv

Improv 2

- Chart Terminology

- Types of Charts

- Creating Charts

- Customizing Charts

- Adding Charts to Presentations

- Printing Charts

Handbook

CHAPTER 12

Working with Charts

Lotus Chart (or simply, Chart) is a program in Improv that lets you create graphic representations of worksheet data. Because it is often easier to understand overall trends or to identify patterns in numeric data when the data are viewed in a graphic format, charts can be especially effective when used for business presentations and in reports.

Chart provides a variety of chart types for your use: Area, Bar, HLCO (High-Low-Close-Open), Line, Pie, and Scatter. Chart's graphing capabilities also let you combine chart types to create a Mixed chart that plots data in different forms on the same page.

> **Note**
>
> Some chart types have three-dimensional (3-D) views, for example, the Bar with Depth and the 3-D Pie. In Chart, chart types that contain the phrase "with Depth" all plot data along two axes, but represent the data in a 3-D view. The 3-D chart types plot data along three axes and represent it three-dimensionally.

You specify chart types from Improv's InfoBox, which appears when you select Settings from the Presentation menu or click the InfoBox icon while you are building your chart.

This chapter explains how to transform your worksheet data into a graphic (chart) format. First you will be introduced to some chart terminology for each chart type to help you become more familiar with Chart. Then, throughout the remainder of the chapter, you will see detailed instructions on how to create, customize, and print charts.

CHART TERMINOLOGY

Before you create a chart, it will be helpful to familiarize yourself with some of the terms used by Chart.

Axis   This is a reference line along which worksheet data is plotted (see the definition of *plot*, just below). Most charts have an x-axis and a y-axis; three dimensional representations also have a z-axis.

Chart   A chart is a graphic representation of numeric data. Charts often include headings and other textual data as well.

Data Points   These are the worksheet values that are plotted in a chart, displayed as small markers, bars, pie slices, and so on. Data points are values from the worksheet which are plotted on the chart (for instance, the amount of sales in one month). These are represented by markers, bars, pie slice, or points on a line.

Grid Lines   Grid lines are optional; when displayed, they extend across the chart area to make it easier to interpret the data values.

InfoBox   The InfoBox lets you select or change chart types and attributes.

Plot   The plot is the area of the chart framed by the x- and y-axes, containing the plotted data. In 3-D chart types, the plot includes a z-axis.

Presentation   A presentation is a document that combines various types of data, such as charts, pictures, drawings, and text, from Improv and other applications.

Legend   The legend is a list of symbols and text that identify the look of plotted data. It is generally placed in a box near the chart.

To change the location of the legend, double-click it—you will be presented with some of the more common choices for locations. Or, just click, and drag it to the desired location. To change specific text within the legend, double-click that text, and you will be allowed to edit it.

Series   A series is a set of related values, such as a column or row of spreadsheet data, plotted on a chart.

Tick Marks   Tick marks are short lines that mark intervals on an axis.

Markers   Markers are used to show the actual data points on a line graph. Markers can be changed by double-clicking the line and selecting a marker from the resulting dialog box.

TYPES OF CHARTS

The various chart types provided by Chart offer a variety of ways to represent your data graphically. You can choose from Area, Bar, High-Low-Close-Open (HLCO), Line, Mixed, Pie, and Scatter (XY) charts, as well as 3-D Bar, Line, and Pie charts.

Because each chart type presents data very differently, you'll want to pick the type of chart that best illustrates the point you are trying to make. The following discussions of the chart types, their SmartIcon representations, and examples of the charts they produce will help you make your chart selections.

Note   In the sections which follow, the Chart Icons for each chart type will be shown next to the related discussion.

Area Charts

Area charts show how values change over a period of time; this chart type emphasizes the size of values rather than their rate of change. For example, you might use an Area chart to see how sales improved over an entire year. Figure 12-1 shows an example of each of these Area chart types:

FIGURE 12-1

Area charts

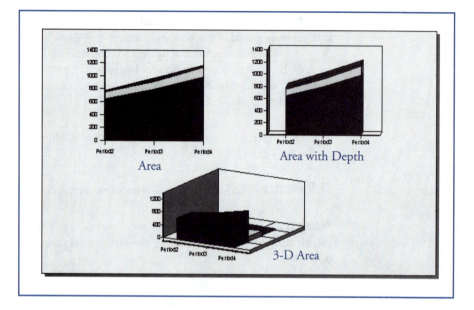

Area

The basic Area chart plots data as it relates to an x-axis and a y-axis. The x-axis is generally used to depict the change in time, while the y-axis shows the actual values being plotted for each time period.

Area with Depth

Like the Area chart, an Area with Depth chart plots the data on an x- and a y-axis, but also draws the chart in three dimensions.

3-D Area

This chart type plots the data on the x-, y-, and z-axes, and displays a three-dimensional view. 3-D Area charts emphasize the totals of the values charted. Chart separates the values into distinct rows, which makes differences easy to recognize.

Bar Charts

Bar charts compare individual items at different points in time, such as monthly or annually. Bar charts also illustrate the frequency of distribution. The size of each bar lets you easily see how values compare to one another. Bar charts are displayed from left to right to give the sense of movement with time.

Chart provides several types of Bar charts, described in the following paragraphs. Figure 12-2 shows the various bar charts available.

Vertical Bar

This chart type tracks individual values at various times, such as motorcycle sales during January, February, and March. You can also use a vertical bar chart to track frequency distribution, for example, the number of motorcycles that come from various manufacturers.

If the selected data has more than one data series, Chart creates a *Clustered* Bar chart and displays each series in a different pattern or color. For example, you could compare motorcycle sales for each week in January at four different retail locations.

Horizontal Bar

Horizontal Bar charts compare individual items at specific times, for example, the return on investment for ten different mutual funds. You can also use this chart type to track frequency distribution—for example, the number of puppies, by breed, sold in 1993.

FIGURE 12-2

Bar charts

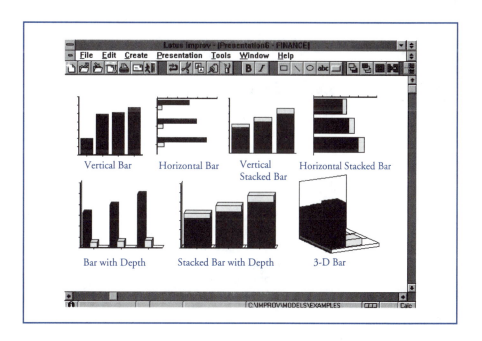

Horizontal charts are used more often when there are only a few sets of data to show. Once the number of bars grows too large, a vertical bar is simpler to read and understand.

Horizontal Clustered Bar If the selected data has more than one data series, Chart creates a Horizontal Clustered Bar chart and displays each series in a different pattern or color. For example, you could compare video rentals during April, May, and June in San Francisco, Oakland, and Berkeley.

 Vertical Stacked Bar This chart type lets you compare totals and individual values at various points in time. The bars represent totals, and the segments of each bar represent individual items. For instance, you might compare the total sales of four brands of cereal, while at the same time viewing the sales of specific brands of cereal within the bar, for each quarter of a year.

 Horizontal Stacked Bar This chart type lets you compare totals and individual values at a specific point in time—for example, comparing the sales of four brands of cereal and the sales of all brands of cereal to the individual and total sales of similar brands sold by a competitor.

Bar with Depth

This chart plots the data in the same manner as the Vertical Bar chart (on x- and y-axes), but draws the chart in three dimensions.

Stacked Bar with Depth

This chart plots the data in the same manner as the Stacked Bar chart (on x- and y-axes), but displays the chart in three dimensions.

3-D Bar

This chart type plots the data on the x-, y-, and z-axes and displays a three-dimensional view. 3-D Bar charts emphasize the totals of the values charted. Chart separates values into distinct rows, which often makes differences easy to recognize. However, be careful using 3-D Bar charts—a tall bar in the front of the chart will make reading the rest of the data difficult or even impossible.

High-Low-Close-Open (HLCO) Chart

Figure 12-3 illustrates an *HLCO (High-Low-Close-Open) chart,* also known as a "stock market chart," which lets you track data that fluctuates over time. The chart uses four series: high, low, open, and close. Vertical lines show the range from *high* to *low* for a specific time period; the longer the line, the greater the high-to-low range. The horizontal markers projecting out from the vertical lines indicate the *opening* and *closing* values during the same period. The left marker indicates the opening value; the right marker shows the closing value.

A typical HLCO chart might track daily changes in pork belly prices over a 30-day period. The vertical lines on the chart would show the high-to-low price range for each day of the month; the horizontal line markers would show each day's opening and closing prices.

If you are charting five data series, Chart plots the values for the fifth series as a Vertical Bar chart below the HLCO chart. If you are charting more than five data series (the HLCO chart option allows up to 23), Chart plots the values for the sixth series on a Line chart in addition to the HLCO chart.

Line Charts

Line charts also show changes in data over a period of time. Similar to Area charts, Line charts emphasize the rate of change over time rather than the size of values. For example, you might use a Line chart to see how sales are improving during the year so far. Each line represents a category of information, and each point along a line depicts a value at a specific point in time.

Line charts are often used for stock quotes. You could have two lines that show the

FIGURE 12-3

HLCO chart

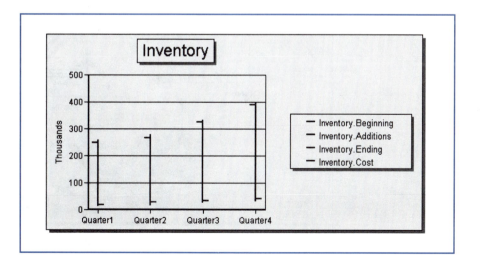

average daily price of two stocks over a 12-month period. Another example is a chart with one line that tracks daily stock prices over one month.

Figure 12-4 shows examples of all the Line charts available within Chart.

Line

The basic Line chart plots data on an x-axis and a y-axis. Several lines may be plotted on the chart at one time. Each of the lines is shown with different markers or colors so that they may be recognized in the group.

Line with Depth

This chart plots the data in the same manner as the Line chart, but displays the chart in three dimensions.

3-D Line

This chart type plots the data on the x- and y-axes in a three-dimensional view. 3-D Line charts use the z-axis to show several values side-by-side rather than horizontally in the

FIGURE 12-4

Line charts

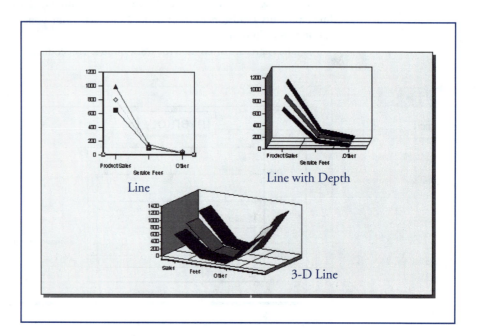

z-dimension. Each range of data thus has its own column within the chart. This is like taking multiple Bar charts and placing them one in front of the other.

Mixed Chart

A *Mixed chart* can combine parts from a Line chart, a Bar chart, and an Area chart, enabling you to display different data in different forms on the same page. For example, you could track ticket sales, attendance, and temperatures for one baseball season at Wrigley Field, with temperature and attendance displayed as lines, and ticket sales as bars.

Each series in the chart can be displayed as a Bar chart, Area chart, or a Line chart. This is changed by double-clicking the series (line or bar) that you want to change, and making your selections from the dialog box shown here:

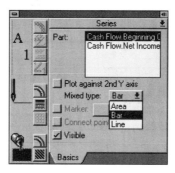

Mixed

This chart is the basic mixed chart, which plots several series of data. Each series, or set of data, can be displayed as a Line, Bar, or Area graph.

Mixed with Depth

This chart plots the data in the same manner as the Mixed chart, but displays the chart with the illusion of depth. This is not as pronounced as the full 3-D effect that is also available.

FIGURE 12-5

Mixed charts

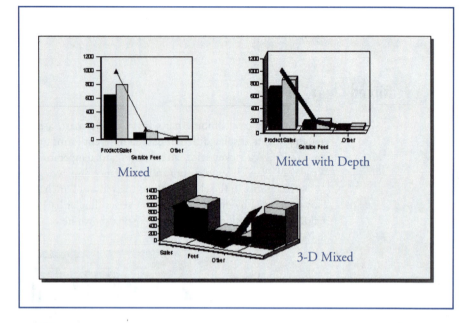

3-D Mixed

This chart type plots the data on the x-, y-, and z-axes and displays a three-dimensional view. As in all 3-D charts, Chart separates values into distinct rows, which makes differences easy to recognize.

Figure 12-5 shows examples of the Mixed chart types available using Chart.

Pie Charts

Pie charts compare different items in one category to the entire category. Each pie slice represents one item, and the size of the slice corresponds to the item's percentage of the total category. For example, you might compare the sales of various brands of chocolate that make up the total chocolate inventory. Figure 12-6 shows the Pie charts available within Chart.

Pie

This is the basic Pie chart, which plots data in a flat, one-dimensional format. Each piece of the pie can be labelled with the actual data, the percentage that the data represents, the item name of the data shown, a combination of these items, or left unlabelled. This is changed when the chart type is selected, using the Layout button.

FIGURE 12-6

Pie charts

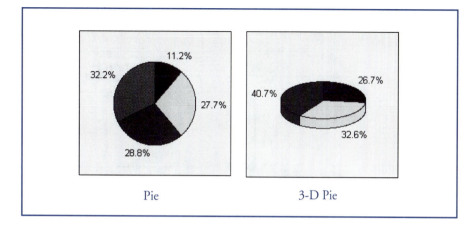

3-D Pie

Chart also provides a 3-D Pie that charts data in the same manner as a regular Pie chart, but with a three-dimensional look.

Scatter (XY) Charts

Scatter charts (also known as XY charts), plot values that change frequently along an imaginary line, to see if a relationship exists between them. If data points appear grouped around the line, then a relationship probably exists; the closer the points come to the line, the stronger the relationship. For example, you could use a Scatter chart to confirm a suspected relationship between night-game attendance at Candlestick Park in October, and wind-chill ranges. Figure 12-7 is an example of a Scatter chart.

CREATING CHARTS

The first step in creating a chart is to select the range of data on which you want to base the chart. Once the data is selected, you use the Create Chart command to create a chart in a new presentation.

Selecting Items to Chart

When you create a chart, first decide which worksheet elements you want the chart to contain: cells, items, category tiles, or formulas. You can create a chart from an entire

FIGURE 12-7

Scatter chart

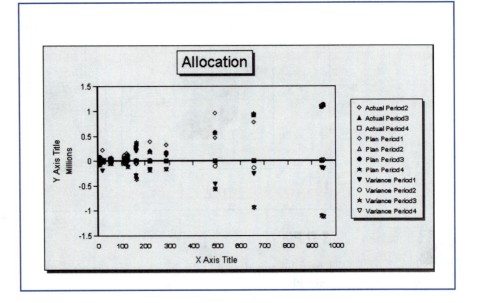

worksheet, or from a range of cells within the worksheet. Within a range of cells, you can select item names, to include item names and their associated cells, or you can select only the data cells.

To make a selection, use one of the following procedures:

- All Items and Cells—click an item; then select Edit Select All. Improv highlights the entire worksheet.

- All Cells—click a cell; then select Edit Select All. Improv highlights all cells that contain values.

- One Cell—click the left mouse button on the item name or cell you want to select.

- Item or Cell Range—click an item name or cell; hold down the mouse button as you drag the cursor over the other item names or cells you want to select.

To select additional data that is not within your selected range, select Worksheet Hide Items to hide the intermediate items (those you want to exclude), then click and drag to select the entire area you want to chart. The hidden items will not be plotted in the chart.

Note

See Chapter 7, "Editing Your Worksheet," or Improv's on-line Help for more information on selecting data.

Creating the Chart

Once you've selected the data from which you want to create a chart, select the Chart option from the Create menu.

Tip

You can also click the SmartIcon that looks like a vertical bar chart to create a chart.

Improv creates a new presentation window and displays a *default bar chart* using the selected data, similar to the chart shown in Figure 12-8. For example, the default Vertical Bar chart contains the following components:

- Title
- Legend
- X-axis
- Y-axis (except for Pie charts)
- Axis titles
- One or more series of data
- Tick marks
- Tick mark labels

FIGURE 12-8

Default bar chart

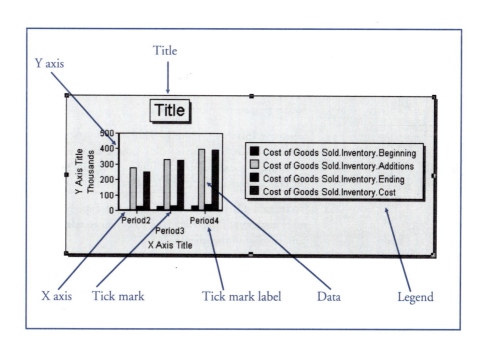

If the default Vertical Bar chart doesn't fit your needs, use the instructions in the next section to customize any chart.

CUSTOMIZING CHARTS

Chart's InfoBox (shown in Figure 12-9) provides you with several ways to customize a chart to fit your needs. You can

- Change the chart type
- Add or change chart components (such as notes and grid lines)
- Change how the data is plotted
- Change chart styles (for chart text, lines, and fills)

Note
For more information on using the InfoBox, see the section, "Improv User Interface," in Chapter 4 or consult Improv's on-line Help.

Changing Chart Types

After you create a chart, you may need to change the default or current chart to another type that illustrates your data more adequately or dramatically. Try applying various chart types until you find the one that best presents your message.

Here are the steps to change the chart type:

1. Select the chart by clicking the chart frame or just inside the chart frame (the border that surrounds the chart).

2. Open the InfoBox (Figure 12-9) by selecting Settings from the Presentation menu or by clicking the InfoBox icon. Or you can double-click directly inside the chart frame to display the InfoBox (be sure not to click any component of the chart, or you will get the InfoBox for that small piece of the chart).

3. To select a different chart type, click the Type box, and then click the representation of the chart type you want to select. (Chart types are explained in detail earlier in this chapter.)

FIGURE 12-9

InfoBox

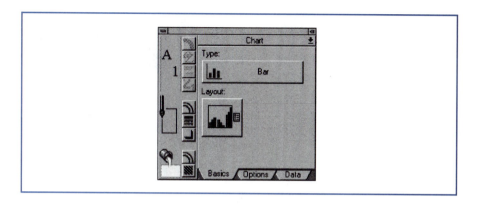

4. Click the Layout box to select a different layout for that chart type. The Layout determines the location of the legend, the location of the title, and whether grid lines are shown.

After you've made your selections, Improv reconfigures the data in the new chart type and layout.

Don't be afraid to experiment. Change the chart type and layout as many times as necessary until you find the format you want, or just to become more familiar with Improv's charting capabilities.

Changing Chart Components

Charts contain several components, such as legends, titles, tick marks, tick mark labels, axes, and axis titles. The components that are available depend on the type of the current chart. You can customize a chart by directly changing its components. You use Improv's InfoBox to do this. Here are the steps:

1. Select the chart you want to modify by clicking either the chart frame or directly inside the chart frame.

2. Select Settings from the Presentation menu, or select the InfoBox.

3. When the InfoBox appears, click the drop-down list next to "Chart" at the top of the Style box. This displays the components associated with the current chart. Here is an example of what you will see:

4. Click the component that you want to add or change; it will display on the selection bar. The settings shown above the Basics tab will depend on the selected chart component. Also, the tools available (on the left side of the dialog box) are based on the component being modified).

5. Click to modify any setting for the component.

6. When the settings are correct, click the Close box in the upper-left corner of the InfoBox to return to the chart display.

Changing Data Assignments

By default, Chart plots the selected data from the worksheet in a row-by-row fashion. To see the information from a different perspective, you can change the way that the chart plots the data.

1. Select the chart by clicking the chart frame or directly inside the chart frame.

2. Open the InfoBox, using the IconBox icon or the presentation Settings main menu option.

Note

If only the Style panel opens (the icons of tools that are shown along the left side of the InfoBox), click the arrow in the top-right corner of the InfoBox to display additional settings for the selected chart.

3. Click the Data tab at the bottom-right of the InfoBox to display the data options for the current chart type, as shown here:

4. Click the Assign Series list box. When the list opens, click the method by which you want the data plotted: By Column or By Row.

    ◪   In all charts except Pie charts, By Column plots each column of data as a series; By Row plots each row of data as a series.

    ◪   In Pie charts, By Column plots each value in a column as a pie slice; By Row plots each value in a row as a pie slice.

Note | Most charts can display up to 23 series. Pie charts can display up to 40 slices.

Changing Chart Styles

Improv's InfoBox also controls a chart's style (that is, its text, line, and fill characteristics). To change parts of a chart's style, follow these steps:

1. Click to select the portion of the chart you want to modify, for example, the title or the legend. Alternatively, select the entire chart to change chart-wide options.

2. Select Presentation Style from the main menu bar. You see the Style dialog box shown in Figure 12-10. You may notice that this is just the left half of the InfoBox!

3. Click any of the following style icons to change style options in the currently selected chart:

    ◪   There are four *text style* icons: Text Color, Font and Point Size, Text Alignment, and Numeric Formats.

FIGURE 12-10

InfoBox style window

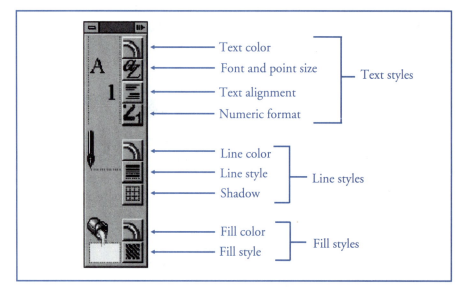

There are three *line style* icons: Line Color, Line Style, and Shadow.

There are two *fill style* icons: Fill Color and Fill Style.

4. When the style options are displayed, click the one you want to modify. Only one option can be modified at a time.

5. When the settings are correct, click the Close box in the upper-left corner to exit the InfoBox and return to the chart display.

Hiding Chart Data

Very often, you may want to give presentations that deal with different parts of your data. Rather than create separate charts, there is a simpler way in Chart.

First create you overall chart, with all the data you need. Then, selectively show and hide the data series in the chart, and print the charts at each step of the way. In this way, you can create a powerful presentation with a minimum number of steps.

To hide data in a chart, and then later show the data, follow these steps:

1. Select the chart by clicking the chart frame or directly inside the chart frame.

2. Select Presentation Settings from the main menu bar.

3. When the InfoBox displays, click the selection bar to display the current chart's components.

4. Click the data series that you want to hide, and then click the Visible box to remove the check mark. Click the box again to redisplay the data.

As a shortcut, just double-click the series you want to change. The InfoBox opens automatically, and you simply select the Visible box to hide or show the data series.

Deleting Charts

If you need to permanently remove a chart, select the chart you want to delete by clicking the chart frame or directly inside the chart frame. Then press Delete, or choose Delete Object from the Edit menu.

ADDING CHARTS TO PRESENTATIONS

Once you have created a chart and adjusted all the components to perfection, you may wish to add it to another presentation. This is a simple procedure, requiring these steps:

1. Select your chart by clicking the border of the chart.

2. Select Edit Copy from the main menu.

3. Move to the presentation into which the chart will be placed, or select Create Presentation from the main menu to create a new presentation.

4. Select Edit Paste from the main menu. You will see the chart appear, and you are now able to move and edit as necessary.

PRINTING CHARTS

Once you've created and customized a chart that you're happy with, or added a chart to an existing presentation, you'll want to print a copy of your work. As with any Windows application, you can print to any printer connected to your computer, or to a file.

The procedure for printing a chart is no different from the procedure for printing a worksheet. Following are some general guidelines; see Chapter 14, "Printing with Improv," for detailed instructions on printing any Improv document.

FIGURE 12-11

Print Preview window

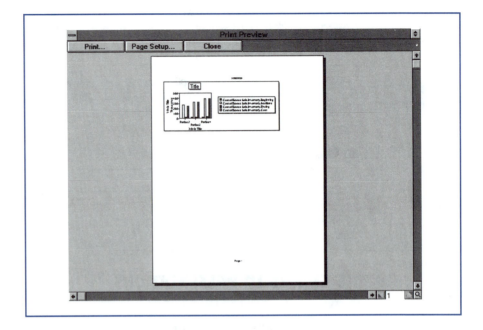

Previewing the Chart

If you wish to preview the chart before printing, select File Print Preview from the main menu.

Figure 12-11 shows a preview of a chart.

Changing the Page Setup

If you preview your chart and it doesn't look right on the preview, click Page Setup in the Print Preview window to open the dialog box shown in Figure 12-12. Here you can

FIGURE 12-12

Page Setup dialog box

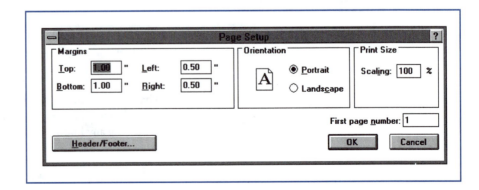

change the Orientation and Print Size settings until the chart is appropriately positioned. Also, change the margins, as well as the Header and Footer, for that final, polished look.

If you forget the meaning of the Orientation settings, look at the icon with an A inside. When you choose a setting, the icon mimics the way the page will look.

Portrait   Choose this orientation to print your chart across the width of the page. This means the printed information on an 8 1/2 × 11-inch page will be taller than it is wide, and the top and bottom margins will be on the short sides of the paper.

Landscape   Choose this orientation to print the chart across the length of the page. The printed information on an 8 1/2 × 11-inch page will be wider than it is tall, and the top and bottom margins will be on the long sides of the paper.

Print Size (Scaling)   To print a larger-than-normal chart, enter a number larger than 100. For example, if you enter 200 in the Scaling text box, the chart prints twice normal size. To print a smaller-sized chart, enter a number smaller than 100. Enter 50, for instance, and you get a half-size chart.

Printers differ in their ability to use scaling. Consult your printer's documentation to determine your printer's capabilities.

When you finish previewing the chart, click the Print command button to print the chart.

Improv 2

- Presentation Objects

- Creating Presentations

- Adding Objects to Presentations

- Refining Presentations

- Printing Presentations

Handbook

CHAPTER 13

Improv Presentations

In Improv, a *presentation* is a combination of different types of documents that present several kinds of data as a unit—such as a quarterly financial report or an enhanced sales presentation.

Improv lets you incorporate both graphics and text from Improv in a presentation; for example, you can create a chart presentation to display data graphically and include all or some of the associated textual data from a worksheet to support the chart.

You can also incorporate information from other applications in your presentation. Improv lets you include a variety of *objects*, which are elements such as charts, text blocks, drawings, and worksheet data that are imported from other Windows applications. For example, you might create a marketing presentation that contains a sales chart created in Improv, a table imported from Microsoft Word that shows past sales statistics, and a flow chart imported from VISIO to illustrate a new sales strategy.

You can print an Improv presentation, or you can display several presentations consecutively on a computer monitor by using buttons on the screen. When you click the button in a presentation, a script is executed telling Improv to open the next presentation. Regardless of what you want to accomplish with a presentation, Improv provides you with the tools to create a lasting impression on clients, customers, or management.

This chapter tells you how to work with Improv presentations. The first part of the chapter explains how to create a presentation, add objects to it, and refine it so that it looks and functions just as you want it to. The remainder of the chapter describes how to print the presentations that you create.

PRESENTATION OBJECTS

Improv refers to each part of a presentation as an *object* and treats each object as one item. Before you create a presentation, you'll want to be familiar with the types of objects Improv lets you include, which are defined just below. Figure 13-1 shows a presentation that includes every type of object.

Button   Buttons are small squares or rectangles that you click to run a script. Buttons are commonly used to present a sequence of presentations, but can be used to start any type of script. Buttons are created from the Create Draw menu.

FIGURE 13-1

Improv presentation objects

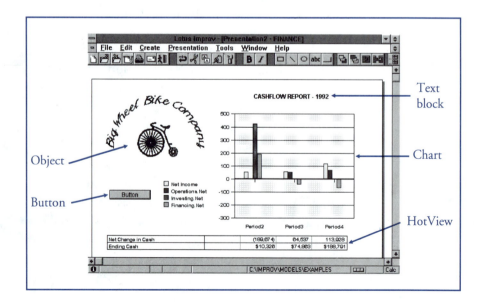

Chart   A chart is a graphic representation of numeric data. Chapter 12 tells you all about creating charts in Improv.

Drawing   Drawings are rectangles, ovals, lines, text blocks, and buttons that you draw and add to your presentation.

HotView   A HotView is a segment of worksheet data that you link to a presentation.

Objects   Presentation objects are pictures, data, text, or sound that you import from other Windows applications.

Text Block   A text block is a frame that you draw, into which you type or paste text.

CREATING PRESENTATIONS

There are two ways to create presentations in Improv: you can create a chart (which opens its own new presentation), or you can create a blank presentation to which you add objects (one of which might be a chart).

Creating Chart Presentations

When you create a chart presentation, Improv stores it in a new presentation window, unless you specify otherwise. Once the chart presentation exists, you can add other objects to enhance it. Charts are more fully discussed in Chapter 12.

Here are the steps to create a chart inside a new presentation:

1. Open the worksheet that contains the data you're going to plot in the chart (if it is not already open).

2. Select the data that you want to chart.

3. Select Chart from the Create menu.

Improv will create the chart and display it in a presentation window, similar to Figure 13-2.

FIGURE 13-2

Improv chart
presentation

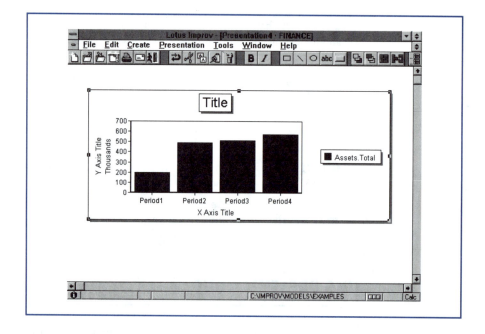

Creating Blank Presentations

A blank presentation starts out as an empty canvas. Beginning with a blank presentation is useful when the presentation you want to create doesn't include a chart. If you change your mind, you can always add a chart to the presentation later.

Here are the steps to create a blank presentation:

1. Select Open from the File menu and select the model for which you want to create a presentation (if it is not already open).

2. Select Presentation from the Create menu.

This creates a blank presentation in your model, ready to be filled with objects.

ADDING OBJECTS TO PRESENTATIONS

As explained earlier in this chapter, Improv treats each part of a presentation as an object. This section explains how to add each type of object to a presentation. Improv lets you have up to 65,536 objects in a presentation!

Adding Charts

If you created a blank presentation without a chart, Improv lets you add one later. To add a chart to an existing presentation, follow these steps:

1.   Select the data in the worksheet that you want to chart.

2.   Select Chart from the Create menu, to display the Create Chart dialog box, shown just below. This dialog box lists a choice called New Presentation, in addition to any other open presentations in the current model.

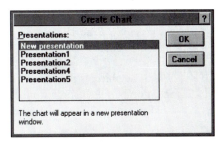

3.   Click the name of the presentation to which you want to add the chart, and then click OK.

If you select an existing presentation, Improv will create the chart object on top of any other objects or charts in the window. You can then click and drag the chart into position. If you chose New Presentation, Improv will create a new presentation window and add the chart.

See Chapter 12 for more information on Improv's charting capabilities.

Improv only lets you add charts to a currently active model; you can't create a chart in one model and copy it to another one.

Adding Drawings

Improv's drawing tools let you add rectangles, ovals, lines, text boxes, or buttons to a presentation. For example, you may want to add a rectangle to frame a group of objects.

Drawing Lines, Rectangles, and Ovals

Follow these steps to add lines, rectangles, or ovals to your presentation:

1. Select the presentation in which you want to draw.

2. Select Draw from the Create menu. On the Draw submenu, click the type of drawing you want to add; or click the Line, Rectangle, or Oval icon on the SmartIcon toolbar.

3. Move the cursor into the presentation window; the cursor changes to cross hairs. (If you select a drawing tool by mistake, press ESC to change the cross-hair cursor back to the arrow cursor, and try again.)

4. Click and drag to create the object in the size and shape you want.

Note

To draw a circle instead of an oval, or a square instead of a rectangle, hold down the SHIFT key while you drag the mouse. As you drag the mouse, a solid line draws the shape of the object.

5. When the object is the size and shape you want, release the mouse button. Selection handles appear around the object, as shown in Figure 13-3. These handles can be used to resize the object.

Note

To deselect a drawing, click anywhere else in the presentation window.

FIGURE 13-3

Selected oval object

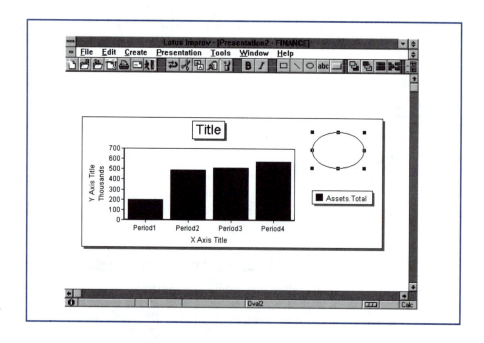

Drawing Text Blocks and Pasting Text

Text blocks are squares or rectangles into which you type or paste text. For example, you can use a text block to add headings, titles, or other information that are not already included in a chart or other object.

1. Select the presentation to which you want to add text.

2. Select Draw from the Create menu and choose Text Block. Or click the Text icon (the one that says "abc") on the SmartIcon toolbar.

3. Move the cursor into the presentation window.

4. When the cross-hair cursor appears, click and drag to create the block in the appropriate size and shape to contain the text you will add. As you drag the mouse, a solid box appears. When you release the mouse, a text cursor appears inside the block.

5. To add new text in the box, just begin typing the desired text at the cursor. Or, if you already have text you want to place in the block, follow the steps below for pasting text.

   To paste existing text into a text block object, follow these steps:

1. Go the application where the text you want to copy is stored. If the application is not running, use the Windows Program Manager to start it. If the application has already been loaded, press ALT+ESC and choose the application from the resulting list.

2. Use the Copy or Cut command to copy the text to the Clipboard.

3. Return to the Improv window. If the text cursor isn't in a text block, double-click the block to edit it (or select the Text icon to create a new text block), and then select Paste from the Edit menu. The copied text appears in the block. The text can now be edited, if necessary.

Adding Buttons

A button is a small square or rectangle that you click in a presentation to run a script (scripts are discussed in Chapter 17 and Appendix B). For example, if you are displaying a series of related presentations on a monitor, you can provide buttons for the viewer to click and move quickly from one presentation to the next. A button might also be used to update values by a percentage, to show future possibilities.

Here are the steps for adding a button to a presentation:

1. Select the presentation to which you want to add a button.

2. Select Draw from the Create menu and choose Button. Or click the Button icon on the SmartIcons toolbar.

3. Move the cursor into the presentation window.

4. When the cross-hair cursor appears, click and drag to create the button in the size and shape you want.

Note

To create a square button instead of a rectangular one, hold down the SHIFT key as you drag the mouse. As you drag the mouse, a solid line draws the button and the name "Button" (which you can't change) appears inside.

5. When you release the mouse, the Attach Script dialog box appears. Follow the steps in the next section to attach a script to the button.

Attaching a Script to a Button

After creating a button, you see the Attach Script dialog box shown in Figure 13-4. You can also select Attach Script from the Tools menu.

Improv stores scripts in library files with the extension .LSS. A script library file can contain one or multiple scripts. The options in the Attach Script dialog box help you select a script to run when you click the button in the presentation. Follow these steps:

1. The File Name list box displays the name of the currently active model and the default script library. Click the list-box arrow to display the list of .LSS files in the IMPROV\SCRIPTS directory, and select the file you want. Or, type in the full path and filename.

FIGURE 13-4

Attach Script dialog
box

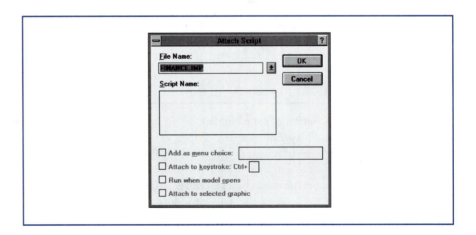

2. The Script Name box lists the scripts for the file selected in the File Name list box. Click the name of the script you want to attach to the button.

3. Verify that the Attach to Selected Graphic check box is checked (because you are attaching the script to a button, this setting will be selected by default).

Note

The other check boxes in the Attach Script dialog box let you add a script as a menu option, associate a script with a hotkey (a CTRL+key combination), or run a script automatically when you open a model. These are settings you might use when you are working with a script in another situation.

4. Click OK to confirm your selections. When the presentation is active, all you'll have to do is click the button to run the attached script.

Adding HotViews

A HotView is data that looks the same in a presentation as it does in the worksheet; that is, the data appears as text rather than as a graphical chart. Use HotViews to add supporting information to a presentation, such as the actual values that a chart represents.

The HotView data is linked to the worksheet, so that when you modify the data in the worksheet, Improv updates it in the HotView, as well.

Caution

You may be tempted to use the Cut/Copy and Paste commands to move a portion of a worksheet into a presentation, but consider this first: when you use Cut/Copy and Paste, you only get a copy of the existing data; if the data gets changed later, your presentation will be out of date! Use HotViews if you want the data to remain current with your worksheet.

Selecting the HotView Data

To select the data for your HotView, use the skills you have already learned for selecting data in worksheets. Using Edit menu options, you can incorporate one cell or many, a combination of item names and cells, just item names, or even the entire worksheet. Or you can click and drag to select the cells and/or items you want. See Chapter 7 or Improv's on-line Help for more information on selecting data.

To select a range of data that is not contiguous within the worksheet, first select Hide Items from the Worksheet menu and hide the items you want to exclude. Then click and drag to select the items you do want to include in the HotView. For example, in a three-column worksheet, to select only the items in the first and third columns, first hide the second column. Then select the first and third columns for the HotView.

Before creating a HotView, select Settings from the Worksheet menu and format the data to be incorporated in the HotView. Once Improv inserts the HotView into a presentation, you won't be able to change the data's text color, font, point size, alignment, and numeric format.

Creating the HotView

Once you select the data that you want for the HotView, select HotView from the Create menu. You will see the Create HotView dialog box shown just below. The Presentations list box lists the item New Presentation, as well as any other presentations that are in the current model.

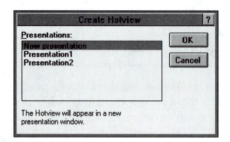

To add a HotView to the presentation, click the name of the presentation to which you want to add the HotView, and then click OK. If you are adding the HotView to an existing presentation, Improv will create the HotView on top of any other objects or charts in the window (the presentation in Figure 13-5 contains a HotView). If the active model doesn't contain a presentation or if you choose New Presentation, Improv creates a new presentation window and adds the HotView.

To move the HotView to a different location or to change its size, use the instructions that appear later in this chapter under "Resizing Objects" and "Moving Objects."

Remember, because the HotView information is linked to the source worksheet, Improv will automatically update the HotView in the presentation if the data is changed in the worksheet.

Adding Objects from Other Windows Applications

You can make your presentation even more dynamic by adding pictures, data, or text from other Windows applications. For example, you could add clip art that you have imported into Microsoft Draw, stylized text created in CorelDRAW!, or a chart created in Lotus Freelance for Windows. You can also use objects from Windows Accessories, such as Paintbrush and Write.

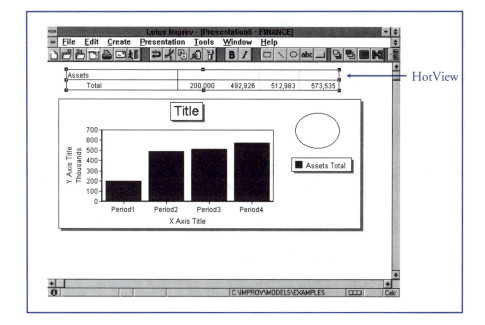

FIGURE 13-5

A HotView in a
presentation

When you import an object from another application, Improv uses the Windows
Clipboard to copy the object, and then uses a Windows feature called *Object Linking and
Embedding (OLE)* to display the object in Improv.

Note

Not all Windows applications support OLE. If you're uncertain whether an application
supports this feature, refer to the application's user manual or your Microsoft
Windows User's Guide for more information.

There are two ways to use objects from other applications in Improv: You can *copy*
existing objects and share them with other applications by creating an OLE link. Or,
while within Improv, you can *embed* in an Improv presentation objects that already exist
or that you create in another application.

To copy an object into Improv from another application, first copy the object to
the Clipboard from the other application. Then choose Paste Special on the Improv Edit
menu. (Any time you Cut or Copy an object within an application, including Improv,
that object is placed on the Clipboard.)

To embed an object, choose Object from the Improv Create menu. In this case,
the application needed to supply or create the new object will be activated. For instance,
if you choose a Word Document object, Microsoft Word for Windows will be started
automatically.

In both of these techniques, OLE allows you to edit the embedded or linked objects
using the original creating application. This adds flexibility to your presentation design
tasks, letting you use the tools that are best for the job.

Before we discuss how to link and embed objects, let's take a closer look at OLE.

About OLE

Windows's OLE feature allows *objects* created in one document, the *source document,* to be used in another document, the *destination document.* Objects are either *linked* or *embedded.* These terms are explained in the paragraphs that follow.

| Note |

This section discusses OLE only as it relates to Improv presentations. See your Microsoft Windows User's Guide for more information.

Object   An object is text, data, or a graphic created in a Windows application. A single cell in a spreadsheet and an entire drawing are both objects. Objects that can be used in OLE operations are determined by Windows, based on the applications that you have installed on your system. These might include Ami Pro Document, Microsoft Excel Chart, Microsoft Graph, Paintbrush Picture, VISIO Drawing, and Word Document.

Source Document   The *source document* is the document from which the object originates. In the discussions in this chapter, the source documents might be created in Microsoft Excel, Lotus Ami Pro, or CorelDRAW!; these applications are also known as *servers.*

Destination Document   The *destination document* is the document into which you will copy or place the object. In the discussions in this chapter, the destination will be an Improv document, and Improv is considered the *client.* You should remember, however, that Improv presentations can also be used by other applications!

Embedding   When an object is *embedded*, Windows takes a copy of the object from the source document and transfers it into the destination document. The copied object does not maintain a relationship to the source document. For example, if you embed a graphic from another application in an Improv presentation and then change the graphic in Improv, the original graphic in the source document is not affected by that change. Likewise, if the drawing is edited in the original application, the copy in your Improv presentation is not affected.

Embedding is similar to using the Cut/Copy and Paste commands, but with one important difference: When you edit an embedded object in the destination document, Windows opens the creating application to let you to make the changes. Embedding lets you modify the object without manually switching between the applications.

Linking   When an object is *linked* (rather than embedded), it maintains a reference to its source document; that is, when you edit the object and save your changes, the same changes are saved in the source document. In addition, changes to the source document are reflected in your linked object. For example, if you link an Excel worksheet into an Improv presentation, you can update and save the worksheet in either application and the changes will be reflected in both documents.

Note

The OLE feature only lets you link objects to an Improv presentation that you've saved as a file in the source application. For example, if you open Windows Paintbrush and create a drawing, you must save it as a file before you link it to an Improv presentation.

Linking ensures that objects remain current in both applications. Be careful, however, that you don't inadvertently change data in an Improv presentation by making changes to the linked data in the source document.

Remember

Changes to linked data update the destination document when you save them in the source document, and update the source document when you save them in the destination document.

Linking an Object

Linking an object allows you to add it to an Improv presentation and maintain a link to the source document in the creating application. To link an object to an Improv presentation, follow these steps:

1. Open the Improv presentation into which you want to add the object.

2. Using the Windows Program Manager, open the application that contains the data or graphic to be linked.

3. Select the item you want to copy, and select Copy from the Edit menu to copy the item to the Clipboard.

4. Return to the Improv presentation.

5. Select Paste Special from the Edit menu. You see a Paste Special dialog box similar to the one shown in Figure 13-6. In the Date Type box, the data type of the object you just copied is highlighted. This is determined by Windows, based on the last application in which a Copy or Cut was performed, and the object that was placed on the Clipboard. In Figure 13-6, the information listed in the Data Type box was generated by copying cells from an Excel worksheet.

6. In the Paste Special dialog box, click the Paste Link command button. Improv retains a link to your source document, and places a copy of the data in your presentation.

FIGURE 13-6

Paste Special dialog
box

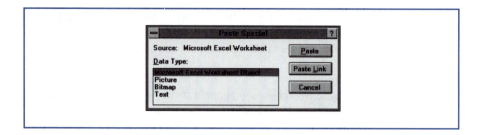

Embedding an Object

You embed an object into an Improv presentation when you only need a static copy of
the object. When an embedded object is changed in Improv, the original object in the
source (server) application is not affected, nor are changes to the document in the source
application reflected in your embedded copy. To embed an object in an Improv
presentation, follow these steps:

1. Select the presentation into which you want the object embedded.

2. Using the Program Manager, open the application that contains the object.

3. Select Copy or Cut from the Edit menu of the source application to copy the
    object to the Clipboard. (If you want the data to remain in the source
    application, select Copy; if you want to remove the data from the source
    application, select Cut.)

4. Return to the Improv presentation.

5. Select Paste Special from the Edit menu. You see a Paste Special dialog box
    similar to the one shown earlier in Figure 13-6. In the Data Type box, the data
    type of the object you just cut or copied is highlighted. As in the procedure for
    linking, this data type is determined by Windows, based on the last application
    in which you performed a Cut or Copy, and on the type of object placed on the
    Clipboard. For example, if you copy an object from Windows Paintbrush, the
    data type will be Paintbrush Picture Object.

6. Click the Paste command button. Improv pastes the object into the presentation.

Creating and Embedding a New Object

To embed an object in an Improv presentation when the object must first be built in
another application, follow these steps:

1. Select the presentation in which you want to create a new object.

2. Select Object from the Improv Create menu. You see the Create Object dialog box shown just below. In the Object Type box are listed the types of objects that you're allowed to create. This list is determined by Windows, based on the software you have installed on your system. For details, see the Microsoft Windows User's Guide or the documentation for the applications that appear on the list.

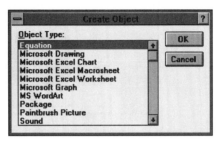

3. Click the object type that you want to create, and then click OK.

4. The Windows application appropriate to the object type you selected will open, and you can create the new object.

5. Once the object is created, to embed it in the Improv presentation choose File Update in the server application (or follow that application's instructions to Update the Object to Improv).

6. Be sure to save the source document (in the server application).

7. Close the server application in which you created the object. The object will appear in the selected Improv presentation.

REFINING PRESENTATIONS

Improv provides you with several ways to refine and enhance a presentation and make it more dramatic or visually effective. You can move and resize objects or object groups, change presentation styles (fonts, lines, colors, and fill patterns), and delete components that are unnecessary or superfluous. This section describes these procedures.

Selecting Objects

The first step in changing an object is to select it. When you select an object, selection handles appear around it, as shown in Figure 13-7.

FIGURE 13-7

Selecting an object
(the chart)

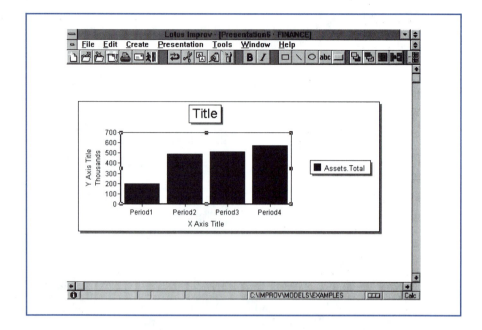

To select an object or several objects, use these selection techniques:

- One object: Move the arrow pointer over the object and click.

- Several objects: Select one object, and then SHIFT+click each of the other objects that are to be selected.

- Several objects in close proximity: Click above and to the left of the first object you want to select, and then drag over the other objects. A box outline appears around the objects, and Improv selects everything inside the box.

- All objects: Choose Select All from the Edit menu.

- Objects with attached scripts: CTRL+click the button or object.

Grouping Objects

Improv lets you classify several objects as a group. This is useful when you need to move or edit several objects at the same time. For example, to change the line style for two objects at the same time, select both objects and classify them as a group. When you select the new line style, Improv will apply it to both objects in the group.

To group several objects, follow these steps:

1. First use either of the following techniques to select objects that you want to group:

   ■ Separate objects: To group objects that are not consecutive or adjacent, hold down the SHIFT key and click each object you want to include. Release the SHIFT key when you've selected the last object.

   ■ Consecutive objects: To group objects that are consecutive or adjacent, click above and to the left of the first object you want to include in the group, and then drag over the other objects. A box outline appears around the objects, and Improv selects everything inside the box.

2. Once you've selected the objects to be grouped, select Group from the Presentation menu. Selection handles appear around the selected objects.

Ungrouping Objects

To ungroup objects that you have grouped, click one of the objects in the group to select the group, and then select Ungroup from the Presentation menu.

Using a Grid to Align Objects

When you need to align several objects, you can use a *grid*. This is useful when, for example, you want the presentation to have a uniform one-inch right margin. When you print the presentation, Improv doesn't print the grid.

Here are the steps for adding a grid to your presentation:

1. Select the presentation, but don't select any of the objects, including the presentation frame.

2. Select Settings from the Presentation menu or click the InfoBox icon. You see the InfoBox shown here:

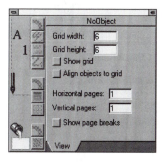

3.   Check the Align Objects to Grid option.

4.   Check the Show Grid option.

5.   In the Grid Width and Grid Height boxes, enter the dimensions of the grid in pixels (pixels are the dots used to place information on your monitor screen). You may want to experiment with this setting to create the most practical grid for your use.

To turn off a grid, uncheck the Show Grid option.

Moving Objects

Caution

If you click and drag the selection handles, you will change the shape and/or size of the object.

One of the easiest ways to customize a presentation is to move objects around to create a more balanced or dynamic look. Improv lets you move objects (or grouped objects) anywhere in a presentation. You can also cut objects and paste them to a different presentation in the same model.

To move objects *within a presentation,* follow these steps:

1.   Select the object (or group of objects).

2.   Click anywhere on the object *except on the selection handles,* and drag it to the new location.

Note

If the object is a button, hold down the CTRL key while you drag.

Tip

A simple way to drag a chart is by clicking and dragging its frame.

To move objects *to a different presentation in the same model,* follow these steps:

1.   Select the object (or group of objects).

2.   Select Cut from the Edit menu.

3.   Open the presentation into which you want to move the object.

4.   Select Edit Paste.

Tip

Once the item has been pasted, use the mouse to drag the item to the best location.

Resizing Objects

If an object is too small to be visually effective or is too large and hides other objects, it's easy to change its size.

First, click the object (or group of objects) to select it. Then use any of these techniques to resize the object:

Widening and Narrowing the Object
To make an object wider, click the *middle* selection handle on either the right or left side of the object, and drag outward. To make an object narrower, click the *middle* selection handle on either the right or left side of the object, and drag inward.

Marking Objects Taller and Shorter
To make an object taller, click the *middle* selection handle on the top edge, and drag upward. To make an object shorter, click the *middle* selection handle on the top edge, and drag downward.

Enlarging or Reducing Objects
To make an object larger, click a selection handle at any corner of the object and drag diagonally outward. To make an object smaller, click a selection handle at any corner of the object and drag diagonally inward. These two motions will change the size but retain the shape of the object. If you drag the selection handles at the sides or center of the item, you will change the size *and* shape of the object.

Changing Presentation Styles

Use Improv's InfoBox Style panel to control the text, line, and fill characteristics of the objects in a presentation. The style elements available in the panel will depend on what object you have selected.

You can use the InfoBox to change a presentation's style at any time. Here is the procedure:

1. Open a presentation, select the object to be modified, and then select Settings from the Presentations menu. You see the Style panel shown in Figure 13-8.

2. Click the style element that you want to add or change.

3. Click the icon for any of the following elements that are available for the currently selected object:

   ◢ **Text style**: Text Color, Font, and Point Size, Text Alignment, and Numeric Format

FIGURE 13-8

InfoBox Style panel

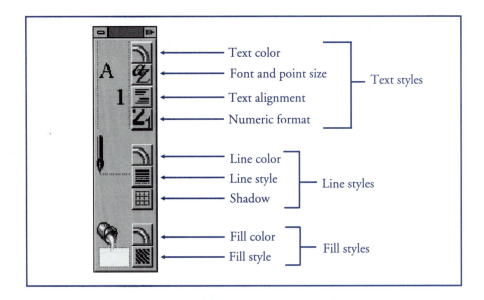

- *Line style:* Line Color, Line Style, and Shadow
- *Fill style:* Fill Color and Fill Style

4. When the options for the style are displayed, click the one you want to modify.

Chart Settings

When you select a presentation chart, the InfoBox will also provide settings specific to customizing the chart. Open the presentation that contains your chart, click the chart to modify, and then select Settings from the Presentation menu. You can also display the Settings panel by clicking the right arrow button at the top of the Style panel. You see the Settings panel shown here:

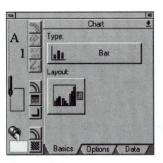

Improv lets you change a variety of chart characteristics, including the chart type, chart components (notes, grid lines, legends, and so forth), and the method used to plot data. The selection bar at the top of the Settings panel displays the currently selected chart component. Depending on the component selected, one or more "pages" of the Settings panel are available, containing the settings available for that component. You select a page by clicking the page Tab at the bottom of the panel.

When the presentation style and settings are as you want them, click the Close box in the upper-left corner to remove the InfoBox from the screen.

Hiding Presentation Data

Hiding certain data in a presentation is often done when you want to print different versions of the same presentation, with some parts hidden or displayed in each version.

To hide objects in a presentation, follow these steps:

1. Select the presentation by clicking on or directly inside of the presentation's frame.

2. Select Settings from the Presentation menu.

3. When the InfoBox displays, click the selection bar to display the current presentation's components.

4. Click the object that you want to hide.

5. Uncheck the Visible box on the Settings panel. You can check the box again to redisplay the data.

Repeat steps 4 and 5 for each item that needs to be hidden.

Deleting Objects

To permanently remove an object from a presentation, click the object you want to delete, and press the DEL key or choose Delete from the Edit menu. If you accidently delete the wrong item, select Undo from the Edit menu.

Creating Pages in a Presentation

If you add objects to a presentation that are too large to fit on one page, Improv will display only what fits. You must create pages in order to include all the data. To add pages (and on-screen page breaks, too, if desired) in a presentation, follow these steps:

1. Open the presentation to which you want to add pages, but *do not* select any objects.

2. Select Settings from the Presentation menu or click the InfoBox icon.

3. In the Horizontal Pages and/or Vertical Pages boxes, type the number of pages you want the presentation to have. Improv adds horizontal pages to the right and vertical pages to the bottom of the presentation.

4. If desired, check the Show Page Breaks option to have Improv display dashed lines as page breaks on screen.

To control what appears on each printed page of a presentation, select File Page Setup to adjust the page scale. See Chapter 14 for more information on printing.

Creating Reports

To create a presentation that can be used as a report, all you have to do is add the elements you want to include on each page of the report, such as a title page, text labels, worksheet data, charts, graphics, and so on, and then insert page breaks in between. Just follow the appropriate instructions in this chapter for all these tasks. There is no limit to the number of pages that a presentation can contain.

PRINTING PRESENTATIONS

Once you have created and refined your presentation, send the output to any installed Windows printer or print file to see a copy of your work. The procedure for printing a presentation is no different from the procedure for printing any other Improv document.

Improv 2

- Getting Ready to Print

- Previewing Documents

- Printing Your Documents

Handbook

CHAPTER 14

Printing with Improv

Once you create an Improv document (worksheet, script, chart, or presentation), you get to see the results of your work. Use any printer installed in Windows to print the document.

This chapter explains how to print professional-looking Improv documents. You can also preview your document onscreen before printing it.

GETTING READY TO PRINT

This section describes the steps you take to prepare your Improv document for printing. This includes verifying your printer setup, adding or changing the document's page setup, and formatting various parts of the document.

Some of the print settings you will use are defaults that you establish through Windows. However, Improv has several additional options for printing; for example, Page Setup, which lets you select the part of a worksheet you want to print as well as control the use of headers, footers, and page numbers.

Setting Up Your Printers

When you install Windows, you have the opportunity to install one or more printers and to specify a default printer and default print settings. These defaults will apply whenever you print from a Windows application, unless you specify differently.

To confirm that the printer you want to use is installed in Windows and set up correctly, you will use Improv's File Print Setup option.

> **Note**
>
> If you don't have a printer installed in Windows or you want to install another printer, click the Printers icon in the Windows Control Panel. See the Microsoft Windows User's Guide for complete instructions on installing a printer.

Selecting a Printer and Designating Its Settings

If you have more than one printer installed in Windows, Improv allows you to select any of those printers for printing your document. You can also change the settings for that printer. At the Improv main menu bar, select File Print Setup; you see the Print Setup dialog box shown in Figure 14-1. The settings in this dialog box are those of the currently selected printer, including its orientation setting and paper size and source.

> **Note**
>
> The Print Setup and Page Setup dialog boxes both contain Orientation options. The Print Setup Orientation options are the defaults for documents printed from any Windows program, including Improv. If you specify a different orientation in Page Setup, Improv will use that setting instead of the one in Print Setup. For instructions on Page Setup, see "Setting Up Pages" later in this chapter.

Default Printer   To select the Default Printer (if it's not already selected), click that radio button. This printer will remain the default for any Windows program, including Improv, until you select a different printer.

FIGURE 14-1

Print Setup dialog box

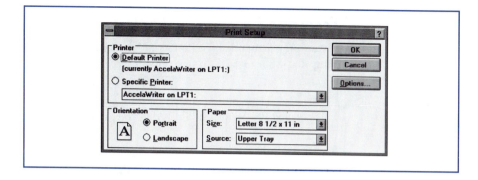

Note
To change the designated Default Printer, click the Printer icon in the Windows Control Panel. See the Microsoft Windows User's Guide for details.

Specific Printer   To select a printer other than the default, click the Specific Printer button. The list box below the button will display a printer name. If you have installed more than one printer in Windows and want to select a printer other than the one shown, click the arrow to open the Specific Printer list box. Use the scroll bar or arrow keys to move through the list, if necessary, and click to highlight the printer you want to select.

Portrait Orientation   Use this Orientation setting to print your document across the width of the page. This means an 8 1/2 × 11-inch page will be taller than it is wide, and the top and bottom margins will be on the short sides of the paper.

Landscape Orientation   Use this Orientation setting to print your document across the length of the page. This means an 8 1/2 × 11-inch page will be wider than it is tall, and the top and bottom margins will be on the long sides of the paper.

Tip

If you forget what portrait and landscape mean, look at the icon with the A inside. When you select an orientation, the icon mimics the way the page will look.

Paper Size   This setting specifies the size of the paper in your printer. To choose a size other than the one shown, click the arrow to open the Size list box, and then click the paper size you want.

Paper Source   This setting tells Improv where to look for paper. If your printer has more than one paper bin and you use a bin different from the one shown, click the arrow to open the Source list box, and then click the paper source you want to use.

Confirming PostScript Printing Options

If your printer supports the PostScript language, click the Options button in the Print Setup dialog box to see additional options specific to PostScript printers (see Figure 14-2).

Print To   These buttons let you send a document directly to the printer, or to an Encapsulated PostScript (.EPS) file that you can print later.

Margins   Click Default to use the default page setup (see "Setting Up Pages" later in this chapter); or click None to exclude margins altogether when the document prints.

Scaling   This option lets you print documents that are smaller or larger than normal. To print the data larger than normal size, enter a percentage number larger than 100; for example, if you enter 200 in the Scaling text box, everything prints twice the normal size. To print data in a reduced size, enter a number smaller than 100; for example, if you enter 50, everything prints one-half normal size.

Color   If your PostScript printer offers color printing, you can click the Color check box to print documents in color. If your printer doesn't print in color, this option will be dimmed.

Send Header with Each Job   A PostScript printer reads a set of generic instructions, known as a header, before printing a document. Click this option to specify that you want Improv to send the header with every print job. (This will add several seconds to the printing time.)

Advanced Options   The Advanced command button displays the Advanced Options dialog box shown in Figure 14-3, which contains additional PostScript settings.

FIGURE 14-2

Print Setup Options dialog box

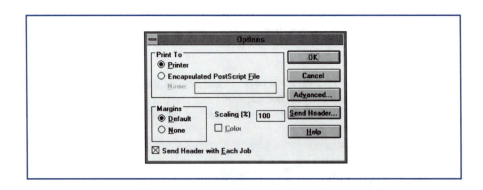

FIGURE 14-3

Print Setup Advanced
Options dialog box

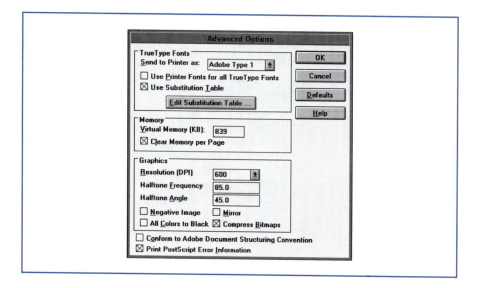

Send Header   This command button offers additional options specific to sending
PostScript header information.

Note

For complete instructions on how to use the settings in the Options and Advanced
Options dialog boxes, see your Microsoft Windows User's Guide and the owner's
manual for your printer. The PostScript options available with the Advanced and Send
Header command buttons are beyond the scope of this book.

Confirming Printer Settings

Once you've chosen the printer you want Improv to use, and all the printer settings are
correct, click OK to confirm your selections and return to the Improv main window. To
exit the Print Setup dialog box without changing any settings, click Cancel.

Setting Up Pages

To get the best results when you print an Improv document, you'll want to confirm that
the overall layout of the page is the way you want it.

To confirm the page setup, select the window you want to print, and then select
File Page Setup from the Improv main menu bar. You'll see the Page Setup dialog box
shown in Figure 14-4. The options in this dialog box let you control how the Improv
document prints. The settings available depend on the Improv document you select.

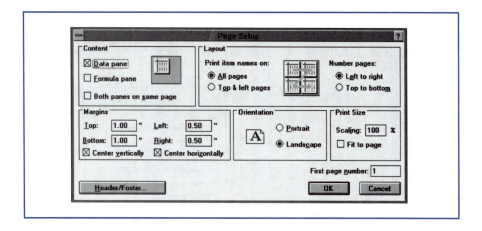

> **Note** Printers differ in their ability to use fonts, graphics, spacing, alignment, and scaling. Consult your printer's documentation to determine your printer's capabilities.

Content

The Content settings are available only when you print a worksheet view. They let you choose how much of the current window you want to print. To enable any of these settings, just click the check box.

Choose the Data pane option to print only the values but not the formulas from which Improv calculates the values. Choose Formula pane to print only the formula pane—for example, if you only want to examine the formulas from which Improv calculates the values in the data pane. Choose Both panes on same page when you want to print both the values and the formulas on one page.

Margins

Margin settings determine the amount of empty space (also known as *white space*) that appears between the printed data and the edge of the page. Improv uses 1 inch as the default top and bottom margins and 1/2 inch as the default left and right margins.

Top, Bottom, Left, and Right   To change any margin, double-click the appropriate text box and type a number (in inches).

Center Vertically or Horizontally   To center the worksheet or chart between the top and bottom margins, click the Center Vertically check box. To center the worksheet or chart between the left and right margins, click the Center Horizontally check box.

Layout

The Layout settings let you specify how you want item names and page numbers to print. To select these settings, just click the appropriate radio button.

Print Item Names on All Pages   Choose this setting to have the row and column item names appear on every page. For example, when you print a large worksheet that takes up several pages, you may want the item names to appear on every page for identification.

Print Item Names on Top and Left Pages   Choose this setting to have row and column items names print only on the pages that represent the top and the left side of the worksheet. For example, if you print a large worksheet and then want to paste it up and reduce it, you can use this setting to print the item names only where they actually appear on the screen view.

Number Pages Settings   When you print a multiple-page worksheet, you can choose how Improv numbers the pages. These settings don't alter what prints on each page; they only affect how Improv orders the printed pages.

Choose Left to right to number printed pages from left to right. Choose Top to bottom to have Improv number printed pages from top to bottom. The following illustration shows how each of these settings will print item names and page numbers:

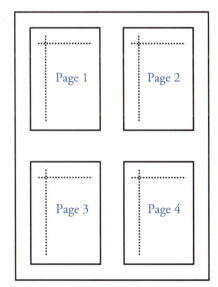
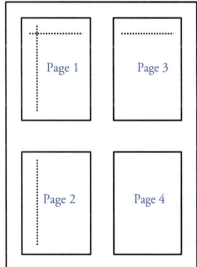

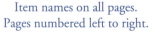

Item names on all pages.
Pages numbered left to right.

Item names on top and left pages.
Pages numbered top to bottom.

There are several ways to control page numbers in Improv documents. Two of these techniques are available in the Page Setup dialog box: To create headers or footers that contain page numbers, use the Header/Footer command button. To begin page numbering with a number other than 1, use the First page number option. (These buttons are explained later in this section.) You can also print a specific range of pages, as explained in the "Printing Your Documents" section later in the chapter.

Orientation

Improv uses the orientation settings in the Printer Setup dialog box unless you specify a different orientation here in the Page Setup dialog box. (See "Selecting Your Printer and Designating Its Settings" earlier in this chapter.) To enable these settings, click the appropriate button.

Portrait   Use this Orientation setting to print your document across the width of the page. This means an 8 1/2 × 11-inch page will be taller than it is wide, and the top and bottom margins will be on the short sides of the paper.

Landscape   Use this Orientation setting to print your document across the length of the page. This means an 8 1/2 × 11-inch page will be wider than it is tall, and the top and bottom margins will be on the long sides of the paper.

Print Size

The Print Size settings let you specify whether you want your Improv document to print in a reduced or expanded size, or to print so that the data fits within the page.

Scaling   To print the data larger than normal size, enter a percentage number larger than 100; for example, if you enter 200 in the Scaling text box, everything prints twice the normal size. To print data in a reduced size, enter a number smaller than 100; for example, if you enter 50, everything prints one-half normal size.

Printers differ in their ability to use scaling. Consult your printer's documentation to determine your printer's capabilities.

Fit to One Page   Click this check box to have Improv make the printed data fit one page whenever possible.

First Page Number

When you want to print a document that is in the middle of another document, use the First page number text box to enter the specific page number you want printed. For example, if you're printing an expense report that appears after page 20 of an annual report, you would click this text box and enter 21.

Headers/Footers

Headers and footers appear at the top (header) and bottom (footer) of each printed page, separate from the body of the document; they contain information such as page numbers, titles, and chapter or section names. The Header/Footer command button lets you control the headers and footers that print in your document.

Click the command button to bring up the Header/Footer dialog box shown in Figure 14-5. Notice that both the Header and Footer boxes contain information.

The Header box contains the code for the default Improv header: {C}{M}. This centers the model name as the header, at the top of each page.

The Footer box contains the code for the default Improv footer: {C}Page {#}. This centers the word "Page," a space, and the page number, at the bottom of each page (for example, "Page 5").

Improv lets you delete the default header and footer and type in your own information, or select automatic text options from the Text Marker list box to create a header or footer. The methods for creating and formatting headers and footers are discussed below.

Excluding Headers/Footers   If you don't want headers and/or footers to print on your document, delete the default codes in the Header and Footer boxes and leave the boxes blank.

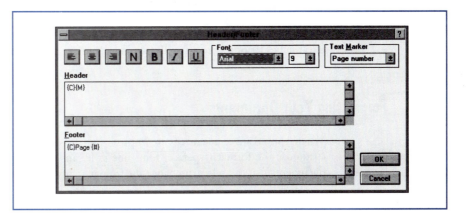

Typing Headers/Footers   To type in your own header and/or footer, highlight any existing text or codes using the text cursor, then press DEL. Type the text that you want to appear. For example, if you're printing a chart that's part of a report, type in the report name.

Automatic Headers/Footers   To create a header and/or footer using the automatic text options in the Text Marker list box, follow these steps:

1.   Use the cursor to highlight the existing header/footer codes or text and press DEL.

2.   Click the Text Marker list box. When the list displays, click the markers that represent the text you want inserted in the header/footer. Improv inserts a code in the header/footer that corresponds to each marker.

3.   Place the cursor in the Header/Footer box where you want additional text, punctuation, or spaces to appear, then type the text, punctuation, or press the SPACEBAR.

For example, to have the footer read "1 of 12," "2 of 12," "3 of 12," etc., click the text markers Page number and Total pages. Place the cursor between the {#} and {P} codes that appear and press the SPACEBAR once. Type **of**, then press the SPACEBAR again. The Footer box should now contain {#} of {P}.

Formatting Headers and Footers   Improv also lets you specify a particular font, alignment, and attribute (bold, italic, underlined) for headers/footers. The Font boxes in the top center of the Header/Footer dialog box (Figure 14-5) list the available fonts and font sizes. The seven icons at the top left represent formatting options: alignment (left, center, and right); and attributes (N for normal—no bold, italic, or underline, B for bold, *I* for italic, and U for underline).

To designate a font, use the text cursor to highlight the text you want formatted. Click to open the Font list box and select the font you want to use.

To change the alignment, place the cursor before the header/footer text and click the icon that represents the alignment you want to apply. Improv inserts a format code into the header or footer that reflects your alignment and attribute selections.

Formatting Your Documents

When you create a document in Improv, use the Improv InfoBox shown below to customize the format (typeface, font, line style, and chart style) before you print the document. You can select or change the format at any time.

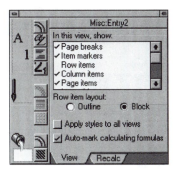

To display the Improv InfoBox, select Worksheet Settings from the main menu bar, or click the InfoBox icon at the left end of the dynamic status bar. For instructions on using the InfoBox, see Chapter 4.

PREVIEWING DOCUMENTS

Improv's Print Preview feature lets you see, before you print, how a document will look. The preview resembles a printed page and includes headers, footers, page numbers, and other elements such as objects and pictures.

To preview, select the worksheet view, chart, script, or presentation that you want to print, and then select Print Preview from the File menu. Improv displays a window similar to the one shown in Figure 14-6.

Using the Print Preview Window

Examine the various parts of your document in Print Preview to ensure that headers, footers, page numbers, and page breaks appear in the correct place.

- *If the document has more than one page,* click the Page Forward and Page Backward buttons at the right of the horizontal scroll bar to preview other pages. The page number appears in the box between the two Page buttons.

- *To enlarge a part of a page so you can examine it more closely,* click the Zoom icon (the magnifying glass at the far-right end of the horizontal scroll bar). Use the scroll bars to move over the page. Then click the Zoom icon again to return to the regular page preview mode.

When you finish reviewing the document, use the following command buttons (at the top of the window) to continue your printing tasks:

FIGURE 14-6

Print Preview dialog box

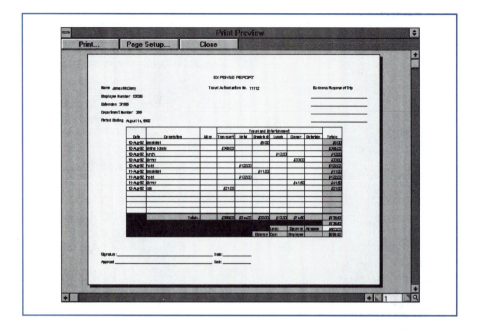

Print   To print your document, click the Print command button to display the Print dialog box. This dialog box is explained in the next section, "Printing Your Documents."

Page Setup   To change the page layout settings before you print, click the Page Setup command button to display the Page Setup dialog box. This dialog box is explained in "Setting Up Pages," earlier in this chapter.

Close   Click this command button to exit the preview window without printing the document and return to the Improv main window.

PRINTING YOUR DOCUMENTS

Once you have selected a printer, entered a document's page settings, and previewed the document, use Improv's Print command to send the document to the printer.

Improv always prints the document in the active window. If you have several views of a document that you want to print, select each window/view individually and issue the Print command for each one.

Selecting Print Settings

When you're ready to print a document, select File Print from the main menu bar. You'll see the Print dialog box shown in Figure 14-7. The Printer line at the top displays the currently selected printer.

Print Range

The settings in this box let you specify whether you want to print the entire document, specific cells, or a range of pages. To enable any setting, click the appropriate radio button.

All   If a document has several pages, choose this setting to print the entire document. Also, choose All to print an entire worksheet and not just specific cells.

Selection   Choose this setting to print specific cells of a worksheet. First, at the main window, click a cell and drag the mouse until the cells you want to print appear within the dotted outline that's displayed as you drag. Then click the Selection radio button in the Print dialog box.

Pages   Choose this setting to print a range of pages; for example, pages 3 through 5 in a ten-page document. Select the Pages option, and then enter the range of pages you want to print. In the From text box, enter the first page you want to print; in the To text box, enter the last page you want to print.

Print Quality

This text box lets you specify the output resolution of your printed document. For example, if you are using a PostScript printer, you can choose a higher resolution in dots

FIGURE 14-7

Print dialog box

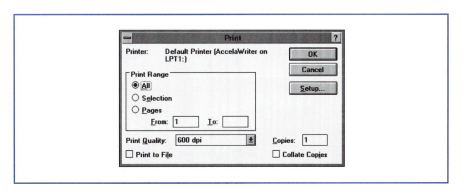

per inch (dpi) for a better-looking document. The selections available will depend on the capabilities of the selected printer. If the selected printer does not support any variation in resolution, this option isn't available.

Print to File

Click this check box when you want to send the data to an ordinary disk file instead of printing it. (This ordinary disk file differs from an .EPS file, which contains special printing instructions for PostScript printers.) For example, you might want to print several documents to separate files, and then use a macro or batch command to print all the files at once.

Note

To print to a file, install a printer driver and configure it to print to a logical port called FILE, instead of the printer port your system usually uses (for example, LPT1). See your Microsoft Windows User's Guide for complete instructions on setting up your system to print to a disk file.

When you select Print to File, each time you print the system will prompt you to enter the location and name of the target print file—for example, you might type in C:\IMPROV\DOCS\WORKSHEET.PRN. Later, you can use the DOS COPY command to print the file. If your printer connects to the first parallel port, you would use the following command at the DOS prompt to print the file:

COPY /B WORKSHEET.PRN LPT1

PART FIVE

More Improv

Improv 2

- Importing Data Files

- Exporting Worksheet Files

- Importing Text Files

- Exporting Text Files

- Exchanging Improv Files

Handbook

CHAPTER 15

Importing and Exporting

Because people use applications other than Improv, it is important to know whether Improv can share data. Importing data involves reading files created by other applications, while exporting data involves writing Improv data into files that can be read by other applications.

Improv allows import and export of data to and from the more popular spreadsheet formats. These include Lotus 1-2-3 files from DOS, Windows, and Macintosh platforms, Microsoft Excel files, and Improv data files from the NeXT machine.

Because Improv reads 1-2-3 and Excel files, you can easily transform those files into Improv format. This means you don't have to rebuild spreadsheets created in 1-2-3 or Excel in order to work with them in Improv. From the other point of view, Improv also writes to 1-2-3 and Excel files, which lets you work with Improv worksheets in those applications. For example, you might *import* a 1-2-3 spreadsheet to take adantage of Improv's dynamic on-screen viewing and analysis capabilities. If you change the data in Improv, just *export* the file back to 1-2-3 or Excel to update the original file with your changes.

If you want to share data with other applications, first save the file as an ASCII text file in your application, and then import the file into Improv. By default, Improv recognizes any file that has a .TXT filename extension as a text file, although other files names can be used. Similarly, to transfer Improv data to a program that can't read the Improv format, you export the worksheet to an ASCII text file.

IMPORTING DATA FILES FROM 1-2-3 AND EXCEL

If you have moved to Improv from 1-2-3 or Excel, or have associates that are still using them, you may be relieved to find out that Improv allows you to read spreadsheets created with these applications.

Improv can read data files in the following formats:

- Lotus 1-2-3 for Windows (Version 1), with the filename extension .WK1

- Lotus 1-2-3 for Macintosh (Version 1), with the filename extension .WK1

- Lotus 1-2-3 for DOS (Versions 2 and 3), with the extensions .WK1 and .WK3

- Lotus 1-2-3 for Windows (Version 4), with extension .WK4

- Microsoft Excel for Windows (Version 4.0), with the filename extension .XLS

Preparing Worksheet Files for Importing

Before you import a worksheet file into Improv, take the following steps to prepare the file. This will help you to achieve the best results when you import the file.

- Redisplay any hidden data that you want Improv to import.

- If you want to import discrete sections of a spreadsheet, assign a range name to those ranges. Improv will import each range name as a separate worksheet within your model.

- If the file contains multiple spreadsheets and you want to import each spreadsheet as a separate Improv worksheet, create named ranges for the data in each sheet. Then, import the named ranges into Improv.

- Rewrite formulas to reference only the cells that you are going to import.

- Delete macros. Since Improv doesn't use macros, this will save space in the Improv file.

- If you create the file in 1-2-3 for Macintosh and want to transfer it to Improv on a PC, create the PC file with the extension .WK3. This can be imported like any other 1-2-3 file.

The Importing Procedure for Worksheet Files

Once you have prepared your file to help ensure that the data will be correctly transferred to Improv, follow these steps to import the file:

1. Select the File menu, and then select Open.

2. Click the List Files of Type list box, which opens and lists the types of files that Improv imports.

   Excel (*.xls)
   1-2-3 (*.wk3)
   1-2-3 (*.wk1)

3. Use the scroll bar or arrow keys to move through the list; find and click the file type that you want to import.

Remember

Another way to move through a drop-down list is to press the first letter of the item you want to select. For example, press L to move to the first item beginning with L.

4. The Directories line displays the current drive and directory. If the file you want to import is in another location, double-click the name of the drive and/or directory you want. The files of the current drive and directory then appear below the File Name text box.

5. Click the name of the file you want to import; the name then appears in the File Name text box.

6. Once the dialog box reflects the specific file you want to import, click OK (or click Cancel to discontinue the procedure). You then see the Worksheet Import dialog box shown in Figure 15-1. Complete the settings in this dialog box as described in the following paragraphs.

Worksheet Import Settings

The two radio buttons in the Import section let you specify what to do with the imported data. Just click to enable one of these settings.

- *As a new model* lets you create a new model with the imported data. You should save the model as a new file.

- *As worksheets added to current model* lets you import the data to a new worksheet in the currently active Improv model.

Import Ranges

Here you will see the *Entire worksheet* choice, along with any range names you created in the source spreadsheet (the one you want to import).

Worsksheet Import
dialog box

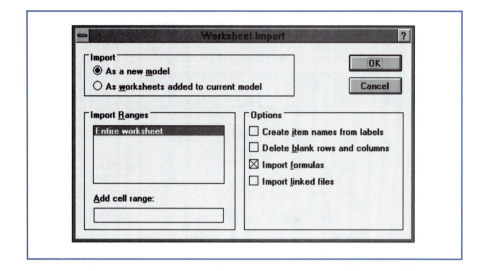

Click *Entire worksheet* to import all the data into one Improv worksheet. Or click the range name that represents the data you want to import. To import several ranges, hold down the SHIFT key and click each name in the list that you want to select. (Remember: Improv imports each range as a separate Improv worksheet.)

Add Cell Range To import an unnamed range, type a range address in this box (using 1-2-3 or Excel syntax) and press ENTER. The range will be added to the Import Ranges box.

Options

The Options box presents several options for how Improv will treat the imported data.

- *Create Item Names from Labels:* Enable this option to have Improv create item names from the labels in the top row and left column of the imported spreadsheet. If you don't enable this option, Improv will name row items 1, 2, 3..., and will name column items A, B, C, and so on.

- *Delete Blank Rows and Columns:* Enable this option to eliminate blank rows and columns from the imported data; otherwise, Improv will import the blank rows and columns along with the data.

- *Import Formulas:* Enable this option to import both cell values and the formulas from which Improv calculates the values. Leave the check box unmarked to import only cell values.

- *Import Linked Files:* Select this option to import, as separate worksheets, all files linked to the imported file. To import only the main spreadsheet, leave the check box unmarked, and Improv will exclude linked files.

Starting the Import Operation

Once your entries in the Worksheet Import dialog box are correct, click OK to start the import operation (click Cancel to discontinue the procedure). When the procedure has finished, the imported data is displayed in one or more worksheet windows, depending on how you chose to import the data.

What to Expect

Figure 15-2 illustrates a sample Excel spreadsheet after being imported into Improv, and the Worksheet Import dialog box settings used for the operation.

Figure 15-2a displays the Excel worksheet, which compares quarterly production profits and calculates the profit margin.

Figure 15-2b shows the settings that Improv uses to import the file. Notice that the Import Ranges box displays the names assigned to the various cell ranges in the Excel file.

Figure 15-2c shows the result of importing the worksheet from Excel into Improv. Improv has removed blank rows and has created item names from Excel worksheet labels. The formula pane shows the formulas that Improv converted from the Excel syntax to the Improv syntax.

Customizing Imported Worksheet Files

When you import data from 1-2-3 or Excel, Improv only formats the column width. Any formatting from the source application, such as special typefaces and borders, are not imported. You will need to modify the imported worksheet to display the data in the format that fits your needs. Here are some guidelines for improving the look and functionality of your imported data files:

- *Rename items:* Use the Cut and Paste options on the Edit menu to move text from the item name cells into the data area, or double-click an item name to edit its name.

- *Rename categories:* Double-click a category tile to edit the text.

- *Group related items:* Click a cell and drag until the cells you want to group together appear within the dotted outline that's displayed as you drag. Select Create Item Group from the main menu bar.

- *Resize rows and columns:* Move the cursor over the line that separates a row or column. When the cursor changes from an arrow to a double-headed arrow, click and drag the line to the width or height you want.

- *Rename the worksheet:* Select Browser from the Window menu. Double-click the worksheet name to edit the text. To add a note about each worksheet, click

FIGURE 15-2

Importing an Excel
worksheet into Improv

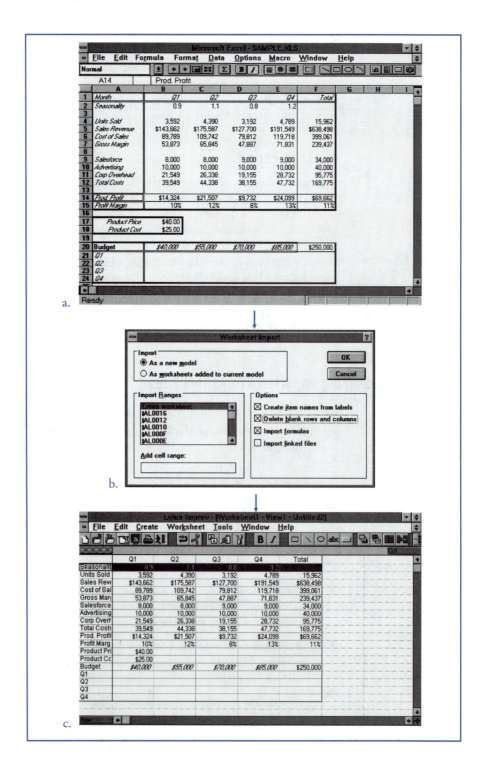

the worksheet name in the left pane, then type the information at the text cursor that appears in the right pane, which is the note area of the Browser.

▨ *Rewrite repetitive formulas:*   If the same formula appears in the formula pane for several cells, change them into general Improv formulas.

▨ *Rewrite commented formulas:*   Improv ignores anything that follows a double slash (//) in a formula line. If a double slash appears before any formula, double-click the formula and delete the //.

Note	See Chapter 8 for complete instructions on using formulas, or position the cursor on any line in the formula pane and press F1 to see Improv's on-line Help topic, "Editing Formulas."

EXPORTING IMPROV WORKSHEET FILES

Not only does Improv allow the importing of data files, it can also export data into other file formats. These formats include the same formats available for import. This allows you to share Improv data with your associates who are still using other spreadsheet programs.

Preparing Data Files for Exporting

If the Improv model that you're exporting contains formula overlaps, use the Edit Clear dialog box to display the values you want to export.

The Exporting Procedure for Worksheet Files

Once you have prepared the Improv model for exporting, follow these steps:

1. Select Save As from the File menu. You will see the Save As dialog box shown in Figure 15-3.

2. Click the Save File As Type list box, which opens and lists the types of files that Improv exports, including the following:

    1-2-3 (*.wk3)
    1-2-3 (*.wk1)
    Excel (*.xls)

3. Use the scroll bar or arrow keys to move through the list. Click the file type that you want to export.

4. The Directories line displays the current drive and directory. If the file you want to create is in another location, double-click the name of the drive or the directory you want. The files of the current drive and directory will appear below the File Name text box.

5. Click the name of the file you want to export. The name appears in the File Name text box. If this will be a new file, enter the name of the file in the File Name text box.

6. Once the dialog box reflects the specific file you want to create through the export, click OK (click Cancel to stop the export). You will see the Worksheet Export dialog box shown in Figure 15-4. Complete the settings in this dialog box as described in the following paragraphs.

Worksheet Export Settings

The three check boxes in the Export section let you specify which elements of the worksheet you want exported. Just click to enable one or more of these options.

☑ Select *Cell contents* to export cell values.

☑ Select *Formulas* to export the formulas from which Improv calculates the values.

☑ Select *Item names* to convert item names to labels in the exported file.

Remember

Another way to move through a drop-down list is to press the first letter of the item you want to select. For example, press L to move to the first item beginning with L.

FIGURE 15-3

Save As dialog box

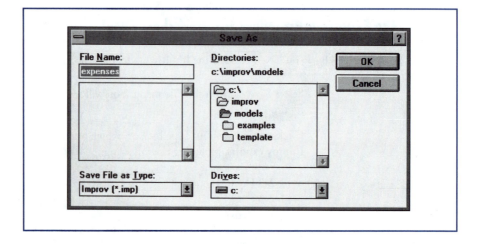

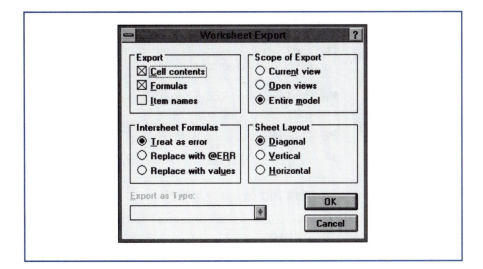

Intersheet Formulas

The buttons in this box let you specify how to handle formulas that refer to cells that did not get exported.

▰ Select *Treat as error* when you want the opportunity to cancel the export procedure if any exported formula refers to a cell that wasn't exported.

▰ Select *Replace with @ERR* to have 1-2-3 or Excel display ERR in any cell containing a formula that refers to a cell that wasn't exported. This allows you to quickly find the errors once you are in 1-2-3 or Excel.

▰ Select *Replace with values* to export the value, but not the formula itself, calculated by a formula that refers to a cell that wasn't exported. In this way, all your information is intact. Unfortunately, you lose any formulas affected.

Scope of Export

The buttons in this box let you specify the amount of data you want to export. For instance, if the model contains a presentation view that you don't want exported, use these settings to exclude the presentation. Just click to select the option you want.

You can choose *Current view* to export only the currently displayed worksheet view, *Open views* to export all open views in the currently active model, or *Entire model* to export one view of each worksheet in the currently active model.

Sheet Layout

The Sheet Layout buttons let you choose how the contents of exported pages or worksheets will be exported.

- *Diagonal* lays out the data in a diamond pattern—that is, diagonally from the upper-left corner to the lower-right corner of the worksheet.

- *Vertical* tiles the data vertically.

- *Horizontal* tiles the data horizontally.

Starting the Export Operation

Once your entries in the Worksheet Export dialog box are correct, click OK to start the export procedure (click Cancel to discontinue the procedure).

IMPORTING TEXT FILES

To import data from a program with a file format that Improv can't read, you need to first save the file in your other application as an ASCII text file, and then import the file into Improv. For example, you might want to export a report created in Quicken and then import it into Improv to use the advanced formatting features to enhance the report.

Improv recognizes any file with a .TXT file extension as a text file. Select the file type All files to import files without extensions, or with extensions other than TXT.

How Improv Imports Text Files

When you import a text file, Improv reads the file as a series of records separated by carriage returns. Each record contains several text fields separated by *delimiters*—symbols such as a tab character, space, or comma that mark the beginning and end of a unit of data. For example, a tab character (produced by pressing the TAB key) can mark the beginning of a string of text.

For each line in the text file, Improv creates a row in the resulting worksheet. For every text field separated by a delimiter in the longest line of the file, Improv creates a column. Improv displays the contents of each delimited text string in a separate cell.

If you enclose a text string in quotation marks, Improv reads the text as a single field, regardless of its contents, and even ignores blank spaces and delimiters. For example, Improv reads

(617 phone numbers)

as three fields, but reads

"617 phone numbers"

as one field.

Preparing Text Files for Importing

Before you import a text file into Improv, take the following steps to format the file and ensure that the text you import appears correctly within Improv. This preparation helps you to achieve the best result when Improv converts the file to a worksheet.

- ◢ Insert carriage returns to separate the lines of text that you want to appear in separate rows in the Improv worksheet.

- ◢ Within each line of text, place delimiters (such as tabs, spaces, or commas) around and between the text you want to appear in separate cells (columns).

- ◢ If the text you want to import into one cell contains spaces and/or the character you're using as a delimiter, enclose the string in quotation marks. For example, to import the string

    Wright, Nicole

  enclose it in quotation marks, thus:

    "Wright, Nicole"

- ◢ If you want text to be enclosed within quotation marks in the Improv file, enclose it in two sets of quotes in the text file. Improv will strip out the first set of quotation marks when it imports the file. For example, to import

    "Reed, Donna"

  enclose it in another set of quotes, thus:

    ""Reed, Donna""

- ◢ If the text file will fill more than 256 columns or 8192 rows of a worksheet, break it up into smaller files and import them separately.

- ◢ If you're using commas as delimiters, make sure you remove comma separators from any numbers that you want to appear within one cell.

- ◢ To have Improv treat numbers as text (for example, to display zip codes or phone numbers), enclose them in quotation marks.

- ◢ Remove non-ASCII characters and empty text fields from the file.

> If you're creating the text file in Ami Pro, click the ASCII Options button in the Save As dialog box. Under ASCII File Options, choose the option called "CR/LF at paragraph ends only," and disable the "Keep style names" setting.

The Importing Procedure for Text Files

The procedure for importing text files begins with the File Open dialog box, just as it does for importing data files. The only difference occurs when you select the file type in the List Files of Type list box; look for these file types:

Text (*.txt)
All files (*.*)

Once you click OK in the Open dialog box, you will see the Text Import dialog box shown in Figure 15-5. Complete the settings in this dialog box as described in the following paragraphs.

Text Import Settings

The two radio buttons in the Import section let you specify what to do with the imported data. Just click to enable one of these settings.

> *As a new model* lets you place the imported text in a new model. You will then save it as a new file.

> *As a worksheet added to current model* lets you import the text into a new worksheet in the currently active Improv model.

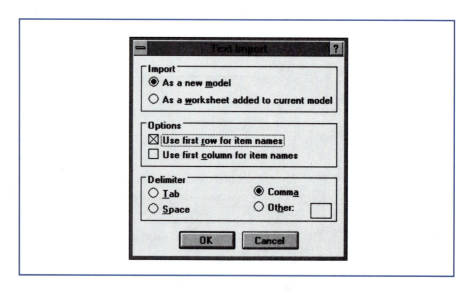

Options

Once you tell Improv how you want to import the text, use the two Options choices to customize the handling of the imported data. To convert the text fields into names for the column items, click the *Use first row for item names* check box. To convert the text fields into names for each row item, click the *Use first column for item names* check box.

Delimiter

Click the button for the delimiter symbol you want to use to mark the beginning or end of a unit of data; for example, a tab character might be used to mark the beginning of a string of text. You can select one and only one character as a delimiter.

▨ *Tab, Space, or Comma:* Surround each field of text within the rows of data that will be imported. Only a single delimiter is used between fields.

▨ *Other:*   If you choose this button, you can type into the text box your own choice for a delimiter character. The text that falls between two of the characters you specify—for instance, two periods—will be imported into a separate cell.

Caution

When you select your delimiter, be sure that your data file does not contain the delimiter within the data. For instance, the description of a sales item might be 42" Fishing Rod. This is innocent enough, except that the import will not read the data correctly—the " symbol, used to mean inches, will make Improv believe a string has started.

Starting the Import Operation

Once your entries in the Text Import dialog box are correct, click OK to start the import operation (or click Cancel to discontinue the process). When the procedure has finished, the imported data is displayed in one or more worksheet windows, depending on how you chose to import the data.

What to Expect

Figure 15-6 illustrates a sample text file after being imported into Improv, and the Text Import dialog box settings used for the operation.

Figure 15-6a is an invoice text file in Microsoft Word for Windows. The file uses commas as delimiters. The delimiters tell Improv which information to put into each column. In addition, the first line of the file supplies the item names for Improv.

Figure 15-6b shows the settings that you want Improv to use to import the text file.

Figure 15-6c shows the result of importing the INVOICE.TXT file from Microsoft Word into Improv. Improv has imported the file into a new model and created item names from the first row of text.

Importing a text file
from Word for
Windows
into Improv

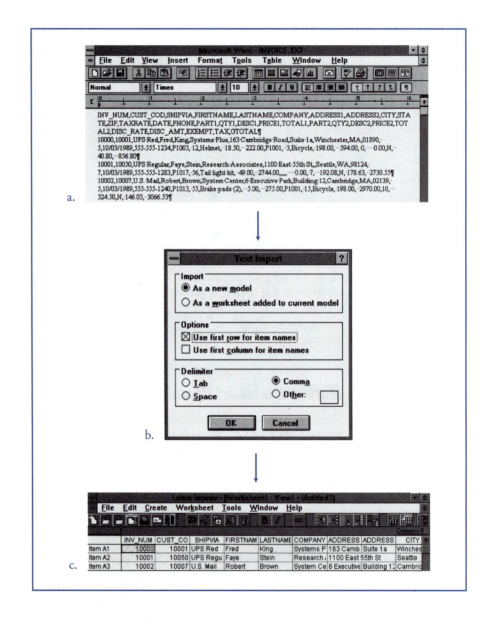

Customizing Imported Text Files

When you import a text file, Improv excludes any formatting from the source application, such as special typefaces. You will need to modify the imported text file to display the data in the format that best fits your needs. Here are some guidelines for improving the look and functionality of your imported data files:

- ▨ *Rename items:* Use the Cut and Paste options on the Edit menu to move text from the item name cells into the data area, or double-click an item name to edit its name.

- ▨ *Rename categories:* Double-click a category tile to edit the text.

- ▨ *Rearrange data:* Click and drag a category tile to a different tile location, to rearrange the data and view the information from another perspective.

- ▨ *Resize rows and columns:* Move the cursor over the line that separates a row or column. When the cursor changes from an arrow to a double-headed arrow, click and drag the line to the width or height you want.

- ▨ *Format numbers:* Select Presentation Style from the main menu bar. Click the Number icon (the fourth icon from the top of the InfoBox) to modify the numeric style. See the Improv on-line Help topic, "Assigning Numeric Formats To Cells," for more information.

EXPORTING TEXT FILES

Improv lets you save a model or worksheet as an ASCII text file. This allows you to transfer analysis results, calculations, and reorganized data from Improv to other applications.

Preparing Text Files for Exporting

Before you export a text file from Improv, prepare the file according to the following instructions. This formats it to ensure that the text you export appears as you want it to in the target application. This preparation helps you to achieve the best results when Improv exports the file as ASCII text.

- ▨ Use Create Category to place at least one category in the column area, if one doesn't already exist. Though not required, it's best to have only one category in the column area.

- Redisplay hidden items: Click the far upper-left corner of the worksheet; then select Worksheet Show All from the main menu bar.

- Remove empty cells from the worksheet: Click the empty cells and press Delete.

- If you want exported text to appear within quotation marks in the target application, enclose it in another set of quotes in the text file. Improv will strip out the first set of quotation marks when it exports the file. For example, to import

    "Reed, Donna"

  enclose it in another set of quotation marks, thus:

    ""Reed, Donna""

Tip

> Save scripts (files with the extension .LSS) as ASCII text files when you edit them in a word processing program. When you save a script as an ASCII text file, Improv doesn't display the Text Export dialog box. To reimport the script to Improv, import it as ASCII text using the instructions in the previous section.

The Exporting Procedure for Text Files

The procedure for exporting text files begins with the File Save As dialog box, just as it does for exporting worksheet files. The only difference occurs when you select the file type in the List Files of Type list box. Look for these file types:

    Text (*.txt)
    All files (*.*)

Once you click OK in the Save As dialog box, you will see the Text Export dialog box shown in Figure 15-7. Complete the settings in this dialog box as described in the following paragraphs.

Text Export Settings

The Text Export settings let you specify the format you want the exported data to have. Just click the check box for the options you want to use.

- To export formatted cell values, select *Styles*.

- To convert item names to the first field in each row or as field heads in the first record, select *Item names*.

- To insert a blank line in between views in the exported file, select *View separator*.

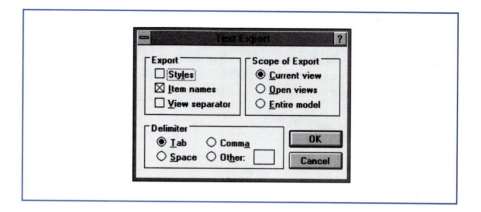

FIGURE 15-7

Text Export dialog box

Delimiter

Click the button for the delimiter symbol you want to use to mark the beginning or end of a unit of data. You can select one and only one character as a delimiter.

▰   *Tab, Space, or Comma:*   Select one of these characters to export text into a text file, using the selected delimiter (a tab, space, or comma).

▰   *Other:*   If you choose this button, you can type in the text box your own choice for a delimiter character. The text that falls between two of the characters you specify—for instance, two periods—will be exported into a separate cell.

Scope of Export

The buttons in this box let you specify the amount of data you want to export. You can choose *Current view* to export only the currently displayed worksheet view, *Open views* to export all open views in the currently active model, or *Entire model* to export one view of each worksheet in the currently active model.

Starting the Export Operation

Once your entries in the Text Export dialog box are correct, click OK to start the export operation (or click Cancel to discontinue the procedure).

What to Expect

Figure 15-8 illustrates a sample Improv worksheet after being exported as an ASCII text file, and the Text Export dialog box settings used for the operation.

Figure 15-8a is the Improv worksheet; it compares loan payment scenarios.

Figure 15-8b shows the settings that you want Improv to use to export the text.

Figure 15-8c shows the result of exporting the Improv LOAN worksheet into Microsoft Word for Windows as an ASCII text file. Improv has formatted the file to include commas as delimiters. The delimiters tell Improv which information to separate as sentences.

FIGURE 15-8

Exporting an Improv worksheet as an ASCII text file

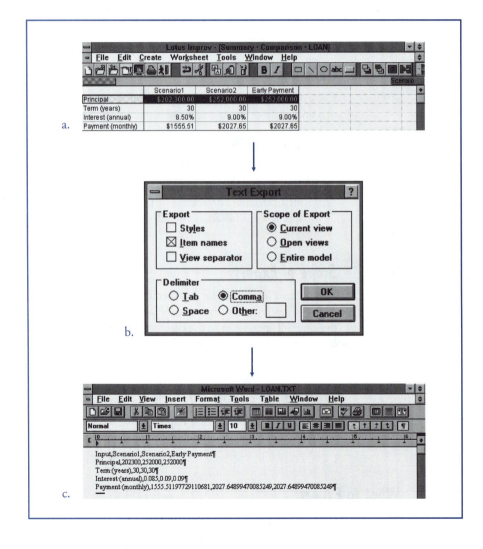

■■■■■■■■■■■■■■■■■■■■■■
EXCHANGING IMPROV FILES

The Improv ASCII file format lets you exchange files between Improv 2.0 for Windows and versions of Improv that run on NeXT computers. Files saved in the Improv ASCII file format have the extension .IMX. You first save information created in Improv 2.0 for Windows as an .IMX file, and then open the .IMX file in Improv 1.0 or 1.01 for NeXT, or vice versa.

Exporting Files to the NeXT Environment

To export an Improv file from Windows to the NeXT environment, follow the same procedure outlined in the previous section, "Exporting Text Files." However, select the Improv text (*.imx) file type in the Save As dialog box's List Files of Type list box.

Importing Files from the NeXT Environment

To open a file created using the NeXT version of Improv, follow the same procedure outlined in the previous section, "Importing Text Files." However, select the Improv *.imx file type in the Open dialog box's List Files of Type list box.

Improv 2

- Working with the User Setup Dialog Box

- Using Templates

- Customizing Improv's SmartIcons

Handbook

CHAPTER 16

Customizing Improv

Improv allows you to customize it in a variety of ways, to help you complete tasks with greater efficiency and get the most out of Improv's features.

This chapter describes

- How to use Improv's User Setup options to customize the program's operating characteristics

- How to customize and use *templates* in Improv to make worksheet creation easier and more efficient

- How to modify the various SmartIcon toolbars to display icons for the tasks that you perform most frequently

WORKING WITH THE USER SETUP DIALOG BOX

Figure 16-1 shows Improv's User Setup dialog box, which lets you customize the Improv screen environment and some aspects of how the program operates. To display this dialog box, select User Setup from the Tools menu.

When you select the User Setup dialog box for the first time, Improv displays the default settings, which remain in effect until you change them, even between Improv sessions. You can return these setup options to their original settings at any time by clicking the Restore Defaults command button.

The Settings Check Boxes

The Settings check box options let you control a number of Improv's program features. These are global options, which are in effect for all models. Any or all of the options below can be enabled at one time.

FIGURE 16-1

User Setup dialog box

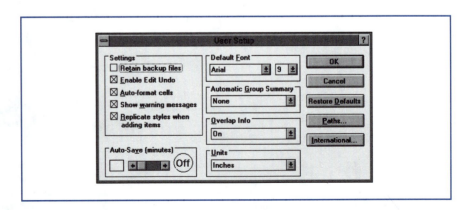

Retain Backup Files

When this check box is enabled, Improv saves a backup version of every one of your Improv model files. These backup files are stored in the directory \IMPROV\BACKUPS (unless you've specified a different backup directory using the Default Paths dialog box, explained later in this section). When Retain Backup Files is not enabled, Improv deletes the backup file when you close a model.

Improv creates a backup file when you first open a model. In this way, you can always return to the way the file was before you started making changes. This is also the copy used if you select Revert to Saved from the File menu.

Improv saves backup files under the model's own filename, adding the extension .BAK; script backup files use the extension .LBK.

Enable Edit Undo

When you turn on this setting, Improv will save previous keystrokes or selections, so that it can activate the Edit Undo and Edit Redo commands. With this setting turned off, execution time improves, but you won't be able to reverse and replicate your Edit commands with Edit Undo and Redo.

Auto-Format Cells

Turn on this setting to have Improv automatically format cells based on the values entered there. For example, if you enter a fraction such as 5/10, Improv will assume you're entering a date and will format the value accordingly; if you enter $350.00, Improv will format the cell as currency with two decimal places. With this decision made, future values entered in these cells will automatically be formatted correctly. When this setting isn't turned on, you have to choose the format for worksheet cells.

You can change the format of an auto-formatted cell at any time using the Improv InfoBox Style panel (see Chapter 4).

Show Warning Messages

When this setting is enabled, Improv will display warning messages in a dialog box; otherwise, most warning messages are suppressed.

Replicate Styles When Adding Items

This setting gives you an alternative to replicating cells using the Edit Cut, Copy, and Paste options. Turn on Replicate Styles When Adding Items, and you can add items and automatically copy their styles from the last existing item. When this setting isn't enabled, you must specify Styles for each new item.

Other User Setup Options

The other options in the User Setup dialog box are list boxes that offer you various choices for customizing Improv for your own working environment.

Auto-Save (Minutes)

You can set the interval at which you want Improv to automatically save open files. (If you enabled the Retain Backup Files setting described above, Auto-Save will only create or update a backup file the first time that it saves a file.)

There are two ways to set the Auto-Save interval:

- Double-click the Auto-Save box at the left of the scroll bar. In the box, type the number that represents how often (in minutes, from 5 to 60) you want Improv to save your work. For example, to save every 15 minutes, type **15**.

- Click and drag the button in the slider bar. Move it to the left or right until the desired interval appears in the Auto-Save box.

To turn off Auto-Save altogether, move the slider button to the far left, or simply type **0** in the box.

Default Font

Improv's default font is Arial 9 point. If you want to use another font and/or point size as the default for your model, first click the Default Font list box to display the list of currently installed fonts. Then just scroll to the one you want and click to select it. To select a point size, follow the same steps: click the Default Font point size box to display the available point sizes, and select the one you want.

Automatic Group Summary

Improv uses your setting for this option to automatically create a group summary item each time you create a group. This summary item appears as the last item in the group and calculates the selected summary type for grouped items in the same category.

To set the Automatic Group Summary option, click to open the list box and then select the type of summary you want Improv to automatically calculate for the group summaries it creates. Your choices are as follows:

- *None:* Improv will not automatically create group summaries.

- *Total:* A sum of the group items.

- *Average:* The average value of the group items.

- *Minimum:* The smallest value in the group.

- *Maximum:* The largest value in the group.

- *Count:* The total number of items grouped.

- *Standard Deviation:* The square root of the variance (that is, to measure the variance of individual group items from the group mean); a standard deviation of zero indicates that all items in the list are equal.

- *Custom:* A value other than the ones provided in the list box. Improv will add a summary item to the group with the default name Custom, but will not add the formula to the formula pane. You type in a formula that references the item name Custom.

Overlap Info

This option controls how Improv handles one formula overlapping another.

Select the option that fits your own needs. Choose On (the default), and Improv will show a list of formulas that the current formula overlaps. If you choose Off, Improv will suppress all overlap information regarding worksheet formulas.

Choose the Audit setting to have Improv display, in the formula pane, specific information on where the overlap occurs, and a list of overlapping formulas. When Audit is selected, Improv's performance may be affected. If you need to use Audit, you may want to enable the setting only for brief periods, and use the On setting the rest of the time.

Units

Improv uses inches as the default unit of measurement. If you prefer to use another unit of measurement, you can choose centimeters, points, or picas for this setting.

The Command Buttons

Following are descriptions of the functions performed by the command buttons in the User Setup dialog box.

Restore Defaults

Click Restore Defaults to restore the User Setup settings to their default status.

Paths

Click the Paths command button to bring up the Default Paths dialog box shown in Figure 16-2. Here you can control the default directory location for Improv models, scripts, backup files (as discussed earlier in this chapter), and the startup model. (The startup model is the worksheet that Improv opens when you start the program or select New from the File menu.) To change any path, just double-click it; when the text cursor appears, type in the new path. Click the OK button to confirm your changes.

International

Clicking the International command button displays the International dialog box. Here you can control how you want to sort data and choose the character set you want to use when you import data. These options are especially useful if you work with firms in Europe and other parts of the world. Following are descriptions of each setting; Figure 16-3 shows the defaults.

Collate Options   These radio buttons let you specify the way that you want Improv to sort letters and numbers when you select Sort Items from the Worksheet menu. The default, International, tells Improv to sort numbers first and then letters. If you select Swedish or Nordic, you can choose whether you want to sort numbers first or last, by

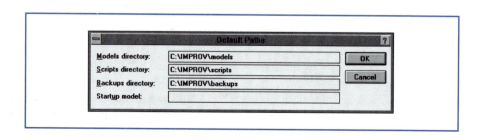

FIGURE 16-2

Default Paths dialog box

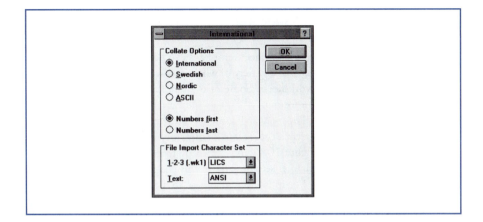

clicking one of the bottom two radio buttons. If you select ASCII, the program sorts letters first and then numbers.

File Import Character Set   The list boxes in this section let you specify the character set Improv should expect when importing Lotus 1-2-3 and ASCII text files. The default for 1-2-3 files is the Lotus International Character Set (LICS); other options are the ASCII and International character sets. For text files, the default is the ANSI (American National Standards Institute) character set; other options are International and Country.

USING TEMPLATES

A *template* is a special type of Improv model that you use as a pattern for other similar models. For example, you can create a worksheet with the item names and format of a monthly budget or quarterly report and save it as a template. Then, when you are ready to do a budget or report for a particular month or quarter, you simply type the relevant data into the template.

When you create templates, include the same elements that you include in any model you create: worksheets, charts, and presentations.

Improv includes a few predesigned templates for you to use. If you chose the default Improv installation, these templates are stored in the directory C:\IMPROV\MOD-ELS\TEMPLATE. If you installed Improv with custom options, the template files only exist in the C:\IMPROV\MODELS\TEMPLATE directory if you chose to transfer the files for Example Models and Templates.

If you can't find the template files in the TEMPLATE directory, use the Improv installation program to install them.

Using Improv's Templates

Improv's worksheet templates can be used as is or customized for your own needs. The templates fit a variety of worksheet scenarios and are easy to use as patterns to build your own worksheets. Some of the templates include formulas; others include only row and column formats.

To open an Improv template, select File Open, and in the Open dialog box double-click the Template directory name. Select the filename of the template you want (see Figure 16-4) and click OK to confirm your selection (see the "Using the Custom SmartIcons" section later in this chapter).

The following table describes each template:

Template File	Worksheet Contents or Function
100BY100.IMP	100 rows and 100 columns.
10BY10.IMP	10 rows and 10 columns.
123WK1.IMP	Two categories; worksheet resembles a .WK1 file.
123WK3.IMP	Three categories; worksheet resembles a .WK3 file.
AGGREGAT.IMP	A recurrence formula that calculates a running total.
BUDGET.IMP	Four categories.
BYMONTH.IMP	Columns for each month in the year.
CATEGORY.IMP	Three categories.
DAILY.IMP	Generates 365 days from the starting date entered.
FINDALL.IMP	A database query to extract all matching values.
FINDONE.IMP	A database query to extract one value.
GROUPS.IMP	Unique item groups.
LOOKUP.IMP	Uses the LOOKUP function across worksheets.
MOVAVG.IMP	Shows how to calculate a moving average.
QTRLY.IMP	Monthly columns grouped by quarter and year.
SERIES.IMP	A recurrence formula.
YRQTRLY.IMP	Months grouped by quarter and years in a different category.

FIGURE 16-4

Displaying template files in \IMPROV\MODELS\TEM-PLATES

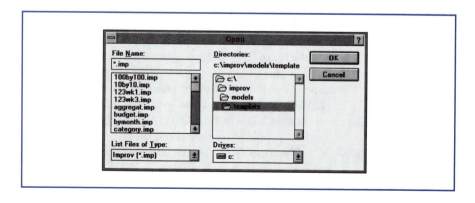

For example, to create a worksheet that keeps a running total of something, use SERIES.IMP; to track company expenses by month and quarter, use the worksheet in QTRLY.IMP.

Some of Improv's templates are quite simple; others are more complex. Open a couple of the template files to get an idea of how the templates look and how to use them. To change the data in existing cells, just click the cell and type your data. Refer to Chapter 7 and Chapter 8 if you need help in adding new row and column items, categories, groups, and formulas.

The following paragraphs explore three of Improv's templates in more detail and make suggestions for ways in which you might use them.

10BY10.IMP

The 10BY10.IMP template, illustrated in Figure 16-5, contains ten rows, ten columns, and two categories. There are no predefined formulas in the worksheet.

You might use this template to track employee information, for example. Each row could contain an employee name, and each column could contain items of information about hire date, pay rate, accrued sick time, and accrued vacation time, for each employee.

BUDGET.IMP

The BUDGET.IMP template, illustrated in Figure 16-6, contains several line items and four categories. In the columns, the Plan category contains the item groups Actual, Budget, and Variance; the Period category contains, within each Plan category, columns for four fiscal periods and a total. In the rows, the Division category contains the item groups Division1, Division2, and Total; the Line Item category contains a line item for each budget item within each Division.

There are four predefined formulas in the worksheet. Click each formula in the formula pane, and look at the data pane to see the items associated with each formula. By adding your own data, you can track actual, budgeted, and variance figures for a company with two departments or two locations.

| Tip |

If you don't want to group the line items into different divisions, delete all but one line item in each division; then click the Division category tile and select Delete Category from the Edit menu. (Improv doesn't allow you to delete categories that contain more than one item.)

MOVAVG.IMP

The MOVAVG.IMP template, illustrated in Figure 16-7, calculates a moving average, using a general recurrence formula for the calculation.

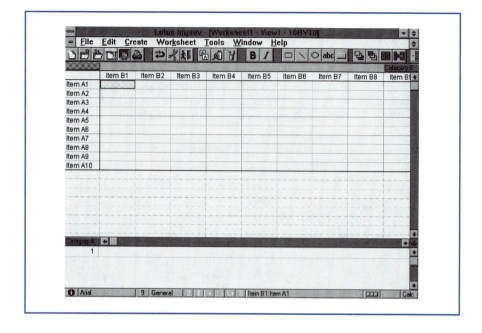

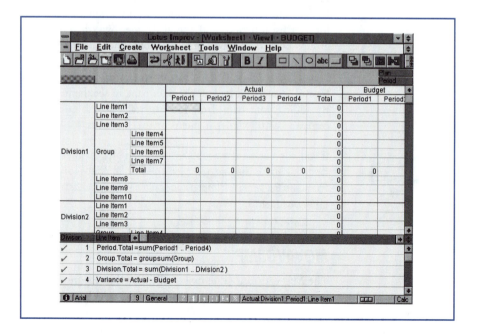

FIGURE 16-7

The MOVAVG.IMP
template

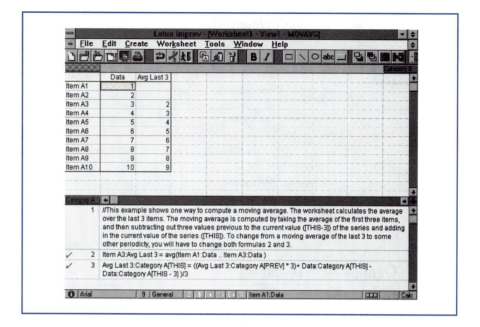

Look at the formula pane. The information for formula 1 is a formula comment, and explains how to use the formula in this template. You might, for example, use MOVAVG.IMP to find the three-month average of sales or returns over a ten-month period.

Customizing Improv's Templates

If any of Improv's templates are similar to one that you will want to use regularly, you can adapt them for your own needs. Improv's intuitive user interface makes it easy to change templates to create a more elaborate structure. For example, in the BUDGET.IMP template, you might add more line items, create additional item groups, or change the period items to months and add additional columns for the other eight months in the year. Just type in your own item names to replace the template item names.

After you customize a template's structure, select Style from the Worksheet menu and use the InfoBox Style panel to change the worksheet's text, number, line, or fill attributes. For more information on using the InfoBox, see Chapter 4 or use Improv's on-line Help.

Saving Customized Templates

Once you have customized a template, be sure to save it under a new name. This leaves the original template unchanged so that you or another user can access it again for other projects.

When you save a customized template, you can save it as a new template and use it as a pattern for future worksheets, or you can save it as a model in which you enter actual data, values, and formulas. To save your work as a new template, select Save As from the File menu; in the dialog box, double-click the Template directory name and then type the new template name in the File Name box. To save your work as a model, double-click the directory name where you want to save the model, and type the new model name in the File Name box. Click OK to confirm your entries.

Creating New Templates

If none of the templates provided by Improv suits your needs, you can create a new template from scratch. Start by selecting New from the File menu.

Enter the item names, category names, and formulas for the new template. (If you need to, refer to Chapter 6, Chapter 7, and Chapter 8 for help with building the elements of your template.) When you finish creating the template, select Save As from the File menu. In the Save As dialog box, double-click the Template directory, type a name for the new template in the File Name box, and click OK to confirm your entries.

Creating a Suite of Templates

A suite of templates is a model that contains several templates for worksheets, views, or presentations. These templates will help streamline your tasks of entering data and creating charts for a favorite model in which the data changes frequently.

Create the first worksheet in the suite of templates using the instructions in the previous section, "Creating New Templates." To create additional templates for the suite, select the appropriate Create menu option—Worksheet, View, Presentation, Chart, or Script—and continue building templates as needed. When you have completed the suite of templates, select Save As from the File menu and save the new templates as a model in the IMPROV\MODELS\TEMPLATE directory. Improv will save the file in the same format as regular Improv models.

Creating a New Startup Model Template

In your work environment, you may work with similar Improv documents every day. You can designate a template or suite of templates as a startup model to appear each time you open Improv or select New from the File menu.

To do this, first use the instructions in the previous two sections to create a template or suite of templates. Once the templates are saved, select User Setup from the Tools menu. In the User Setup dialog box, click the Paths command button to display the Default Paths dialog box (refer back to Figure 16-2). This dialog box lets you specify the default directory path for your models, scripts, backups, and the startup model. Click the Startup Model text box, and type in the drive, directory, and name of the template or suite of templates that you have created for this purpose.

For example, suppose you frequently use Improv to enter your company's financial information. Following the instructions for "Creating a Suite of Templates," design a suite of templates that record company sales, expenses, assets, inventory, and so forth. Select Save As from the File menu, and give the model a name that's meaningful to you, such as FINANCE.IMP in the directory IMPROV\MODELS\TEMPLATE (remember to use the file type *.imp). Next, select User Setup from the Tools menu, and in the User Setup dialog box click the Paths command button. In the Default Paths dialog box, click the Startup Model text box and type in the full path and name of the model you created. For our example, you would type

C:\IMPROV\MODELS\TEMPLATES\FINANCE.IMP

Once you have created the new FINANCE.IMP model, saved it, and specified that you want Improv to use it as the startup model, Improv will open that model each time you start the program or select New from the File menu.

CUSTOMIZING IMPROV'S SMARTICONS

Improv provides you with three predefined sets of SmartIcons: the Worksheet, Presentation, and Script SmartIcon sets (see Appendix C). When you first open Improv, the default Worksheet SmartIcons display in a toolbar at the top of the screen. Improv lets you customize the SmartIcon sets to fit your own work environment, so you can remove the SmartIcons for functions you don't often use, and add others that perform the tasks you need to do frequently.

Working in the SmartIcons Dialog Box

To modify Improv's SmartIcons, select SmartIcons from the Tools menu. You see the dialog box shown in Figure 16-8.

On the left, under Available Icons, is a list box containing all the icons that are available for you to use.

In the box at the top-center is the name of the SmartIcon set that's currently selected. The icon list below the set name shows you the SmartIcons currently included in the selected set. When you first use Improv, the list box will include only the names of the default sets: Presentation, Script, and Worksheet. However, Improv also lets you create your own SmartIcon sets for individual worksheets, scripts, or presentations, as explained in a later section. For example, you may want to exclude some of the icons for chart-related tasks when you're using a worksheet.

You can also change the position of the SmartIcon toolbar, using the Position list box. And, using the dialog box command buttons, you can attach scripts to SmartIcons, add and delete entire sets of SmartIcons, and change the displayed size of SmartIcons. All these and other SmartIcon tasks are described in the sections that follow.

Modifying Existing SmartIcon Sets

To add, delete, rearrange, or group icons from one of Improv's SmartIcon sets, select SmartIcons from the Tools menu. You see the SmartIcons dialog box, shown in Figure 16-8.

FIGURE 16-8

SmartIcons dialog box

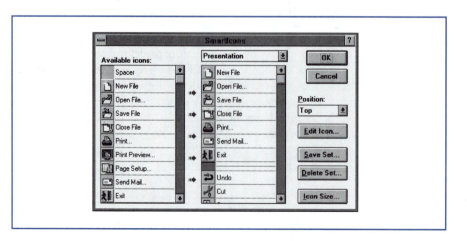

Adding and Deleting Icons

To add a SmartIcon, start by clicking the list box at the top of the dialog box to display the list of SmartIcon sets, and click the name of the set to which you want to add an icon. The list of icons below the set name shows you what SmartIcons are already included. In the Available Icons list, click the icon that you want to add, and drag it into the desired position in the icon list.

Improv lets you use icons created in other Windows applications. Create an icon and save it as .BMP file in the \IMPROV\ICONS directory. The new icon then appears on the Available Icons list.

Following the same steps listed above for adding an icon, display the list of SmartIcons for the set you want to change. Click the icon you want to delete, and drag it anywhere off the list.

Rearranging Icons

It's convenient to arrange the SmartIcons within a set so that related tasks are grouped together. For example, you might want to have the SmartIcon that represents the Cut command at the opposite end of the toolbar from the one that represents the Paste command. To move an icon from one location to another in the selected list, click the one you want to move and drag it to the desired location. Figure 16-9 shows the Exit icon being dragged to a new location.

FIGURE 16-9

Dragging a SmartIcon to new location

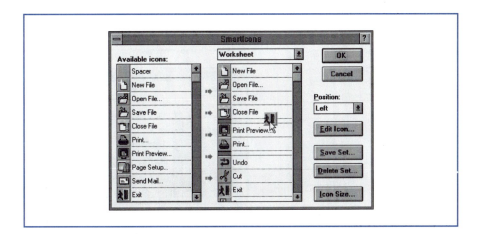

Grouping Icons

Use the Spacer icon (in the Available Icons list) to separate icon groups. When the SmartIcon toolbar is displayed in the Improv window, the icons that were grouped using the Spacer icon are separated by a space.

First arrange the icons in the selected set the way you want them. Then click the Spacer icon and drag it to the place where you want a space to appear between two other icons. To remove a space between icons, just click the space and drag it anywhere off the list.

Using the Custom SmartIcons

Select the Edit Icon command button to bring up the Edit SmartIcon dialog box (Figure 16-10), which lets you attach Improv scripts to custom icons that Improv provides or to icons you create in other Windows applications. Once you've added the custom Smart-Icon to a SmartIcon set, you can display that set in the Improv window and click the custom icon to run the attached script.

The Edit SmartIcon dialog box offers eight custom icons, shown in the Available Icons list; you can add these icons to any SmartIcon set. You can attach any script provided by Improv or a new script of your own to any of these icons. Three of the custom icons already have scripts attached:

Load@Functions Icon This icon runs the ADDINS20.LSS script for registering Improv's add-in functions. Before you can use add-in functions, you must first run this script to register the functions to make them available to Windows and Improv. If you frequently use add-in functions, it's a good idea to include the Load@Functions icon in your Worksheet SmartIcon set. Then you can just click the SmartIcon to ensure that add-in functions are available (see Appendix A for further information on these functions).

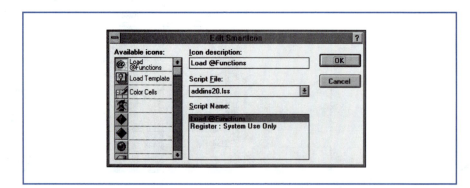

FIGURE 16-10

Edit SmartIcon dialog box

Load Template Icon The script attached to this icon displays the Load Template dialog box shown in Figure 16-11; here you can select the worksheet template that you want to use. If you're exploring several templates, or you find that you are using templates frequently, it's a good idea to include this custom icon in your Worksheet SmartIcon set; that way, you can quickly access templates in one step, instead of using the File Open command and selecting from a file list.

Color Cells Icon The script attached to this icon displays the Color Cells dialog box shown in Figure 16-12. Use this dialog box to change the color of certain cells based on values and conditions that you specify. You may want to include this icon in your Worksheet SmartIcon set, to let you quickly emphasize certain worksheet data by changing the data's color when it reaches a certain value, or when it is recalculated.

Attaching a Script to an Icon

Use the following procedure to attach a script to an icon and then add it to a SmartIcon set:

1. In the Edit SmartIcon dialog box (Figure 16-10), click one of the icons in the Available Icons list.

2. Click in the Icon Description text box and type in a short description of the script you're attaching.

3. Open the Script File list box, and then click the name of the script you want attached to the icon. Some script files contain multiple scripts. If more than one name appears in the Script Name box, click the name of the script you want to run.

FIGURE 16-11

Load Template dialog box

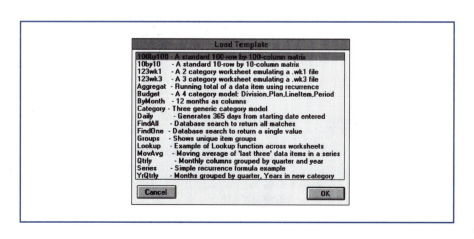

FIGURE 16-12

Color Cells dialog box

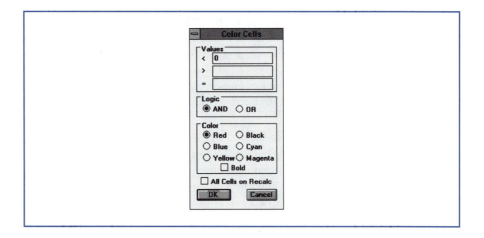

Note For a script to appear on the Script File list, you must have saved it with an .LSS filename extension in the \IMPROV\SCRIPTS directory.

4. When your entries are correct, click OK to confirm your selections and return to the SmartIcons dialog box.

5. To add the new custom icon to the selected SmartIcon set, select it from the Available Icons list, and drag it to the appropriate place on the icon list.

Changing SmartIcon Size

Click the Icon Size command button to bring up the Icon Size dialog box, which lets you change the size of displayed SmartIcons. There are two choices: Medium (the default) and Large. Click the appropriate button to select or deselect either size. Click OK to confirm your changes.

The Large size displays SmartIcons approximately 60 percent larger than the Medium size. When you choose the Large option for displayed SmartIcons, keep in mind that this will affect the number of icons Improv can fit on the screen!

Positioning the SmartIcon Toolbar

The Position list box in the SmartIcons dialog box displays the location in the Improv window where the selected SmartIcons toolbar appears. Click the box to see a list of available choices—Top, Bottom, Right, Left, and Floating—and click to select the position you want. The new position becomes the default position for all SmartIcon sets.

Keep in mind that the position you select, along with the icon size (Medium or Large), affects the number of icons Improv can display on the screen.

- *Top:* This is the default position setting for the SmartIcon toolbar; it displays a maximum of 27 medium-size icons or 16 large-size icons across the top of the Improv window. (Remember: You can choose the Medium or Large size for SmartIcons by clicking the Icon Size command button in the SmartIcons dialog box.)

- *Bottom:* This position setting displays a maximum of 27 medium-size icons or 16 large-size icons across the bottom of the Improv window.

- *Right:* This position setting displays a maximum of 18 medium-size icons or 11 large-size icons vertically down the right side of the Improv window.

- *Left:* This position setting displays a maximum of 18 medium-size icons or 11 large-size icons vertically down the left side of the Improv window.

- *Floating:* This position setting displays SmartIcons in a separate window that is not attached to the Improv window; this floating SmartIcon window can be resized.

If a set contains more icons than Improv can display on the SmartIcon toolbar, select Floating; you can then resize the floating window in which they appear so that all of the icons in the set can be seen.

Creating and Saving New SmartIcon Sets

To create an entirely new SmartIcon set, modify the list of icons in the selected set until it is structured the way you want. Be sure the icons that you want in the new set are in the correct position in the list.

If you want to save a new SmartIcon set under the same set name, just click OK to confirm your changes.

To save the set under a new name, click the Save Set command button in the SmartIcons dialog box. You see the dialog box shown here:

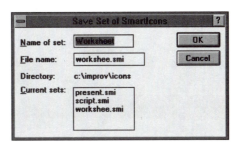

Click in the Name of Set text box and enter the new set name; then click in the File Name text box and enter the filename. If you want to save the new set under a different but existing set name, click the name you want to use in the Current Sets list.

When your entries are correct, click OK.

Deleting SmartIcon Sets

If you want to permanently delete a SmartIcon set, click the Delete Set command button in the SmartIcons dialog box. When the Delete Set dialog box appears, click the name of the set you want to delete and then click OK. Or, just select the set in the SmartIcons dialog box and then click Delete Set.

When you delete a SmartIcon set, it is permanently erased from your system. You will have to re-install Improv to retrieve the deleted set.

Improv 2

Handbook

CHAPTER 17

Creating Scripts

With the LotusScript programming language you can create *scripts* that automate the tasks you perform routinely in Improv. As you set up worksheets in Improv, you will probably notice that you perform some tasks frequently on a given worksheet—switching between a group and a detail view of your data, for instance, or performing "what-if" analyses with your product mark-up, or entering deposits and subtracting checks from your checking account register. These are the frequently repeated tasks that you can automate with scripts.

A script can be as simple as a recorded series of steps you take to perform a familiar task, which Improv then carries out without your intervention. A more complex script is one that automatically performs functions that might take dozens or even hundreds of manual steps.

CREATING A SCRIPT

There are two ways to create a script: You can record a series of key sequences and mouse events, or you can write a script from the ground up.

Recording a script is a very straightforward process. You should start by having firmly in mind the steps you need to take to complete your task. On Improv's Create menu you select the Script command, then click a button to tell Improv to start recording your steps as you actually perform a task. Save that recording, then, when you want to perform the task again, you simply play back the script and the script performs the task without your intervention.

You can play back a recorded script by choosing the Run Script option on the Tools menu, or by attaching the script to a menu item, a keystroke, or a graphic object. This is discussed in more detail later, in "Attaching and Running the Script."

In contrast to recording, writing a script requires more familiarity with the Improv script language and the concepts of programming. One way to get familiar with the LotusScript language and how it is used is to study your recorded scripts and the script examples provided with Improv. This will give you a good start at learning the language. Once you begin to understand the language, you can modify the scripts you record and make them more flexible and powerful. Appendix B describes some the LotusScript functions available when you write your own scripts.

After you have created a script for a worksheet, you can run it by attaching it to a menu choice for that worksheet, to a button or an object in a presentation, or to a keystroke. You can also choose Run Script from the Tools menu to start your script.

Usually, scripts are only available in the model in which they were created. After you have recorded a number of scripts, you may begin to notice that some of your scripts are similar in purpose, and only vary by some task or element that is specific to the worksheet you use it with. Once you learn the tricks of modifying individual scripts to make them "general-purpose," you can store them in a *script library*, where they will be accessible to all your models.

You can also use the Lotus Dialog Editor to create a *dialog box*, a tool that allows you to gather worksheet-specific information to use with your general-purpose scripts.

In the sections that follow, you will work through the process of recording a script and attaching it to a menu choice, button, or keystroke sequence. You will also learn the fundamentals of general-purpose scripts, including how to modify and debug them, and how to use the Lotus Dialog Editor to create a dialog box for user input.

RECORDING A SCRIPT

If you are not familiar with programming, the easiest way to create a script is to record it. As soon as you recognize that a particular operation is being repeated frequently in

FIGURE 17-1

The NEWSLTR worksheet

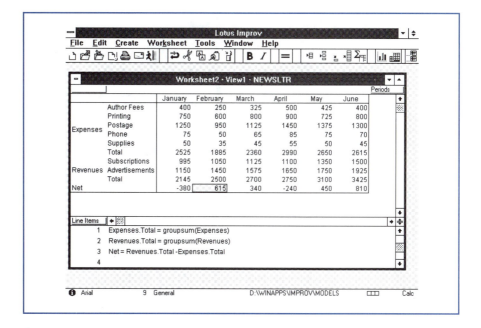

your Improv work environment, you should consider recording a script to automate that task.

Suppose you run a small consulting business, and as part of your business you publish a monthly newsletter that forecasts trends for your industry. You have created a worksheet file, named NEWSLTR, that itemizes the monthly expenses for the newsletter, such as payments to writers, and all of the expenses associated with printing and mailing. On the same worksheet, you track revenues from the publications, including subscription payments, and fees collected for advertising. The formulas in the worksheet calculate the total expenses, total revenues, and net income. Figure 17-1 shows this worksheet with some data.

As you use the NEWSLTR worksheet, you notice that you frequently hide the line items in the expense and revenue categories and analyze only the category totals and the net income. By recording two scripts, you can easily switch between the detail and the summary views.

Each time you switch between the detail and the summary views, you repeat the same series of actions: you highlight the detail lines under Expenses, select the Worksheet menu, and choose the Hide Item option; then you highlight the detail lines under Revenues and select Worksheet Hide Item again. To record a script that will automatically perform these functions for you, follow these steps:

1. Be sure that the correct worksheet is displayed. Then, select Script from the Create menu. You will see the following dialog box:

2. Be sure the Start Recording button is selected, then click OK to start recording your script. You see the words "Recording Script" appear in the status bar.

3. Using your mouse, highlight the detail lines in the Expenses group (Author Fees through Supplies), and select Hide Items from the Worksheet menu.

4. Highlight the detail lines in the Revenues group (Subscriptions and Advertising), and again select Hide Items from the Worksheet menu.

5. Now select Stop Recording from the Create menu. Improv brings up a *script window* showing your newly recorded script, something like this:

The script will be displayed in a Script Window when you are done recording. Scripts that are recorded in this way are stored as part of the model file. (If you wish to save the script for use by other models, use the Save As option from the File menu, and save the script as an LSS file. This is described is the "Writing a Script" section of this chapter.)

This may seem like a fairly simple procedure to record as a script, but remember that you now have the power to record, with the Create Script feature, almost any action you perform in Improv. If a particular menu choice cannot be recorded, it will be disabled while the recorder is running (for instance, you cannot start recording another script).

If you accidently press the wrong keystrokes while you are recording, or perform incorrect actions with the mouse, you have two choices for correcting the script. One option is to re-record the entire script. However, if your script is long and you don't want to perform all the functions again, you can directly edit the script in the Script Window, removing the incorrect items.

Once you have recorded the steps of a script, you can run it, as described next.

ATTACHING AND RUNNING THE SCRIPT

There are several ways to run your script after you have recorded it. One way is to create a new item in the Tools menu that will run the script whenever you select that option. Or you can attach the script to a keystroke sequence (CTRL plus any alphabetic key) so that the script runs whenever that key combination is pressed. You can also run a script automatically when you open a worksheet or when a button or other graphic object is selected in a presentation. All these choices are available in the Attach Script dialog box (Figure 17-2).

The steps to access the Attach Script dialog box depend on where you are in the script recording process.

After you stop recording your script, or any other time the script window is on the screen, the menu options at the top of your worksheet will change; the option to the right of Create becomes Script. Open the Script menu, and you'll see an option called Attach, which displays the Attach Script dialog box.

Or, if the script window is closed, you can select Attach Script from the Tools menu. This also brings up the Attach Script dialog box.

FIGURE 17-2

Attach Script dialog box

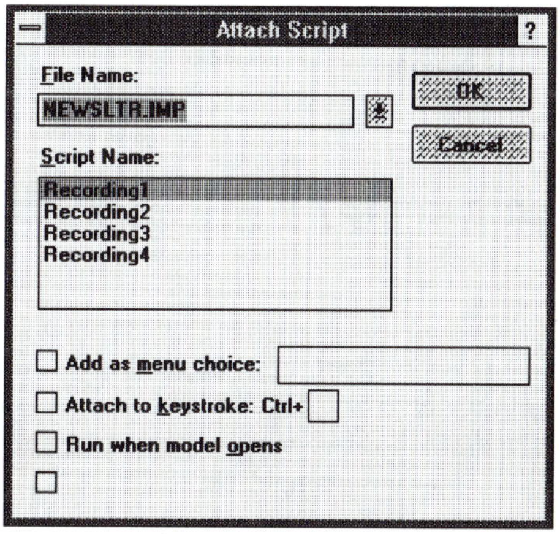

Attaching a Script to Menu Choices and Keystrokes

In the Attach Script dialog box, you designate how you want to access the recorded script. First, select the script you want to attach. Then select the options as described here:

- ◪ If you want to add the script as a menu item, click the Add as Menu Choice check box; in the box to the right of that option, type the name of the item. The name you enter here will be added to the bottom of the Tools menu.

- ◪ If you want to attach the script to a key-combination, click the Attach to Keystroke: Ctrl+ option and enter the desired character in the box to the right. Remember that you have to press the CTRL key and your selected character to activate the script.

- ◪ If you want the script to run automatically each time the model is opened, be sure to select the Run When Model Opens checkbox.

To remove a script from the Tools menu or detach it from an assigned key-combination, just return to the Attach Script dialog box, select the script in the Script Name list box, and click to uncheck the appropriate options.

Attaching a Script to a Button or Graphic Object

You can also attach a script to a button (or other graphic object) in a presentation. First activate the presentation that contains the button you want to use. Then select the button, and choose Attach Script from the Tools menu. From the list of script names in the Attach Script dialog box, click on the name of the script you want to attach to the button, and select Attach to Selected Graphic. Confirm all your selections in the dialog box, and click OK.

When you create a new button in a presentation, you will automatically be given the option to attach a script.

WRITING A SCRIPT

When you write a script, you are simply enumerating and recording the series of steps necessary to perform an action. Any task you perform repeatedly is a candidate for a script. In the first part of this chapter, you explored the steps required to record a simple script and attach it to a menu choice or keystroke, but scripts can be far more complex than that previous example.

Your Improv software includes five example scripts, with the filename extension .LSS, located in the subdirectory SCRIPTS under your IMPROV directory. You can access these scripts as you would any file, study their format, and use them as models for the more complex scripts you want to write.

To open an existing example script, choose Open from the File menu. In the List Files of Type box, select LotusScript (*.lss). Listed in the File Name box, you will see the names of the five script files that come with Improv.

Let's take a look at one of these scripts. Double-click the COLORCEL.LSS file to display the COLORCEL script file in a script window on your screen. You might find it easier to study the file if you print a copy; select File Print, and Improv will print the script just as it does any other file.

Note

COLORCEL.LSS is the most extensive of the example scripts provided with Improv and will give you the most exposure to script techniques; but it is also the most difficult to understand. You may wish to examine SEARCH.LSS, LOADTMPL.LSS, and the other scripts provided, for a less challenging introduction to LotusScript.

Understanding LotusScript

When you have a hard copy of a script to study, you will see that the LotusScript language is rather cryptic, and only somewhat English-like. It is similar to the BASIC language. This will not be as simple to understand as Improv formulas! The scope of this book does not allow for a full programming tutorial in LotusScript. However, it is important that you know the capabilities that are available. You or an associate may at some some point want to extend your copy of Improv with scripts. Therefore, the following sections are an overview of the features and capabilities available in LotusScript. For additional information and instructions, refer to Appendix B, the LotusScript chapter in the Improv Handbook, and the extensive online LotusScript Help, available from the Help menu within Improv.

Constants and Variables

When you write a script, you want to be able to use it with many spreadsheets, not just one. Don't identify cell names, formulas, and so on by using their names in a particular spreadsheet; if you do, the script will only work with that spreadsheet. To write a "general-purpose" script, you must identify items in general terms, and let the script substitute specific names in each individual case as needed. The generic terms for these values are called *constants* and *variables*. The value of a variable can be changed by a script, but a constant cannot be changed (examples of these declarations are shown below, in reference to the COLORCEL script).

When you refer in a script to a constant or a variable, you must declare its *data type*, such as *string, date, number,* and so forth. (Data types are discussed further in Appendix B.) Each data type allows certain actions that are logical for that type. For instance, strings can be alphabetized; numbers can be added together. At the beginning of the COLOR-CEL script, you will see three string variables "declared"—that is, they are named and memory is allocated for them. Look for these lines in the script:

```
string ltcond
string gtcond
string eqcond
```

In the lines after the string declarations you will see declarations of *integers* and constants (*consts*). You can determine what the cryptic names mean by finding them in one of the tables in Appendix B, and then reading the definition; look for *string* under data types, and *const* under numeric value-handling functions. Some examples of declarations are:

```
integer logand%
integer trig%
integer clr

const BLACK=255
const RED=128
const YELLOW=50
```

Performing Actions

In order to apply to all spreadsheets, *actions*, too, must be described in general terms. If you wanted to add the total of a column of figures, for example, you might say: "Add *cell1* to *cell2*, add that total to *cell3*, and give me the grand total." In a spreadsheet with only three rows of cells, you would get the desired total. But you might be unpleasantly surprised if the spreadsheet has five rows, because you did not say, "Now add the total of the first three cells to *cell4*, and add that total to *cell5*."

The solution to this problem is to describe the action in more general terms: "Add the cells together until there are no more cells." This might involve the use of a DO WHILE loop, as shown here:

```
DO WHILE OK_var = 1
   ' Here is where the calculations would occur
   Total = Total + 1
   IF Total > 10 THEN
      OK_VAR = 0        ' This will end the DO WHILE loop
   END IF
LOOP
```

Other constructions that control action are IF-THEN-ELSE and SELECT CASE, which define *conditions* for the action; and GOTO, which defines a method for moving around within the script in an unstructured way.

Conditional statements are used to perform an action only under specified conditions. For instance, in the code example above, OK_VAR is assigned a value of zero (the action), but only if Total is greater than 10 (the condition).

Functions and Subroutines

Functions and *subroutines* are parts of the script that are called to perform their action repeatedly. They are another way to keep your scripts succinct: The script can repeat a function as many times as necessary. A function and a subroutine are both a series of statements, but a function always returns a value. You can find functions in several of the example scripts: They begin with the word *function* and end with *end function*.

Here is a function from COLORCEL:

```
Function NumberP (string cellvalue) as BOOLEAN
' This function determines whether a given string
'    can be converted to a number

on error ERR_COERCE
   NumberP = FALSE
end on

NumberP = TRUE
s# = Number(cellvalue)    ' If this operation triggers an
   '                        ERR_COERCE error, then the value
   '                        is not a number, and FALSE will be
   '                        returned by the "on error" above.
   '                        Otherwise, the default TRUE value
   '                        will be returned.

end Function
```

Types of Commands and Functions

The LotusScript language can be divided into three sections:

▪ *Core LotusScript:* A core set of commands and functions used to describe your objects and actions, the order in which you want actions performed, error handling, built-in functions that perform common computations, and commands to build your specialized functions.

- ☑ *Improv-Specific Functions:* Functions that reproduce the effects of Improv actions, such as displaying a dialog box for your input.

- ☑ *C Functions:* Functions that can be used within the C programs you write, and that must include certain C-language conventions and must link to a library file.

All of the LotusScript commands and functions are listed in Appendix B, organized according to the command function category. Improv's on-line Script Help lists the exact spelling for the Improv-specific functions and the arguments each one expects.

Combining the LotusScript functions with an understanding of basic programming concepts will allow you to develop elegant and powerful Improv applications.

Seeing a Script in Action

Try running all the example scripts on a worksheet to see what they do in that worksheet. Select Run Script in the Tools menu. In the Run Script dialog box, highlight COLOR-CEL.LSS. As the script runs, you will see a dialog box that lets you enter values specific to the spreadsheet you are working with. The important point is that the COLORCEL script will run with any spreadsheet; you add model-specific information in the dialog box.

Writing a Script of Your Own

When you are ready to try writing a script of your own, choose Script from the Create menu. In the Create Script dialog box, click on the Create New Script Window radio button and click OK. You will see a blank script window, where you can begin typing in your script.

An easy way to write a script of your own is to first record the major functions you wish to perform using the script recorder (choose Create Script and click the Start Recording button). After you finish recording the script, open the script window (using the Browser) and work with the script that Improv generated, making the necessary adjustments. This saves time and prevents simple typing errors for much of your script code.

Debugging a Script

The first time you write a complex script of your own, you may find that some minor errors and defects (commonly known as *bugs*) exist in your script. The best way to determine whether this has occurred is to test the script on some simple data and then examine the results to see if they are what you anticipated. The process of testing your script and finding and eliminating any errors is called *debugging*.

The Debug Window

Improv provides one very useful method of debugging: the Debug window. One of the challenges of debugging is determining what line of a script has caused the unexpected results. With the Debug window activated you can watch the script execute, and monitor it along the way. As you step through the script line by line (the current line is displayed), you can watch the effect of each command on your worksheet. The Debug window also gives you a way to monitor the value of variables that would otherwise be hidden from you.

Here's how to activate the Debug window:

1. Choose Run Script from the Tools menu. The dialog box that appears will be similar to the one shown below, except it will contain your worksheet name and a list of the scripts that are attached to it.

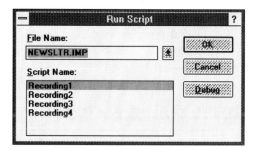

2. Select the script file you want to debug, and click on the Debug button.

The Debug window appears at the bottom of your screen, with a message in the upper section telling you that Improv is *compiling* your script file. (Compiling means converting the relatively English-like terms of your script into a form that Improv can understand.)

The lower area of the Debug window is divided into two sections (see the illustration just below). On the left is a running display of the line of script currently being executed. On the right is a group of four push buttons; each button executes the script at a different rate. To step through the script one line at a time, click the Step Into button. To run a function or subroutine that is on the current line, without looking at each line within it, click Step Over. To run the script until it encounters a STOP statement or until the script ends, click Continue. Use the Edit/Halt button to stop the debugging process.

```
┌─────────────────────────────────────────────────────────────────┐
│ ▭              Debugging Recording3 · NEWSLTR                     │
├─────────────────────────────────────────────────────────────────┤
│ Compiling D:\WINAPPS\IMPROV\MODELS\NEWSLTR.IMP,Recording2      ▲  │
│ Module loaded: D:\WINAPPS\IMPROV\MODELS\NEWSLTR.IMP,Recording2    │
│ Module unloaded: D:\WINAPPS\IMPROV\MODELS\NEWSLTR.IMP,Recording2▒│
│                                                                ▼  │
│ ◄ ▒                                                            ► │
├─────────────────────────────────────────────────────────────────┤
│ Module Recording3 is about to be executed now   Step Into  Continue│
│                                                  Step Over  Edit/Halt│
└─────────────────────────────────────────────────────────────────┘
```

CREATING SCRIPT LIBRARIES

Once you've begun to write more scripts and make them generic, you will want them to be accessible from all of your worksheets, rather than only in the worksheet in which they were created. For this purpose, individual scripts can be collected in a script library file.

When you save a script you have written and debugged, choose the File Save As command and give the file a name with the extension .LSS, the file extension reserved for script library files. You will probably want to store all of your script library files in the same subdirectory. By default, Improv stores script files in the Scripts subdirectory, but you can change this location if you wish (see Chapter 16 for more details).

THE LOTUS DIALOG EDITOR

The Dialog Editor is a separate program that is included with your Improv software. It is used to create dialog boxes for user input. With the Dialog Editor, you assemble input boxes that contain push buttons, data input fields, and so forth. (This same Editor can be used to customize other Lotus products, such as the word processor, Ami Pro.)

The Dialog Editor assigns a number to each object you draw in the dialog box. Once you have finished drawing, you have what looks like a dialog box, but without any intelligence. Save the box as a dialog box file, and return to Improv.

Next, within an Improv script you associate the dialog box to a script, assigning an action to each object. Each object is referred to by the number assigned in the Dialog Editor. In this way, your dialog box can be made to perform the desired actions.

As you develop a library of general-purpose scripts, dialog boxes can be used to make those scripts more flexible. Specifically, if you can pass information to the script or get the needed user input for a script, a particular script could serve in more situations and be more versatile. Use dialog boxes, just like the ones used in Improv, to get user input for your scripts.

PARTSIX

Instant Improv:
Using the Example Models

Improv 2

- Opening the Model

- Using the Browser

- Using the Worksheet

- Using the Dialog Box Manager

- Using Scripts

- Customizing the Model

Handbook

CHAPTER 18

Creating a Check Register

Tracking your personal or business finances is a very serious task. You depend on the money in your checking account to pay for the things you need. Therefore, accurate records are imperative.

Improv comes with a sample model that is patterned after your checkbook, called CHEK-BOOK.IMP. Not only does this model teach you about using some of Improv's features, it also provides a basis from which you can design your own checkbook model.

The first part of this chapter explains how to open the Checkbook model, and briefly describes each element that's displayed on the screen. The second part of the chapter discusses each element in greater detail and suggests activities that you might consider in improving the model for your own use.

OPENING THE CHECK REGISTER MODEL

To open the Checkbook model, select File Open from the main menu bar. In the Open dialog box, click on the Examples directory. In the list of Examples directory files that appears under the File Name text box, click CHEKBOOK.IMP, and then click OK to confirm your selection. Improv loads the check register model shown in Figure 18-1.

The first time you open the Checkbook, all of the following elements are displayed in their own windows on the Checkbook screen:

▨ Checkbook Dialog Box Manager: Each of the command buttons in this dialog box (except Exit) runs a common check register transaction, prompting you for the necessary information.

▨ Checkbook Browser: The Browser is essentially a table of contents listing each element in the Checkbook model. Use it to rename elements, to open or move among the various elements in the model, and to add, copy, and delete any element a model contains.

FIGURE 18-1

The Checkbook
(CHEKBOOK.IMP)
model,
with all its windows

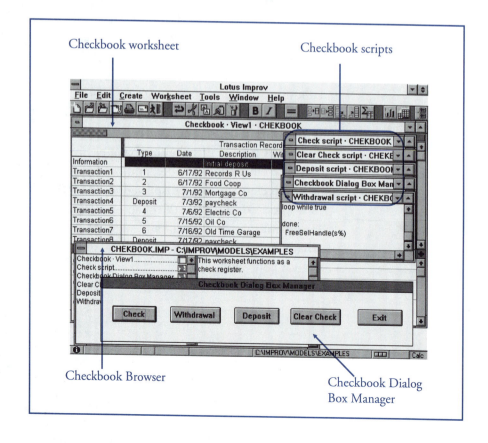

Checkbook worksheet

Checkbook scripts

Checkbook Browser

Checkbook Dialog
Box Manager

Note

See Chapter 17 for complete instructions on working with LotusScript in Improv.

☑ CHEKBOOK Scripts: The five Checkbook are used to display the Checkbook Dialog Box Manager and to respond to the Check, Withdrawal, Deposit, and Clear Check buttons. Each script window contains the actual code that is executed for each of these operations.

☑ Checkbook Worksheet: The top half of the worksheet is the data pane, which displays the actual check register details and values. The bottom half of the screen is the formula pane, containing formulas from which Improv calculates the values in the data pane.

USING THE BROWSER

To move the Browser to the front of the Checkbook window for further examination, click the Exit command button in the Checkbook Dialog Box Manager; this removes the Dialog Box Manager from the screen and allows you to see all of the Browser window.

If you cannot find the Browser on the screen, select Browser from the Window menu, and the Browser will be displayed.

Tip

The Browser, illustrated below, is an effective tool for managing a model that contains several elements.

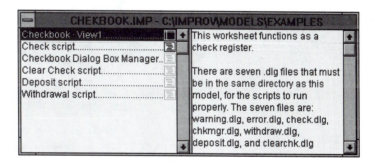

The left side of the Browser window displays the name of each element in the Checkbook model, along with an icon that identifies the element type. The icon to the right of "Checkbook - View1" identifies this element as a worksheet; the remaining five icons identify their elements as scripts. When an element is closed, the icon is dimmed. When you select (highlight) an element in the Browser, a note associated with that element appears on the right side of the window.

Try the activities in the following sections to become more familiar with how the Browser works.

Adding Another Checkbook View

By creating different views of the same Checkbook worksheet, you can display the same information in various ways without having to reenter the data or maintain a separate worksheet. To see how easy it is to create another view of an existing worksheet, follow this procedure:

1. In the Browser, click on the Checkbook - View1 icon; this displays the Checkbook model.

2. Select View from the Create menu. Improv creates a new view of the worksheet and adds it to the Browser list as Checkbook - View2. The new view becomes the active window.

3. Select Settings from the Worksheet menu. Try changing some of the settings for the components in the worksheet, such as the number format. Notice how Improv updates the Checkbook worksheet display as you select various settings.

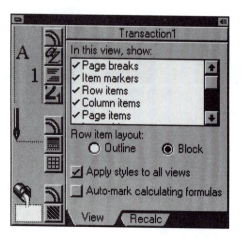

If the Apply Styles To All Views check box on the Settings View page contains a check mark (as shown above), Improv applies your changes to all views of the currently selected worksheet. To have your changes apply only to the selected view, disable the Apply Styles To All Views option.

Viewing and Adding Notes

Use the notes section in the Browser to document the different items in your model. This will help to maintain continuity when several people use a model. It also provides reminders for yourself if you work only occasionally on a particular model. Follow these steps to explore the Browser's note capabilities:

1. Select one of the script elements from the list in the left side of the Browser window, and read the information that appears in the note pane on the right to learn more about using the script with the worksheet.

2. Click in a spot in the note pane where you'd like to add a note. When the text cursor appears, type in a new note, or modify any note that already exists.

When you are done experimenting, you can remove the Browser from the screen by clicking on the Close box in the Browser's upper-left corner.

When you create a New model and select Browser from the Window menu, the worksheet has no notes and the note pane doesn't display in the Browser. To add a note, click on the Note icon that appears in the lower-right corner of the Browser. Improv opens a blank note pane, where you can type a description of the worksheet or add information that might be helpful to other users.

USING THE CHECKBOOK WORKSHEET

If it's not already active, select Checkbook - View2 from the Browser by double-clicking the Checkbook - View2 icon or by selecting Checkbook - View2 - CHECKBOOK from the Window menu. (If you didn't create a second worksheet view in the previous section's activity, select Checkbook - View1.)

Figure 18-2 shows the worksheet for Checkbook - View1. The top half of the worksheet displays actual checkbook transactions, and the bottom half displays the formulas from which Improv calculates the values. As in the paper check register that you may carry with your checkbook, each row in the data pane represents a single transaction; in Figure 18-2, notice the row names in the column at the far left of the worksheet (Information, Transaction1, Transaction2, etc.). The columns are for the details of each transaction, such as a transaction type (for example, a check number or the word *Deposit*), date, and amount, and a Cleared? field so you can mark when a transaction has cleared the bank.

Improv uses formulas to calculate the values for Balance and On Account (On Account is not shown in Figure 18-2. It is the column to the right of Balance used to track the balance of uncleared items. You need to move the cursor to the right to see it).

FIGURE 18-2

The Checkbook
worksheet

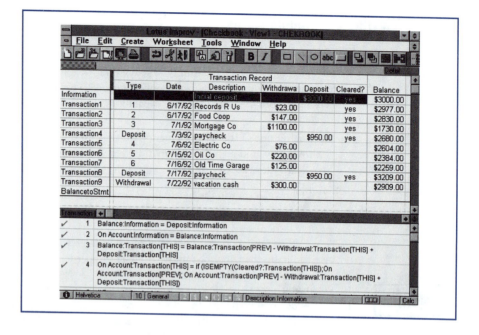

The formulas are shown at the bottom of Figure 18-2. Each time you enter or change a transaction, Improv calculates and updates the worksheet. All you have to do is enter the transaction details. To see this function in action, click on a row in the data pane, and then select Mark Formulas from the Worksheet menu. The corresponding formula is highlighted in the bottom pane.

Entering a New Transaction

To enter a transaction in the Checkbook worksheet, you add a new item and type the transaction details in the data pane. (You can also use the Checkbook Dialog Box Manager to enter transactions, as explained later in this chapter.) As an example, try the following cash withdrawal transaction:

1. Click on the last item, with the row name Transaction9.

2. Select Items from the Create menu. Improv creates a new item, Transaction10, and adds it to the worksheet (see Figure 18-3). You could also highlight Transaction9 and press ENTER to automatically add another item.

3. Click the new item's row name (Transaction10) to highlight the cell; then type **ATM** to replace the system-generated item name.

FIGURE 18-3

The Checkbook worksheet with added item

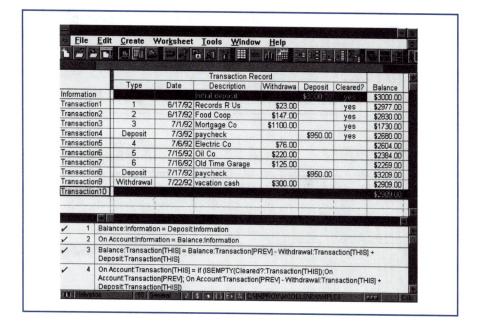

| File | Edit | Create | Worksheet | Tools | Window | Help |

	Type	Date	Description	Withdrawa	Deposit	Cleared?	Balance
			Transaction Record				
Information			Initial deposit		$3000.00	yes	$3000.00
Transaction1	1	6/17/92	Records R Us	$23.00		yes	$2977.00
Transaction2	2	6/17/92	Food Coop	$147.00		yes	$2830.00
Transaction3	3	7/1/92	Mortgage Co	$1100.00		yes	$1730.00
Transaction4	Deposit	7/3/92	paycheck		$950.00	yes	$2680.00
Transaction5	4	7/6/92	Electric Co	$76.00			$2604.00
Transaction6	5	7/15/92	Oil Co	$220.00			$2384.00
Transaction7	6	7/16/92	Old Time Garage	$125.00			$2259.00
Transaction8	Deposit	7/17/92	paycheck		$950.00		$3209.00
Transaction9	Withdrawal	7/22/92	vacation cash	$300.00			$2909.00
Transaction10							$2909.00

✓	1	Balance:Information = Deposit:Information
✓	2	On Account:Information = Balance:Information
✓	3	Balance:Transaction[THIS] = Balance:Transaction[PREV] - Withdrawal:Transaction[THIS] + Deposit:Transaction[THIS]
✓	4	On Account:Transaction[THIS] = if (ISEMPTY(Cleared?:Transaction[THIS]);On Account:Transaction[PREV]; On Account:Transaction[PREV] - Withdrawal:Transaction[THIS] + Deposit:Transaction[THIS])

4. Move to the Type column and type **Cash**, and in the Date column enter today's date.

5. In the Description column, enter **Bingo Bucks**; in the Withdrawal column, type the amount **$100.00**.

Note

For each transaction, you must enter a value in either the Withdrawal or Deposit column.

6. Let's assume that you know the transaction has cleared the bank (that is, it has shown on your bank statement). Type **Yes** in the Cleared? column and press ENTER. Notice that Improv updates both the Balance and On Account values.

Reconciling the Account

To ensure that your checking account records are up to date and accurate, you will need to reconcile your check register against a monthly bank statement, accounting for additional debits and credits to your account (such as service charges). You can do this with Improv's Checkbook by following these steps:

1. In the Cleared? column, type **Yes** for each item that appears on your bank statement.

2. Create new Items for monthly service charges, check order charges, and interest earned.

Notice that when you clear items (by entering Yes in the Cleared? column) and add new transactions, Improv continues to update the Balance and On Account values.

USING THE CHECKBOOK DIALOG BOX MANAGER

The Checkbook Dialog Box Manager, shown below, is another way to enter check register transactions. This window appears at the front of the screen when you first open the Checkbook model. Each command button in the Dialog Box Manager executes a CHEKBOOK.IMP script that performs one of the check register functions. (You can also run any of these scripts by selecting their names from the Tools menu.)

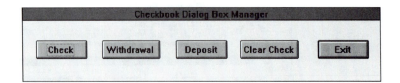

To close the Dialog Box Manager and work with other elements in the Checkbook, click the Exit button. Once you close the Dialog Box Manager, you can redisplay it by selecting Manager from the Tools menu. The purpose of each button and script is shown here:

Button	Related Script	Purpose
Check	Check Script	Write a check
Withdrawal	Withdrawal Script	Make a non-check withdrawal
Deposit	Deposit Script	Make a deposit
Clear Check	Clear Check Script	Mark a transaction as having cleared the bank
Exit	none	Exit the Manager (button) menu

Entering Transactions with Dialog Box Manager

Using the Checkbook Dialog Box Manager, here are the steps to enter a new check:

1. If the Checkbook Dialog Box Manager isn't displayed as the top window in the Checkbook screen, select Manager from the Tools menu.

2. When the Checkbook Dialog Box Manager appears, click on the Check command button. You will see the Check dialog box, as shown here:

Check		
Bank: Cod Bank		**7**
Account: 20804365	**Date [MM/DD/YY]:**	03/07/93
Pay to the order of:		**Amount:**
		$
For:		
Balance: $2909.00	☐ Cleared?	Exit

3. Your system's date appears as the default entry in the Date text box. To change it, click the Date text box and type in the desired date.

4. Click the Pay To The Order Of text box, and type the name of the recipient of the check (for this activity, just type any name). Use TAB or RIGHT ARROW to move to the Amount field, and type the check amount. Move to the other fields in the dialog box, and enter appropriate information in each field.

5. When your entries are correct, click on the Exit button, and watch Improv update the worksheet with the new transaction details.

6. The Check dialog box reappears on the screen. Enter another check, or click Exit to return to the Checkbook Dialog Box Manager.

Experiment with the other transaction buttons in the Checkbook Dialog Box Manager. Click Withdrawal, Deposit, and Clear Check, and examine the dialog boxes that appear for entering data for those transactions. When you finish, click the Exit command button to return to the worksheet.

USING CHEKBOOK.IMP SCRIPTS

The Checkbook model contains five predefined scripts. The first time you open the model, each of these five scripts displays in its own window, where you can view or modify it (the script windows are stacked, as shown in Figure 18-1). When each CHEK-BOOK.IMP script runs, it brings up a dialog box that lets you perform various procedures. To remove any script window from the screen, double-click the Close box in the upper-left corner of the script window. If you want to redisplay the script, select it from the Tools menu.

Assigning a Hotkey to a Script

LotusScript lets you assign a script to a keystroke, which you can then use to execute the script. The keystroke is always a combination of CTRL and a letter key from *A* to *Z.* Attaching a hotkey to a check register script lets you quickly run the script from the worksheet window, without having to use the Tools menu or Checkbook Dialog Box Manager.

Try the following procedure to assign a hotkey to one of the scripts:

1. Select Attach Script from Tools menu. You see the Attach Script dialog box shown here:

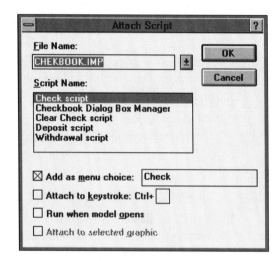

2. In the Script Name list box you'll see the name of each script in the Checkbook model. Click to highlight the scripts one at a time, and notice which settings are selected for each.

3. Click the Checkbook Dialog Box Manager script.

4. Click the Attach To Keystroke check box; then, in the Ctrl+ text box, type **D**.

5. Click OK to confirm your changes and return to the worksheet.

Now you can press CTRL+D at any time when the Checkbook worksheet is active to display the Checkbook Dialog Box Manager.

CUSTOMIZING THE CHECKBOOK MODEL

You can use the Checkbook model as a basis for designing your own personalized check register; you don't have to create an entirely new worksheet. Because the check register formulas are already set up, you only have to replace the sample data with your own. *But before you do this,* save the worksheet model under a new name; then customize the new copy of the model to fit your own needs. This way, you can retain CHEKBOOK.IMP as a template for future check registers that you may wish to create for other accounts.

Here's how to save CHEKBOOK.IMP under a new name and customize it:

1. If you do not have the CHEKBOOK model loaded (or open), select Open from the File menu to open the model.

2. When the Checkbook model appears, select Save As from the File menu, and enter a new filename for your customized version of the check register. The new check register then appears.

3. In the new worksheet, type in your own data to replace the sample check register data. To edit the data cells, just click them. Type your own transaction information in each row to replace the existing sample data.

4. Edit the row and column item names to fit your own needs; for example, you might want to Check, Cash, Fee, or Deposit for each of your check transactions.

5. If you want to change any of the worksheet attributes, such as the number style or item name font, select Worksheet Settings.

To review your entries in printed form, select Print from the File menu to print a copy of the register.

ON YOUR OWN

The Checkbook model contains sample data that allows you to see some of the capabilities available in Improv. In addition, the model demonstrates the use of scripts to automate processes within Improv, and how to customize Improv worksheets to your own tastes.

Now that you have completed this chapter, and received an introduction to the Checkbook model, you may want to further explore the model on your own. If the check register resembles one that you would normally use, you are ready to customize it for your own needs, or use it as is to manage your checkbook.

As you continue to work with this model, you may wish to refer to Chapter 7 and Chapter 8 for additional guidance.

Improv 2

- Opening the Model

- Using the Browser

- Exploring the Worksheet

- Customizing the Worksheet

- Exploring the Printer View

Handbook

CHAPTER 19

Creating an Expense Report

Companies and individuals commonly record and analyze expenses and often submit the information in report form. Improv provides EXPENSES.IMP, a model which illustrates the real life use of a worksheet to track expense transactions. The worksheet also shows an example of how to use a cross-checking formula. In addition, the model contains a printer view that generates an expense report using the data collected.

The first part of this chapter explains how to open the model, and briefly describes each element that's displayed on the screen. The second part of the chapter discusses the elements in more detail and suggests what activities to try.

OPENING THE EXPENSE REPORT MODEL

To open the expense report model, select Open from the File menu. Click the Examples directory, then click EXPENSES.IMP in the list that is displayed. Click OK or double-click the filename to open the model. Improv loads the expense report model shown in Figure 19-1.

The first time you open the model, these elements are displayed on screen.

◪   EXPENSES.IMP Browser

The Browser is a window that contains a list of each element in the Expense Report model, like a table of contents. Use it to rename elements, to open or move between different elements in the model, and to add, copy, and delete any element the model contains (see Chapter 5 for more information on Browse windows).

◪   Expense Report - Complete View

This view shows the complete worksheet. You see the data pane, which displays row and column item names and the worksheet values. You also see the formula pane, which contains the formulas on which Improv calculates the values in the data pane. Enter expense amounts in this view.

FIGURE 19-1

Expense Report model

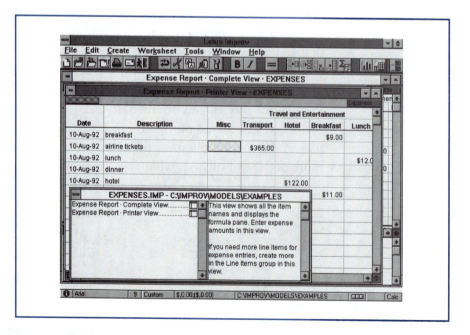

🔲   Expense Report - Printer View

This view prints out a standard report; the item names and the formula pane are not displayed. The printer view shares the same data with the worksheet, but doesn't share the same display. This means that changes you make to the worksheet values or calculations will also update the report view (and vice versa), but rearranging the data in one view doesn't affect the worksheet.

USING THE BROWSER

If the Browser isn't on the screen, select Browser from the Window menu. You see the Browser shown here:

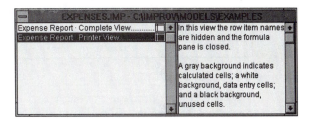

The left side of the window displays a list of the elements in the model, along with their names and icons that identify each element as a worksheet view, chart, script, or presentation. When you highlight an element in the Browser, a note associated with the selected element appears on the right side of the window. To remove the Browser from the screen, click the close box at its upper-left corner.

EXPLORING THE WORKSHEET

If it's not already active, select Expense Report - Complete View from the Window menu. You see the display shown in Figure 19-2. Keep this display handy as you learn about the elements shown below.

Worksheet Contents

The top two-thirds of the worksheet, called the data pane, displays the expense transactions. The bottom third of the screen, called the formula pane, displays the formulas from

FIGURE 19-2

Expense Report -
Complete View

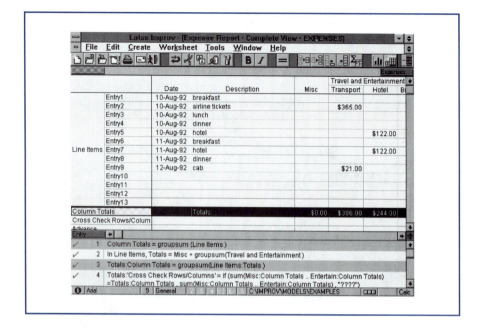

which Improv calculates some of the values that appear in the data pane. If you click a row in the data pane, and then select Mark formulas from the Worksheet menu, you will see the formulas that correspond to that row.

The Expense Report worksheet has two categories: "Entry" for the rows and "Expenses" for the columns.

Entry   The Entry category is used to maintain the expense transactions. Each line records one expense activity. It includes a date, description, and an amount in one or more of the expense categories.

Expenses   The Expenses category contains transaction details. Each column represents a different facet of the expense transaction, such as the date, description, and separate columns for each type of expense. The final column calculates transaction totals.

Using Cross-checking Formulas

Improv uses general formulas to calculate the column and row (transaction) totals. Each time you enter or change a transaction, Improv calculates the new values and updates the worksheet. All you have to do is enter the transaction details.

The Expense Report worksheet contains a cross-checking formula that uses the IF function. The formula confirms that the column totals and transaction totals balance.

Click Formula 4 in the formula pane, then select Mark Cells from the Worksheet menu to highlight the value associated with that formula. Use the scroll bar to move down the worksheet until the display looks like Figure 19-3.

The formula adds together the total for each column and compares that value to the Column Totals value. If the two values are the same, that value is entered into the Cross Check Rows/Columns cell. If the two values are not the same, a series of question marks is entered in the cell. This alerts you to a possible problem. Use this formula as a reference to create cross-checking formulas in your own worksheets.

Adding a New Expense Type

The worksheet's cross-checking formula specifies a data range: (Misc:Column Totals .. Entertain:Column Totals). When you add a new expense column after the last existing expense type column, you also have to edit the cross-checking formula to include the new column in the range. To do this, follow these steps:

1. Click Entertain to select that column.

2. Select Edit Add Item from the Edit menu. Improv adds a new column item, as shown in Figure 19-4.

3. Click the new column's default item name, type **Tips**, then press ENTER.

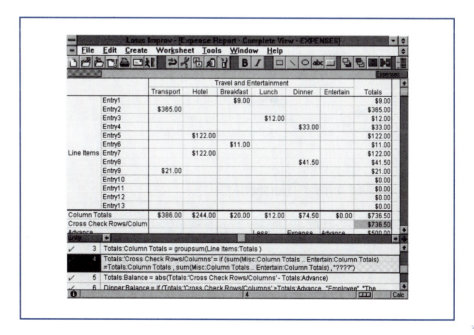

FIGURE 19-4

Expense Report - Insert Column Item

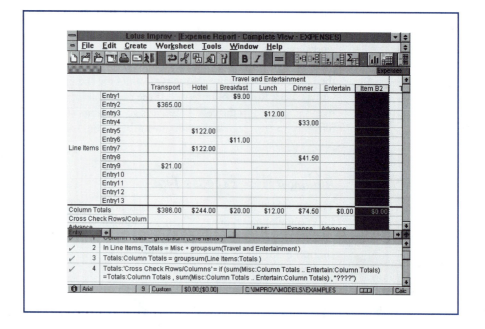

4. Double-click Formula 4 in formula pane. Find the first occurence of the range (Misc:Column Totals..Entertain:Column Totals).

5. Use the mouse to position the text cursor after the last letter in "Entertain," press BACKSPACE repeatedly to delete the word, then type **Tips**.

6. Find the second occurence of the range (Misc:Column Totals .. Entertain:Column Totals) and repeat step 5. Figure 19-5 shows how the data pane and cross-checking formula look after your edits.

If you don't change the formula, the Tips column won't be included in the cross-checking calculation and the Cross Check Rows/Columns:Totals cell will always display four question marks (????).

Adding a New Transaction

Now, to become more familiar with the data entry process, enter a transaction for the new expense type. Once you add the new expense type, it's easy to enter a transaction for that expense.

1. Click the last item row name "Entry13."

FIGURE 19-5

Revised
Cross-checking formula

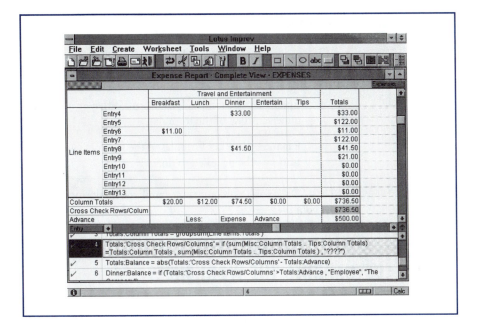

2. Select Add Item from the Edit menu, or simply press ENTER while Entry13 is highlighted; a new item will be created automatically.

    Fill in the expense information. Press TAB or RIGHT ARROW to move to the next data field. Use LEFT ARROW to move to a previous field.

3. Click the new item name to edit the text and type **VISA**. Press TAB to move to the Date field.

4. Enter a date. If you enter a date using a slash, for example, 3/5, when auto-formatting is turned on, Improv assumes that you're entering a date. It converts the fraction and enters it with a date format, for example 3-Mar-93 (you can use User Setup from the Tools menu to confirm whether or not the Auto format check box is marked in the User Setup dialog box).

5. Press TAB or RIGHT ARROW to move to the new Tips column. You can also click the Tips cell in the current row.

6. Enter the amount **$10.00**.

    Notice how Improv updates the relevant total values.

Examining Formulas

After you explore this worksheet, try the following activities to learn more about the formulas provided.

1. Enter a cross-checking formula in a different worksheet to test your understanding of the formula.

2. Examine the other formulas in the formula pane and determine exactly what Improv is being asked to do.

Once you've become more familiar with the model, it's easy to customize it to better fit your own needs.

CUSTOMIZING THE WORKSHEET

To use the EXPENSES model for your own expense report, save the model to a new name, then customize the new model. Because the expense report formulas are already set up, you only have to replace the data, instead of creating an entire new worksheet.

Saving the New Model

Before you replace the sample data with your own, save the EXPENSES worksheet with a new name. This lets you customize the new model and leave the sample model unchanged for future reference.

1. If the expense report worksheet is not the active window, select it from the Window menu or select File Open to reopen the model.

2. Once EXPENSES.IMP has been opened, select File Save As and enter the filename and location for your new, customized expense report model.

The new model will be displayed now in the main window.

Replacing the Sample Data

Once you are using the new model, type in your data to replace the sample expense transaction data.

1. Click the data cells to edit them, then type your own transaction information in each row to replace the existing sample data.

2. Click the row and column item names and type in new names to fit your own needs. For example, replace "Entry#" with "Check#" or the name of a credit card used for an expense transaction.

If you want to delete all of the sample data at once, select the data area (all the Entry lines and columns Date through Tips) and press DEL. In the resulting dialog box, select Clear Data Only. All the data will be erased, leaving the worksheet open for your own data.

Customizing the View

Improv's InfoBox provides you with several ways to easily customize how your worksheet displays. Worksheets views contain several elements: the rows, columns, item names, values, lines, etc. These elements can be customized using the InfoBox.

The right side of the InfoBox is the Style panel and controls a worksheet's elements, as shown here:

▨   Text Styles (color, font, alignment, numeric formats)

▨   Line Styles (color, style, shadow)

▨   Fill Styles (color, pattern)

You may want to customize the printer view of the expense report to explore the InfoBox. Select Expense Report - Printer View - EXPENSES from the Window menu. Highlight an element that you want to change, and click the InfoBox icon. You will see an InfoBox similar to the one shown here:

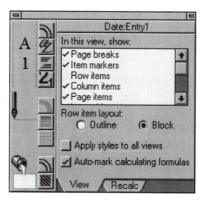

EXPLORING THE PRINTER VIEW

The Printer View displays the Expense Report as a standard form. The row item names and the formula pane don't display.

The Printer View uses background color to highlight important areas of the report. Data entry cells have a white background; calculated cells have a gray background; and unused cells have a black background. The view is formatted for a printed document and contains headers and footers.

If it's not already active, select Expense Report - Printer View - EXPENSES from the Window menu. You see the display shown in Figure 19-6.

Hiding Worksheet Data

Improv lets you "hide" certain worksheet settings to enhance the display or to just exclude superfluous settings from the view. The left side of the InfoBox is the View page and controls the elements that display in the current view. Notice that in the Printer view "Row items" isn't checked because in this view the row item names are not shown.

Elements can be hidden or redisplayed by changing the status (checked or unchecked) of each element.

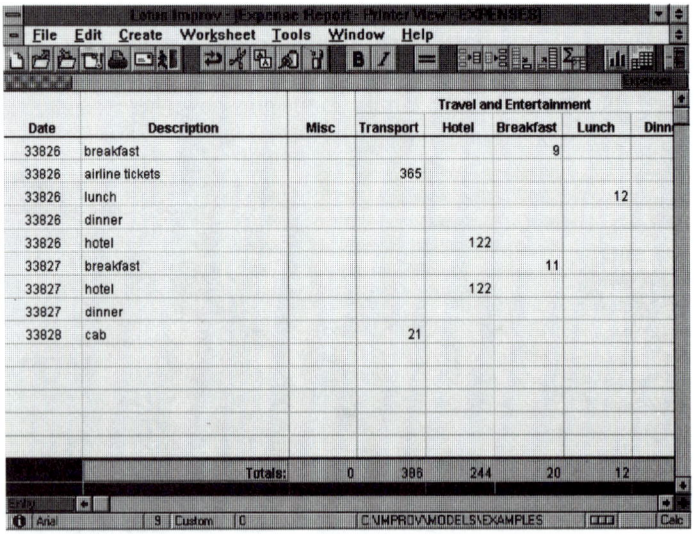

FIGURE 19-6

Expense Report -
Printer View

Printing the Report

Note

See Chapter 14 for detailed instructions on printing any Improv document.

You can print the expense report on a regular basis for your own records or to submit it for reimbursement. Send the output to any installed Windows printer or print file.

The procedure for printing a formatted worksheet view is no different from the procedure for printing any other Improv document.

1. To preview the expense report before printing, select Print Preview from the File menu.

   Figure 19-7 shows the preview window.

   When you finish previewing, click the Print command button to print the report.

2. If you don't want to preview the report, select File Print from the main menu bar to print the chart.

ON YOUR OWN

The EXPENSE model provides a full-featured expense reporting system. This chapter has introduced you to the major features and capabilities that are provided. Now, explore the sample data, along with this chapter, to better understand how the model was designed and how it can work for you. Then, if the model looks like something that is applicable to you, adapt it to meet your own needs and expectations.

FIGURE 19-7

Expense Report print preview

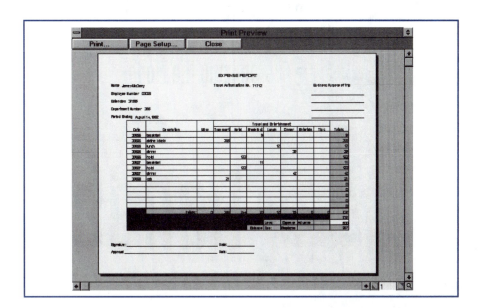

Improv 2

- The Loan Model and Browser

- Exploring the Summary Comparison Worksheet

- Exploring the Amortization Schedule

- Using Loan Qualification Ratios

- Exploring the Payment Table

- Customizing the Model

Handbook

CHAPTER 20

Analyzing Loans

When you want a lending institution to grant you a business or personal loan, it helps to do some homework first. If you research various loan scenarios (for example, the effects of different principal amounts and interest rates on monthly payments), it can help you to determine the amount of money you want to borrow and the payments that work best within your personal or business budget. With this information in hand, you'll be able to express your financial needs to a lender much more precisely.

Improv provides you with a Loan model, LOAN.IMP, that makes this process much easier. The Loan model contains loan qualification and comparison worksheets, a payment table, and an amortization schedule. (*Amortization* is the process of converting the cost of an intangible asset to an expense over its useful life, and is discussed in more detail later in the chapter.)

The Loan model also illustrates how to create Improv worksheets that share data. When worksheets share data, you enter information one time; then you use formulas in another worksheet to reference the same information. This saves time and eliminates data-entry errors.

The first part of this chapter provides an overview of the Loan model. The remainder of the chapter explains each of the model's elements in more detail, and describes the Improv features illustrated by the model. You'll also learn how to customize the model so you can adapt the worksheets to fit your own personal and business loan scenarios.

THE LOAN MODEL AND BROWSER

To open the model, select Open from the File menu, and select LOAN.IMP from the Examples directory. Improv loads the Loan model, shown in Figure 20-1. The first time you open the model, all of the following elements are displayed on screen.

▧ *Loan Model Browser:* The LOAN.IMP Browser displays a list of each element in the Loan model, like a table of contents. Use it to open or move among the elements of the model, and also to add, copy, or delete elements.

FIGURE 20-1

Loan model and
Browser

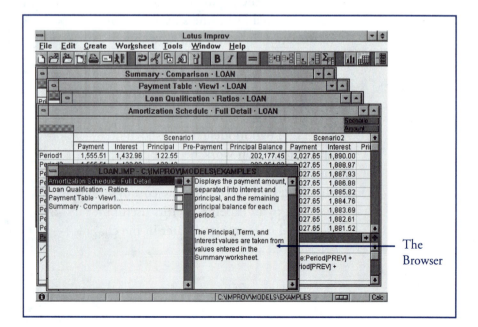

The
Browser

- ☑ *Amortization Schedule:* This worksheet examines each payment period during the life of the loan, including monthly payments, the amounts of principal and interest, extra payments, and the remaining balance. In accounting terms, this schedule illustrates how mortgage payments convert to an expense over the life of the loan.

- ☑ *Loan Qualification - Ratios:* This worksheet lets you calculate ratios that lenders use to determine if potential borrowers qualify for a loan.

- ☑ *Payment Table - View1:* This worksheet view lets you enter principal and interest amounts to create a monthly payment schedule.

- ☑ *Summary Comparison:* This worksheet lets you calculate and compare monthly payments for various loan scenarios, that is, loans with different principal amounts and interest rates.

As stated earlier, the Browser lists each component in the model, like a table of contents. If the Browser isn't already at the front of the Improv screen, select Browser from the Window menu. The Browser window for the Loan model is shown here:

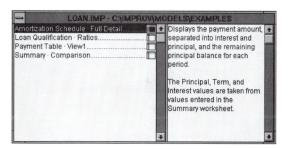

See Chapter 2 for more information on using the Browser.

EXPLORING THE SUMMARY COMPARISON WORKSHEET

The Summary Comparison worksheet lets you enter principal amounts, terms, and interest rates for one or more loans; then Improv calculates the monthly payment. Use the worksheet to compare the monthly payment for several loans with the same principal amount at various interest rates, or several loans with different principal amounts and various interest rates.

If it's not already active or displayed in the Improv window, display the worksheet by selecting Summary Comparison from the Window menu or from the Browser. The worksheet will look similar to Figure 20-2.

FIGURE 20-2

Summary Comparison
worksheet

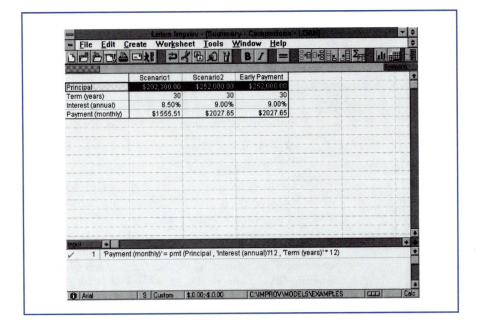

The Loan model's Summary Comparison worksheet and the Amortization Schedule share data. You enter loan variables in only one place, the Summary, and Improv then references the variables in formulas that appear in the Amortization Schedule.

Worksheet Contents

The top half of the Summary Comparison worksheet (the data pane) displays values. The bottom half (the formula pane) contains the formulas from which Improv calculates some of the values that appear in the data pane.

The worksheet has two categories: Input for the rows, and Scenario for the columns.

Input The Input category contains values for loan components. Each row represents a different component, such as loan principal, term of the loan, annual interest rate, and monthly payment.

Scenario The Scenario category represents the various loan scenarios for which you want to compare data. Each column is treated as a different loan.

Worksheet Formulas

The Summary Comparison worksheet illustrates how Improv lets you use one general formula to calculate every instance on a worksheet. For example, Formula 1 calculates the monthly payment for every loan scenario in the worksheet, including new scenarios you add later. When you enter or change the principal, term, or interest amounts, Improv recalculates the payment and updates the worksheet.

Using the PMT Function

The Summary Comparison worksheet uses the PMT function to calculate the monthly payment. This function calculates loan payments at a given interest rate per period, for a specified number of payment periods. PMT calculates payments for an ordinary annuity (that is, loans you pay yearly or at other regular intervals).

Suggestions for Practice

The Summary Comparison worksheet lets you quickly see how different loan variables affect the monthly payment. Change the interest rate and principal to view the effects of using this feature.

- ▰ Click the Interest (annual) percentage under Scenario2, type **.11**, and press ENTER. Be sure to type the decimal point in front of the number; otherwise, the interest rate will be 1100%. Notice that the monthly payment for Scenario2 changes to $2399.85.

- ▰ Click the Principal amount in Scenario2, type **225000**, and press ENTER. It's not necessary to type the decimal point when you enter whole numbers unless the number includes cents. Notice that the monthly payment for Scenario2 changes to $2142.73.

Look at how the Scenario2 and Early Payment scenarios on your screen differ from Figure 20-2. Originally, there was no difference in these two situations because the Principal, Terms, and Interest values were the same. Now that you've altered the scenarios, the monthly payment compares the smaller loan at a higher interest rate with the larger loan at a lower interest rate.

Select Revert to Saved from the File menu to save the Summary Comparison with its original values for future reference.

Use the Revert to Saved option with caution. This actually removes any changes that you have made to the model since the last File Save was performed.

EXPLORING THE AMORTIZATION SCHEDULE

Tip

Consult your accountant to determine the useful life of intangible assets.

The Amortization Schedule illustrates the process of converting the cost of an intangible asset (a mortgage in the Loan model), to an expense over its useful life (the payments and interest that are accumulated and paid). To explore this worksheet, select Amortization Schedule - Full Detail from the Window menu or the Browser. You see the Amortization Schedule shown in Figure 20-3.

What Is Amortization?

As stated earlier, amortization is the process of converting an intangible asset to an expense over its useful life, or over the life of the loan. An *intangible asset* can't be readily seen or touched and doesn't have physical substance; examples are mortgages, leaseholds, licenses, and copyrights. For it to quality as an intangible asset, you must own the item and it must have a monetary value. The period of time over which you amortize an intangible asset depends on the period of time the asset is of value to you.

FIGURE 20-3

Amortization Schedule
- Full Detail

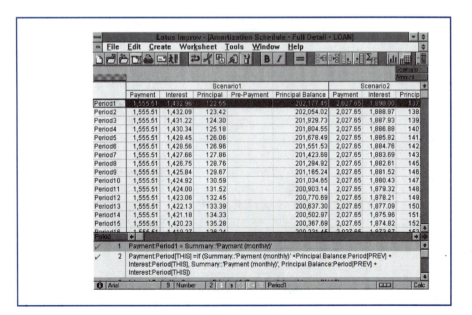

Worksheet Contents

Figure 20-3 displays the full details of the Scenario1 loan from the Summary Comparison worksheet: the standard monthly payment, the amounts applied to principal and interest during each month, any extra payments, and the remaining principal balance after each payment.

The Amortization Schedule worksheet illustrates how Improv enables worksheets to link data. You enter loan variables (principal, terms, and interest) for three scenarios in the Summary Comparison. The Amortization Schedule uses the same Scenario categories. Improv references the Summary's variables in the Schedule's formulas for each scenario to calculate the Amortization values.

Look at Formula 1 and notice the double-colon mark (::). Double colons in a formula indicate a reference to values stored in another worksheet. The name before the mark is the other worksheet's name; the name after the mark is the cell in the worksheet being referenced. For example, Formula 1 references Summary::'Payment(monthly)'. This tells Improv to use the Payment(monthly) item values in the Summary Comparison worksheet. See Chapter 8 for more information on using intersheet formulas.

You might also notice in Figure 20-3 the use of the words THIS and PREV in Formula 2 (as in Payment:Period[THIS]). THIS and PREV are special keywords used by Improv to represent the current line (THIS) and the previous line (PREV) in the data pane. These words are very useful when you're writing formulas where one value depends on the previous value.

Suggestions for Practice

In the Summary Comparison worksheet, change one of the loan scenarios; for example, change the principal or interest. Then select Amortization Schedule - Full Detail from the Window menu or from the Browser. Notice how Improv has updated the worksheet using the new information you entered.

Select Revert to Saved from the File menu to save the Summary Comparison with its original values for future reference.

USING LOAN QUALIFICATION RATIOS

The Loan Qualification Ratios worksheet lets you experiment with various down-payment scenarios and calculate the top and bottom ratios. Lenders use these ratios to determine if a borrower qualifies for a loan. The Loan Qualification Ratios worksheet does not link to other worksheets in the model. Improv lets you easily modify this worksheet to research your own loan qualification scenarios.

To open the worksheet shown in Figure 20-4, select Loan Qualification Ratios from the Window menu or the Browser. (If the Loan model isn't open, select File Open and open the model from the Examples directory.)

Worksheet Contents

The Loan Qualification Ratios worksheet lets you analyze whether you qualify for a loan from two perspectives: your perspective, and the lender's perspective. The Column category on the worksheet defines the method used for each perspective.

The first column, Calc%Down, analyzes the scenario from your perspective; you enter the down-payment amount that's affordable to you. The second column, Input%Down, analyzes the scenario from the lender's perspective; here you enter the percentage of the purchase price that the lender requires as a down payment. For both columns, you enter the purchase price, the interest rate, the yearly term of the loan, and your monthly income and expenses. Improv calculates either the percentage down to display your perspective, or the down payment to display the lender's perspective. Improv also calculates the loan amount and the top and bottom ratios. These values allow you to examine your options before you approach a lending institution.

FIGURE 20-4

Loan Qualification
Ratios worksheet

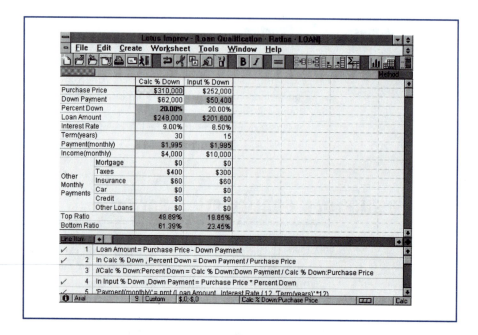

Suggestions for Practice

Improv's flexible editing features allow you to easily modify the Loan Qualification Ratios worksheet to examine your own qualification scenario.

Note

The values displayed in this worksheet are in a format that helps you quickly distinguish between items that you enter and items that are calculated using formulas. Worksheet cells with a white background contain data that you enter. Cell values that have a gray background are calculated by Improv. Each time you enter or change a value in a white cell, Improv recalculates the worksheet formulas and updates the affected gray cells.

Let's modify the data to examine how this worksheet functions. The worksheet uses a 30-year home loan for the borrower's scenario (Calc%Down) and a 15-year home loan for the lender's scenario (Input%Down). You can change the values to represent any loan you want to examine.

First, let's examine a scenario from your perspective. In the Calc%Down column, first enter the Purchase Price. Next, enter the Down Payment. Improv calculates the percentage of the purchase price that the down payment represents. Finally, change the income and expense items, and notice how the ratios change based on your entries.

Next, examine the scenario from the lender's viewpoint. In the Input%Down column, enter the Purchase Price you want to use. Then enter the Percent Down (the percentage of the purchase price required by the lender). Be sure to type the decimal point before the number, or the percentage rate will be incorrect. Improv calculates the down payment. Again, try changing the income and expense items, and notice how the ratios change based on your entries.

Tip

You may want to talk to your banker about the use of ratios in determining loan qualifications.

EXPLORING THE PAYMENT TABLE

The Payment Table worksheet lets you enter different interest rates and principal amounts; then it creates a customized payment table based on those values. This lets you compare the monthly payment for several principals at a variety of interest rates. The sample data in the Loan model is for a 30-year mortgage loan. The Payment Table worksheet does not link to other worksheets in the model.

To explore this worksheet, select Payment Table View1 from the Window menu or from the Browser. You will see the worksheet shown in Figure 20-5.

FIGURE 20-5

Payment Table

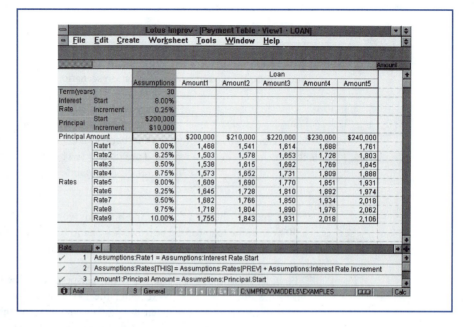

FIGURE 20-5

Payment Table

Like the Loan Qualification Ratios worksheet, the Payment Table uses a display format that helps you distinguish between items that you enter and items that Improv calculates. However, here the format is the opposite of the Loan Qualification Ratios worksheet: You enter values in cells with a gray background, and Improv calculates the values in cells with a white background.

You enter the values for your loan in the Assumptions column: a starting principal, and a dollar amount by which to increase the principal. You also enter a starting interest rate and the increments by which the interest rate will increase.

Once you've entered your data, Improv calculates the monthly payment for each principal and interest combination and displays the values in the table at the bottom of the data pane. This worksheet enables you to quickly see how principal and interest compare as they increase.

If you want, enter your own data in the worksheet to examine various assumptions. Click each of the first five values in the Assumptions column and type in a different value; notice how Improv updates the payment table using your changes.

CUSTOMIZING THE MODEL

To use the Loan model to research and analyze your own prospective loan scenarios, be sure to save the model first to a file with a new name, before you change any sample data.

Then you can modify the new model and leave the sample model unchanged for future reference. Just select Save As from the File menu, and enter a filename and location for your customized loan model.

Afterward, change any element in the new model to fit your own needs. Because the formulas already exist, you only have to replace the sample data and add new items, instead of creating an entire new worksheet. Improv recalculates the values and updates the worksheets based on your entries.

Modifying the Worksheets

Improv's flexible editing features let you easily change the model worksheets to examine your own loan scenarios—all you need to do is replace the sample values with your own information. Click the item names and data cells, and type your own names and values in each column and row to replace the existing sample data. For example, you might replace Scenario1 in the Summary worksheet with the name of your prospective lender.

To add additional items, such as another loan scenario to the Summary Comparison worksheet or more personal expense items to the Other Monthly Payments item group in the Loan Qualification Ratios worksheet, click a column or row and select Add Item from the Edit menu to add an item to the right of your selection.

To remove unnecessary columns or rows, click the column or row and select Delete Item from the Edit menu.

Customizing the Format

Improv's dynamic formatting features give you the tools to easily customize the Loan model's worksheets. Select the Style and Settings options on the Worksheet menu to bring up Improv's InfoBox. The InfoBox's Style panel and Settings pages let you control text attributes, numeric formats, line styles, and fill patterns. See "Improv User Interface" in Chapter 4 or Improv's on-line Help for more information on using the InfoBox.

Improv 2

- The Accounts Receivable Model

- Exploring the Model

- Customizing the Model

Handbook

CHAPTER 21

Analyzing Accounts Receivable

When you sell goods or services on credit, you need to track amounts that have not yet been paid by your customers, known as your *accounts receivable*. Often, a portion of your accounts receivable may prove to be uncollectible, and it's important to recognize these "bad debts" quickly. That way you're able to create a realistic allowance for bad debt and stay in control of your company's lifeblood: its incoming cash flow.

Improv's Accounts Receivable (ACCTREC.IMP) model helps you manage your receivables by calculating *aging information* and providing you with the tools to identify overdue accounts. The model also illustrates the advantages of using linked worksheets; that is, worksheets that share data. You only have to enter data once, and Improv updates any associated values in linked worksheets.

This chapter gives an overview of the Accounts Receivable model, and then discusses each part of the model in greater detail. The chapter also contains suggestions on how to customize the model for your own use.

THE ACCOUNTS RECEIVABLE MODEL

To open the model, select File Open and select ACCTREC.IMP from the Examples directory. Improv loads the Accounts Receivable model shown in Figure 21-1. The first time you open the model, all of the following elements are displayed on screen.

- *Accounts Receivable Model Browser:* The Browser lists each element in the model, like a table of contents. Use it to rename elements, to open or move among the model's elements, and to add, copy, and delete any element the model contains.

- *Account Summary:* This worksheet view summarizes accounts receivable information by customer account, including outstanding amounts and days open. Improv calculates all items except the company name.

FIGURE 21-1

The Accounts Receivable model

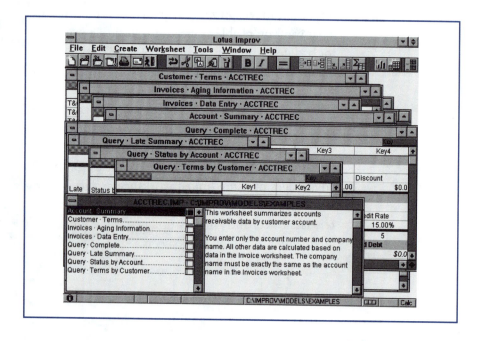

▰ *Customer Terms:* This worksheet view contains payment terms and special conditions for specific customer accounts. The model lets you assign more than one set of payment terms to customers. You enter all items except Select Key.

▰ *Invoices Aging Information:* This worksheet view stores accounts receivable aging information for individual invoices, including collection data and time outstanding.

▰ *Invoices Data Entry:* Use this worksheet to enter invoice information, such as invoice date and amount.

▰ *Query Complete:* This query consolidates all information contained in the Late Summary, Status by Account, and Terms by Customer views.

▰ *Query Late Summary:* This query displays the number of late invoices, the total late amount, and the estimated bad debt for each account. Improv calculates all items.

▰ *Query Status by Account:* This query displays the account total, late amount, and late charges for each account. Improv calculates all items except Customer name and Invoice class.

▰ *Query Terms by Customer:* This query displays the discount rate, discount period, credit, and default rates for each customer. Improv calculates all items except Customer name and Invoice class.

As stated earlier, the Browser lists each element in the model, similar to a table of contents. Figure 21-2 shows the ACCTREC.IMP Browser. If the Browser isn't active on your screen, select Browser from the Window menu.

The Accounts Receivable model contains many elements, and the Browser lets you quickly move among them to quickly examine accounts receivable information from different perspectives.

See Chapter 2 for more information on using the Browser.

FIGURE 21-2

The ACCTREC.IMP
Browser

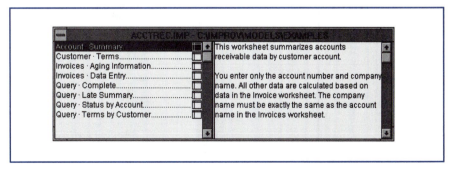

EXPLORING THE MODEL

Improv arranges the model's accounts receivable information in four worksheets: Customer, Invoice, Account, and Query. Each worksheet relates to a specific task. Figure 21-3 illustrates the interaction among the worksheets, as well as the other views of the Invoice and Query worksheets available in the model.

Following are descriptions of the four worksheets.

Customer Worksheet The Customer worksheet has one view, Terms. Here you enter a customer's payment terms and any special conditions that apply to the account.

Invoices Worksheet The Invoices worksheet has two views, Date Entry and Aging Information. You enter new invoices in the Data Entry view. Improv uses a formula to refer to the Customer Terms worksheet to verify the customer's payment terms. Then it calculates accounts receivable aging information and displays it on the Invoices Aging Information view, using formulas to reference the data in the Customer Terms and Invoices Data Entry worksheets.

FIGURE 21-3

Interaction among
ACCTREC.IMP model
worksheets

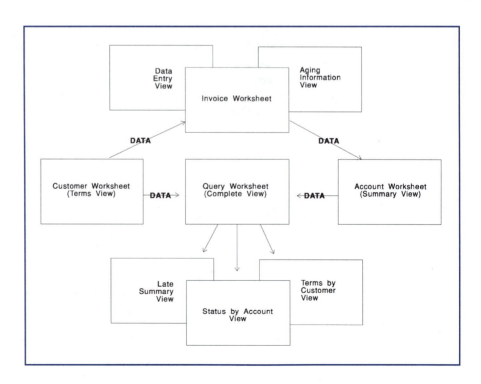

Account Worksheet The Account worksheet has one view, Account Summary. Improv uses formulas to reference the Invoices Aging Information view to calculate the values in the Account Summary.

Query Worksheet The Query worksheet has four views: Complete, Late Summary, Status by Account, and Terms by Customer. Each view lets you extract data from the model to isolate specific accounts receivable information and display it from a different perspective.

The Accounts Receivable model's four worksheets interconnect. You enter payment terms in the Customer Terms worksheet. When you enter new invoices in the Invoices Data Entry worksheet, Improv uses formulas to reference the Customer Terms worksheet and determines terms and conditions for the invoice. After you enter invoice details, Improv uses those values to perform calculations in the Account Summary and Query worksheets.

The remainder of this section describes each worksheet in detail. If you decide to customize the model for your own business needs, use this information for reference.

Entering Customer Terms

You enter terms and conditions (T&C) for your customers as the first step in analyzing accounts receivable information. Customer terms and conditions identify the circumstances under which you accept payment from each customer. You enter this information in the Customer Terms worksheet, shown in Figure 21-4.

There are two categories in this worksheet. The T&C category has one row for each set of terms and conditions being maintained. The Specifics category has one column for each peice of information available about a specific T&C entry.

Complete one row for each of your customers. After you've entered the terms and payment conditions, you can go on to enter invoice details in the Invoices Data Entry worksheet.

Company Enter the customer's company name.

Class Enter codes that you designate to indicate various classes of payment terms and conditions for one customer. When you enter an invoice on the Data Entry worksheet, you also enter its corresponding class, which must exist in the Customer Terms worksheet.

Discount Enter the percentage by which you reduce a customer's invoice when it is paid within the time specified in the Disc Days column.

Select Key Because a customer can have more than one class of payment, invoices need a unique identifier. Improv uses Formula 1 (SelectKey=Company&Class) to join the entries in Company and Class to create a unique identifier for invoices. Improv maintains the entries in this Select Key column.

FIGURE 21-4

Customer Terms
worksheet

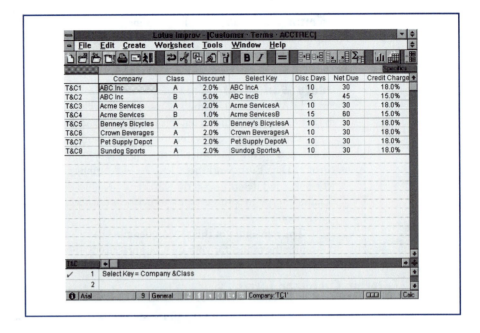

This type of identifier, known as a concatenated key, is based on the use of the concatenate (&) operator in Improv. This operator is used to join two character strings into one long string. For instance, 'ABC Inc' and 'A' become 'ABC IncA', as shown in the Select Key column of Figure 21-4.

Disc Days   Enter the number of days within which a customer must pay to have an invoice reduced by the percentage in the Discount column.

Net Due   Enter the number of days within which the customer must pay invoices to avoid a late payment charge.

Credit Charge   Enter the annual interest rate you charge for late payment of invoices.

Default Rate   Enter the percent chance that a customer will default on payment of an invoice, based on your prior experience. The Default Rate column is not shown in Figure 21-4, but is located to the right of the Credit Charges column in your worksheet.

Entering Invoice Details

The Invoices Data Entry worksheet is one of the two views of the Invoices worksheet. It only displays the items where you enter data; that is, items that aren't relevant to entering invoices have been excluded from the display using the Hide Items command on the

Worksheet menu. Select Invoices Data Entry from the Window menu or from the Browser. You see the screen shown in Figure 21-5.

Notice the gray bar to the right of the Date column. This is the marker that Improv uses to indicate hidden items. Double-click the marker to redisplay the hidden items. When you do, the worksheet displays customer aging information, which isn't relevant until you've entered invoices. The aging information displays on the Invoices Aging Information worksheet view, which is discussed in the section that follows this one.

The worksheet has two categories: Invoice for the rows and Detail for the columns. The Invoice category contains transactions; each row records one invoice. The Detail category contains transaction details; each column represents particular information about an invoice. All open invoices (Invoice1 through Invoice13) belong to the Open group. Notice that a group sum (Total) appears at the bottom of the group, and that Open appears to the left of the invoice names.

Tip

To personalize the Invoices Data Entry worksheet, change the row item names (Invoice1, Invoice2, etc.) to actual invoice numbers. When you add new line items, Improv recognizes the previous items as a series and automatically increases the item number sequentially in each new item name (Invoice14, Invoice15, and so on). See "Working with Items" in Chapter 9 for more information about using series that Improv recognizes.

Once you've entered all of the customer invoice details, you'll be ready to analyze accounts receivable information. Improv uses formulas that reference the customer and invoice data to calculate the accounts receivable aging information and account summaries that display in the remaining worksheets and views.

Now here are descriptions of the information in the Invoices Data Entry view.

FIGURE 21-5

Invoices Data Entry worksheet

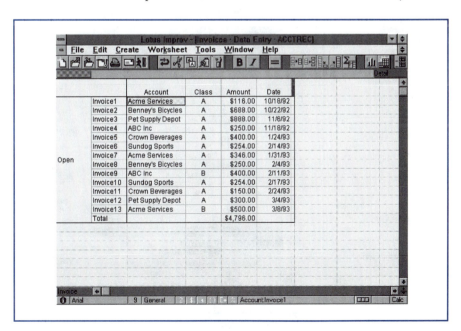

Account   Enter the customer's account name, which should be the same as the company name in the Customer Terms worksheet.

Class   Enter the class that represents the payment terms for the invoice. The class must already exist in the Customer Terms worksheet.

Amount   Enter the original invoice amount.

Date   Enter the original invoice date.

Viewing Invoices Aging Information

The Invoices Aging Information worksheet is another view of the Invoices Data Entry worksheet. The Aging Information view displays all items of the Invoices worksheet, including the items that were hidden in the Data Entry view—items that calculate and display accounts receivable information for each open invoice.

Select Invoices Aging Information from the Window menu or from the Browser. You will see a screen similar to that shown in Figure 21-6.

Improv calculates all cells in this worksheet. Each time you enter an invoice in the Invoices Data Entry worksheet, Improv automatically updates the Invoices Aging Information

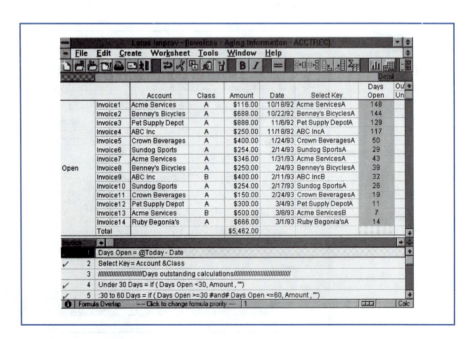

FIGURE 21-6

Invoices Aging
Information worksheet

worksheet with the new data. The first four columns display the information you entered in the Data Entry worksheet. The remaining columns are described in the paragraphs that follow. Note that not all these columns are shown in Figure 21-6 because of screen width restrictions. You will need to scroll right in the model to examine them all.

Select Key   This column displays the invoice's unique identifier. Improv creates this identifier using Formula 1 to concatenate the entries in the Account and Class columns.

Days Open   This column shows the number of days since the invoice was sent—that is, how long the invoice has been open. Improv calculates this as the number of days from the original invoice date to the current system date.

Outstanding (Under 30, 30 to 60, 61 to 90, Over 90)   The formula for the items in this group uses the values in the Days Open column to calculate the aging period in which the invoices fall. For example, if an invoice has been open for 7 days, Improv displays the invoice amount in the Under 30 Days column; if the invoice has been open for 50 days, Improv displays the invoice amount in the 30 to 60 Days column.

Improv provides all the above aging information as a powerful tool to aid you in collection efforts and to help you stay in control of your cash flow. In the Invoices Aging Information worksheet the information is in a format that emphasizes individual invoice details. In addition, the Loan model provides the Account Summary worksheet (described in the next section) so that you can view the same information summarized by account.

The items in the Collections group (to the right of the Outstanding group) display a variety of information to help you identify bad debt. Several of the Collection group formulas reference items in the Customer Terms worksheet. Look at Formula 10 and notice the double-colon mark (::). A double-colon in a formula indicates a reference to values stored in another worksheet. The name before the marks is the other worksheet's name; the name after the marks is the cell in the worksheet being referenced. See Chapter 8 for more information on using intersheet formulas.

Disc Days   This column uses the Disc Days and Select Key values in the Customer Terms worksheet to calculate the number of days within which a customer must pay the invoice for you to classify the payment as early.

Net Due   This column uses the Net Due and Select Key values in the Customer Terms worksheet to calculate the number of days after which you classify the payment as late.

Status   This column shows the invoice's status, which Improv determines using the information in the Disc Days and Net Due columns.

Late Key   This column displays the invoice's unique collection identifier. Improv creates the identifier using Formula 13 to join the entries in the Account and Status (from the Collections group) columns. Formulas in the Account Summary worksheet reference this key to calculate values in the Late Charges, Discount Offered, Invoices Late, Max Late, and Total Late columns.

Late Fees   This column shows the late fees outstanding for the invoice.

Total Due   This column displays the total invoice amount due, which includes any late fees and discount.

Est Bad Debt   This column shows the portion of the invoice that you're unlikely to collect, based on the account's Default Rate in the Customer Terms worksheet.

Collectible   This column shows the portion of the invoice that you're likely to collect, calculated as the Total Due amount less Est Bad Debt.

Viewing the Account Summary

The Account Summary worksheet uses the two Invoices worksheet views to calculate and condense accounts receivable information and display it by customer account. Improv calculates all cells in this worksheet except for the Company name, which you enter. Improv updates the Account Summary values each time you enter a new invoice in the Invoices Data Entry worksheet or modify information in the Customer Terms worksheet.

Select Account Summary from the Window menu or from the Browser. You see the screen shown in Figure 21-7.

Notice that several formulas in this worksheet reference items in the Invoices worksheet. Look at Formula 1 and notice the double-colon mark (::). A double-colon in a formula indicates a reference to values stored in another worksheet. The name before the marks is the other worksheet's name; the name after the marks is the cell in the worksheet being referenced. See Chapter 8 for more information on using intersheet formulas.

The Account Summary columns are described in the paragraphs that follow. As with the Invoices Aging Information worksheet, use the scroll bar to examine all the Account Summary columns.

Company   Enter the company's name, which must already exist in the Customer Terms worksheet.

Note   The Company column is case sensitive. In order for Improv to transfer or update the account information, the Company name must appear in the Account Summary exactly as it does in the Customer Terms worksheet, with the same uppercase and lowercase letters. Otherwise, Improv will not recognize the name.

FIGURE 21-7

Account Summary
worksheet

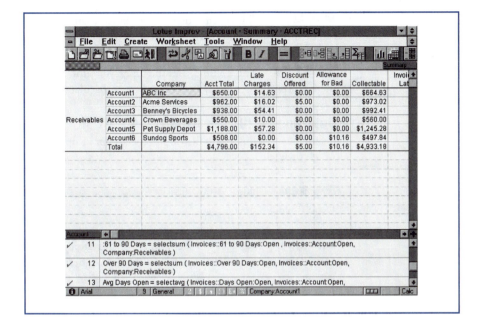

Acct Total   This column shows the account's total unpaid invoices.

Late Charges   This column uses the Late Fee and Late Key values in the Invoices Aging Information worksheet to calculate the total late charges owed on the account.

Discount Offered   This column uses the Discount, Late Fees, and Late Key values in the Invoices Aging Information worksheet to calculate the total discount available if the customer pays its outstanding invoices within the number of days that lets you classify the payment as early.

Allowance for Bad   This column calculates the amount you should allow for bad debt against this account, based on the Est Bad Debt value in the Invoices Aging Information worksheet.

Collectible   This column shows the amount that you can expect to collect from this account, based on the Collectible value in the Invoices Aging Information worksheet.

Invoices Late   This column uses the Days Open and Late Key values in the Invoices Aging Information worksheet to calculate the total number of late invoices.

Max Late   This column uses the Open Amount, Late Fees, and Late Key values in the Invoices Aging Information worksheet to calculate the largest late amount.

Total Late   This column uses the Open Amount, Late Fees, and Late Key values in the Invoices Aging Information worksheet to calculate the total late amount.

Outstanding (Under 30, 30 to 60, 61 to 90, Over 90)   The formula for the items in this group distributes the account's open invoices to the aging period in which they fall.

Avg Days   This column displays the average number of days that invoices for this account remain open.

Late Query Keys   These columns display system-assigned unique account keys that enable Improv to generate query information. Queries are discussed in the following section.

Performing Queries

A *query* is a question that you ask the model; for example:

- What is the status of every account?

- What are the terms for every customer?

- What are the late summaries for each account?

The Query worksheets illustrate how you create questions that request and extract specific information from the Accounts Receivable model data. Improv uses the SELECT function to retrieve values that meet a question's specified criteria. See Appendix A or Improv's on-line Help for more information on the SELECT function.

The Complete view of the Query worksheet consolidates the other three Query worksheet views: Status by Account, Terms by Customer, and Late Summary. The model lets you view all this information on one worksheet, or on individual worksheets. Because Improv has already set up the accounts receivable queries, all you have to do is type in the Key information.

In order for the queries to work, Improv must have generated unique account keys for the Query worksheet and for accounts with overdue invoices in the Account Summary worksheet. Improv has generated these keys for you; they appear in the last column (Late Query Keys) of the Account Summary worksheet.

Using Query Worksheets

Select Query Complete from the Window menu or from the Browser. You see the screen shown in Figure 21-8.

As stated previously, this worksheet consolidates the queries that appear in the three other Query worksheet views. The Late Summary view only displays the information shown on the bottom third of the Complete view; the Status by Account view only displays the information from the top third of the Complete view; and the Terms by Customer view only displays the information shown in the middle third of the Complete view.

Notice the top item in each column (Key1, Key2, and so on). These items are used to request information in each of the queries. Look at the gray background lines, labeled Key name, in each query—these tell you what information needs to be entered in each column. For example, in the Terms by Customer query, enter the Customer Name and Invoice Class. Improv immediately updates the resulting information from the query.

CUSTOMIZING THE MODEL

To use the Accounts Receivable model for your own company, first select the File Save As command and save the model to a file with a new name. This lets you work with the new model and leave the ACCTREC.IMP model unchanged for future reference. Then

FIGURE 21-8

Query Complete view

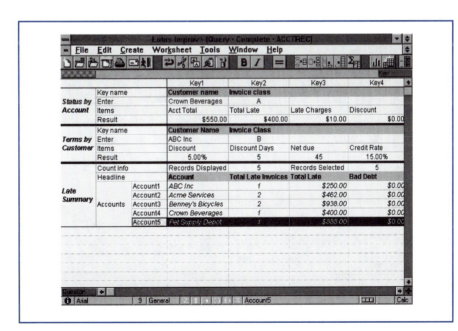

go ahead and customize any element in the new model to fit your own business needs. Because the formulas already exist, you need only replace the data and add new items, instead of creating an entire new worksheet. Improv recalculates the values and updates the model's worksheets based on your entries.

Modifying the Worksheets

Improv lets you easily change the Accounts Receivable worksheets to display your own data and, if need be, to accommodate a more elaborate receivables structure. You'll need to modify the items in the Customer Terms and Invoices Data Entry worksheets with your own information. Once you do this, Improv automatically updates the information in the other worksheet views. If you need help editing the worksheet, see Chapter 7.

Improv's InfoBox provides you with several ways to customize the display of text, numbers, lines, and fills in your Accounts Receivable worksheets. See Chapter 4 or Improv's on-line Help for more information on using the InfoBox.

Once you customize the ACCTREC.IMP model and begin using it on a regular basis, you have a powerful tool at your disposal to help you recognize potential bad debts and stay in control of your company's cash flow.

Improv 2

- Opening the Financials Model

- Exploring the Financials – Complete Worksheet

- Exploring the Financials Reports

- Customizing the Model

Handbook

CHAPTER 22

Creating Integrated Financials

Imagine a worksheet that gives you the total picture of your personal financial status, or that of your company. Then imagine generating dynamic reports automatically from that worksheet. Improv's Financials model, FINANCE.IMP, lets you do just that. The model contains a worksheet and three report views that illustrate how easy it is to combine balance sheet, income statement, and cash flow data into a complete financial picture, and to generate detailed reports from the same data.

The first part of this chapter briefly describes the Financials model. The remainder of the chapter discusses each element of the model in more detail, as well as the Improv features that the model illustrates.

OPENING THE FINANCIALS MODEL

To open the Financials model, select FINANCE.IMP from the Examples directory in the File Open dialog box. You will see a screen similar to Figure 22-1. The first time you open the model, all of the following elements are displayed:

◪ *FINANCE.IMP Browser:* The Browser lists each element in the Financials model, similar to a table of contents. Use it to open or move among the elements in the model, to rename elements, or to add, copy, and delete any element the model contains.

◪ *Financials - Complete View:* The integrated financial worksheet combines the data from the other elements in the Financials model (balance sheet, income statement, and cash flow reports) to present a total financial picture. The data in the reports are linked to the worksheet. When you change a worksheet value, Improv updates the associated values on the report views, as well as the worksheet.

◪ *Balance Sheet Report:* This report shows assets, liabilities, and equity for a specific accounting period and is formatted as a printed report.

◪ *Income Statement Report:* This report summarizes revenue and expenses for each period in the year, and is formatted as a printed report.

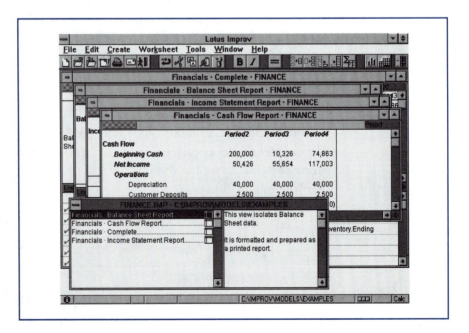

▨   *Cash Flow Report:* This report provides information about cash receipts, cash payments, and investment and financing activities during each accounting period.

EXPLORING THE FINANCIALS - COMPLETE WORKSHEET

The Financials - Complete integrated worksheet contains a complete financial picture for one company, combining all the data and values from the report views of the FI-NANCE.IMP model. Let's take a look at this model worksheet; if it's not active in your Improv window, select Financial - Complete from the Window menu or the Browser. You see the integrated Financials worksheet shown in Figure 22-2. To enlarge the worksheet to its maximum size for a better view, click the Maximize button in the upper-right corner of the worksheet window.

Worksheet Contents

The top half of the Financials worksheet, the data pane, displays financial values, in a format that helps you distinguish between values that you enter and values that Improv calculates using formulas. Worksheet cells with a gray background contain data that you

FIGURE 22-2

The integrated Financials worksheet

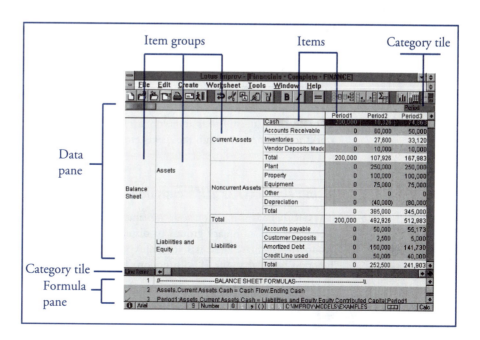

enter; cells with a white background contain values that Improv has calculated.

The bottom half of the screen, the formula pane, displays the formulas from which Improv calculates values in the data pane. When you click on a cell with a white background in the data pane, you can look at the formula pane to see the highlighted formula that calculates the selected value.

Worksheet Structure

The Financials - Complete worksheet illustrates how to structure a worksheet and organize data in meaningful way. Improv organizes data in a hierarchy of classifications: items, item groups, and categories. Each classification is subordinate to the one above it in the hierarchy. Each item is part of a larger category. You classify related items within a category as item groups.

Item Groups

A balance sheet shows business assets, liabilities, and equity as of a specific date. *Assets* are items of value that a business uses to generate revenue, such as inventory and accounts receivable. *Liabilities* are the obligations a company incurs as a part of doing business, such as accounts payable or bank loans. *Equity* represents the owner's investment in the business. When you analyze a balance sheet, remember that assets should equal liabilities plus equity.

In Improv, a group is a series of items identified by a common name. There are three major groups in the Finance model: Balance Sheet, Income Statement, and Cash Flow. Each of these is called a *nested group* because they contain further group breakdowns. For instance, the Balance Sheet group has two nested groups: Assets, and Liabilities and Equity. These are broken down even further. To classify related item groups *within* another group, select the related item groups and select Item Group from the Create menu. Improv creates a nested group, within which the selected item groups fall. For example, the Current Assets and Noncurrent Assets groups on the Financials - Complete worksheet are nested within the Assets group.

Using the GROUPSUM Function

The GROUPSUM function adds the values in a group or range. The integrated Financials worksheet uses summary groups to display group subtotals. When you use summary groups to calculate subtotals for items in the same category, use the GROUPSUM function rather than the SUM function. This prevents Improv from including subtotals in total calculations.

In Figure 22-3, Formulas 5 and 6 use the GROUPSUM function to calculate totals for the Current Assets and Noncurrent Assets groups. Formula 7 uses the GROUPSUM function to calculate the total of the Assets group, which contains the two nested groups Current Assets and Noncurrent Assets. The Assets total is calculated correctly by including every cell in the Assets group, except those cells that use the GROUPSUM function. If Formula 7 were to use the SUM function to calculate the Assets total, the result would be incorrect; SUM would include every cell in the Current Assets and Noncurrent Assets groups, including the group sums, and the total would be twice its expected amount.

Categories

In this model, two categories are used. The Line Items category, which is made up of each row in the model, is used to list the specific amounts being tracked. The Period category (columns) lists the periods of time for which financial data is being collected.

What to Try

You have learned that when Improv worksheeet groups have summary items, you can collapse the group to display only the group name and its total. Collapsing a group doesn't affect worksheet data; it only displays the data differently. In the Financials model, you

FIGURE 22-3

Formulas using the
GROUPSUM function

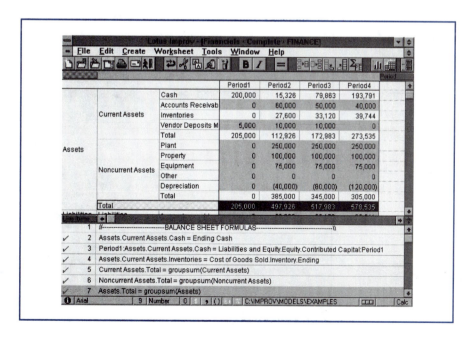

can use this feature to isolate subtotals and totals and focus on the worksheet's "bottom line." Try collapsing some of the Financials worksheet groups and notice the effects of using this feature.

First, click Current Assets to select that group, and select Collapse Group from the Worksheet menu. Improv collapses the selected group, as shown in Figure 22-4. Notice that the Cash, Accounts Receivable, Inventories, and Vendor Deposits line items are no longer visible. Next, select the Noncurrent Assets group and collapse it. Notice that the collapsed view emphasizes the financial status of your company's assets and not the individual assets themselves.

To redisplay individual items in a collapsed group, click to select the group and select Expand Group from the Worksheet menu.

EXPLORING THE FINANCIALS REPORTS

The reports in the FINANCE.IMP model make it easy to isolate data from the integrated Financials worksheet and display it in several different views: the Balance Report, the Income Statement Report, and the Cash Flow Report. Creating a worksheet with an organized structure facilitates this process.

Each view prints as a standard report; the item names and formula pane are not included. The reports share the same data with the integrated Financials worksheet, but

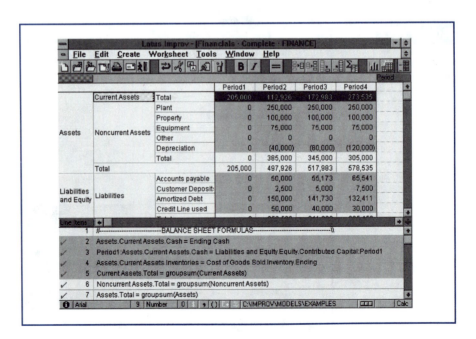

FIGURE 22-4

The Current Assets group, collapsed

do not share the same display. This means that changes to the worksheet values or calculations will be reflected in the reports, and vice versa; however, rearranging the data in one report doesn't affect other reports or the worksheet.

The Balance Sheet Report

To display the Balance Sheet Report, select Financials - Balance Sheet Report from the Window menu or from the Browser. Figure 22-5 illustrates a Balance Sheet Report.

Each report view in the Financials model uses a format appropriate for a report. Notice in Figure 22-5 that the integrated Financials worksheet's item names and item, cell, and worksheet grid lines do not appear in the Balance Sheet Report. Enhanced text is used to emphasize report headings.

Select Settings from the Worksheet menu. Notice in Figure 22-5 that the selected Row Item Layout setting is Outline. This layout indents the item names, similar to headings in an outline. Click the radio button for the Block layout setting and notice how the report changes—the item names are displayed in block form, which takes up more space on the screen. When you're done, change the layout back to Outline.

In the Settings panel, examine the list box of elements at the top and notice which ones are checked. These are the elements selected to appear in the current view; items without a check mark don't display. Use the scroll bar to move down the list to the Item Grid, Cell Grid, and Worksheet Grid items—notice that they are not checked. These are the settings you need to exclude in order to display the report without grid lines. Click

FIGURE 22-5

Balance Sheet Report

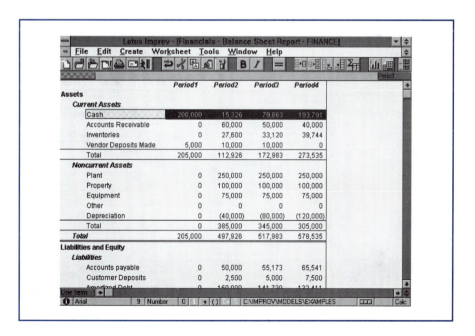

the Cell Grid item, and notice the difference in the report display. When you're done, click Cell Grid again to remove the grid lines.

The Income Statement Report

The Income Statement Report summarizes your company's revenues and expenses for a specific period. Because an income statement's net income for one period equals the change in owner's equity shown on a balance sheet between the same period and the next, the information on the Income Statement Report helps to explain how assets, liabilities, and equity change between balance sheets.

Select Financials - Income Statement Report from the Window menu or the Browser. You will see an Income Statement Report like the one in Figure 22-6.

Select Style from the Worksheet menu. Click the Font icon, which is the second icon from the top of the Style panel. In the Font window, you'll see the available text attributes (bold, italic, and so on), font sizes, and typefaces. Notice the selected text attributes (the ones with check marks beside them) and the highlighted font size and typeface for the Cost of Goods Sold item: 9 point Arial, bold, and italic. (Also notice that indicators in the dynamic status bar at the bottom of the Improv window display the style for the currently selected item. You'll get a chance to work with the status bar in the next section, about the Cash Flow Report.)

Try changing the font size or typeface for the Cost of Goods Sold heading to see

FIGURE 22-6

Income Statement
Report

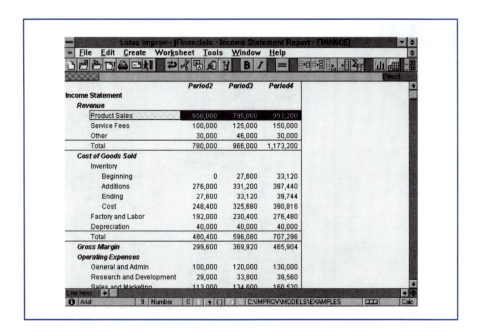

the difference in the report display. When you're done, click the original settings to restore the original style.

The Cash Flow Report

The Cash Flow Report provides information about your company's cash receipts, cash payments, investments, and financing activities during an accounting period. The report has three major sections: Cash Flow from Operations, Cash Flow from Investing activities, and Cash Flow from Financing activities. This report is a valuable tool for assessing a company's ability to generate positive future cash flow and its ability to meet obligations.

Select Financials - Cash Flow Report from the Window menu or from the Browser. You see a Cash Flow Report like the one in Figure 22-7.

As you examine the Cash Flow Report, look at the dynamic status bar. Click Arial on the status bar. A list of other available typefaces displayes. Click a couple of different typefaces to see how they look in the report. When you're done, you may wish to return to the Arial default.

Printing the Reports

The Balance Sheet, Income Statement, and Cash Flow Reports display data in a report

FIGURE 22-7

Cash Flow Report

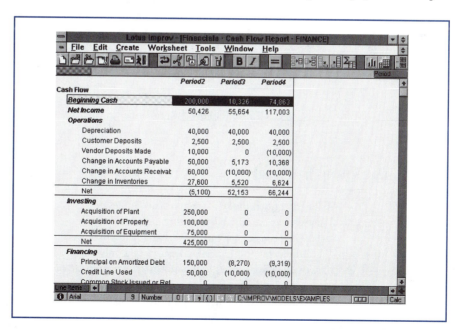

format. The row item names and the formula pane are excluded, and the views print as standard reports. The report titles are Improv headers.

You can use Improv's Print function to print your financial reports on a regular basis, for analysis or for submitting to a lending institution or board of directors. You can send the output to any installed Windows printer or print file. The procedure for printing a formatted worksheet view is no different from the procedure for printing any other Improv document.

Note	See Chapter 14 for detailed instructions on printing Improv documents.

CUSTOMIZING THE MODEL

To use the Financials model for yourself or your company, be sure to save the worksheet with a new name first. Then go ahead and customize any element in the new model to fit your own needs. Because the formulas already exist, you need only replace the example data, instead of creating an entire worksheet. Improv will recalculate the values and update the worksheet based on your entries. The original sample model will remain unchanged for future reference. Here is the procedure for saving the model with an filename that you can customize:

1. If the Financials model is not open, select Open from the File menu and choose FINANCE.IMP from the Examples directory.

2. When the model displays, select Save As from File menu, and enter a new filename and location for your customized Financials model. The new model appears in the main window.

3. Select Browser from the Window menu, then select the first element you want to customize. Follow the guidelines in the section just below.

Modifying the Model

The integrated Financials model categorizes data by Period and Line Item and illustrates just one approach to organizing financial data. Improv's features, many of which this chapter discusses, let you easily change the worksheet and associated reports for a different or more detailed financial structure. You only need to replace the items in the Financials - Complete worksheet with your own data; Improv then updates the report views.

Select the Financials-Complete worksheet from the Browser or the Window menu. Click each row item, and type in the names of your own assets, liabilities, revenue, expenses, and so on. Use the TAB key to move from column to column. To add new line items to the item groups, use Add Item from the Edit menu or Items from the Create menu; for example, you may have other current assets to include in the Current Assets group. Use Delete Item from the Edit menu to remove unnecessary line items. For more information on editing a worksheet, see Chapter 7.

Once you've modified the integrated Financials worksheet to fit your own situation, you may wish to further customize the model's four reports. Use Improv's InfoBox Style panel and Settings options to easily change the reports, including the text, line, and fill attributes, the numeric format, and any colors that you want to add to the report. The discussion in Chapter 4, "Improv User Interface," and Improv's on-line Help offer additional information on using the InfoBox.

Once you have customized the Financials worksheet and report views and begin using them regularly, you'll see the benefits of having your personal or company financial data located in one file. The worksheet's complete financial structure means you never have to open and close several files to generate your important financial reports on a regular basis.

PART SEVEN

Appendixes

Improv 2

- Function Categories
- The Add-In Functions
- Conventions Used
- Calendar Functions
- Financial Functions
- Group Functions
- Logical Functions
- Mathematical Functions
- Select Functions
- Special Functions
- Statistical Functions
- String Functions

Handbook

APPENDIX

A

Function Reference

As you work with Improv, you will want to become more familiar with the formulas you use to manipulate your data. Improv has many *built-in functions* that simplify your work by performing common but specialized calculations. These built-in functions are not restricted to numeric calculations; some perform calculations (or *transformations*) on logical, date, or character data.

ABOUT IMPROV FUNCTIONS

Think of a function as a "black box": You enter data, and Improv will perform the necessary calculations or transformations and produce a predictable outcome. Each function must have an *argument,* which is the object on which Improv acts when it performs the calculation or manipulation. It is important to remember that a function always returns a *value.*

Many functions perform calculations on numeric data. Some of these are simple calculations you could perform yourself: the SUM function totals the numeric values in a list, for example. Other functions perform more complex calculations you probably learned in math classes, such as calculating the square root of a numeric value, which is done by the SQRT function. Other functions perform even more complex operations: the VDB function calculates the variable-rate declining depreciation allowance of an asset.

Some functions work on non-numeric data. *Logical functions* make calculations based on true or false *conditions. String functions* manipulate text, and are used primarily to format your worksheet. A few other special functions will give you information about your worksheet or the computer you're using.

USING IMPROV FUNCTIONS

Improv uses some rather cryptic abbreviations to name its functions, but, luckily, you don't need to remember them. When you click the Functions button on the formula bar, an alphabetical list pops up—simply use your mouse to scroll through the list and click the function you want to use. Improv will automatically enter the function name into your formula.

When you pop up the function list, you will see the *argument placeholders* (that is, the words that represent the argument values you need to supply) in parentheses after the function name. To supply the argument values, you can replace the placeholder with your data, or point and click the data pane cell that contains the data you want to enter.

FUNCTION CATEGORIES

There are nine categories of Improv functions; they are grouped according to the type of calculation performed:

Function Category	Type of Calculation
Calendar	Calculation of values associated with dates and times
Financial	Analysis of investments and annuities; depreciation; calculation of cash flow and loans
Group Summary	Statistical calculations on values in groups and ranges
Logical	Calculations based on conditions that are either true or false
Mathematical	Calculation of values using trigonometry, logarithms, and numeric operations
Select	Statistical calculations on values that meet specific criteria
Special	Information about the contents of a worksheet
Statistical	Statistical calculations on numeric values
String	Text evaluation and manipulation

······················
THE ADD-IN FUNCTIONS

Improv includes about 50 very specialized *add-in functions*; *add-in* means that you must register at the beginning of your work session if you want to use them. If Improv fails to recognize a function that you invoke, it may be because you haven't yet registered the add-in functions file. For thorough instructions for loading these functions, consult your Improv manual.

The add-in functions are as follows, and are also defined in this chapter:

ACCRUED	DATEDIF	NORMAL	PUREVARS
ACOSH	DATEINFO	NPER	PVAL
ACOTH	DB	PAYMT	RANK
ACSCH	DECIMAL	PERMUT	ROUNDDOWN
ASECH	ERF	PPAYMT	ROUNDUP
ASINH	FACT	PRICE	SECH
ATANH	FDIST	PUREAVG	SINH
BETA	FVAL	PURECOUNT	SKEWNESS
BINOMIAL	GAMMA	PUREMAX	SUMSQ
CHIDIST	HEX	PUREMIN	TANH
COMBIN	IPAYMT	PURE	TDIST
COSH	IRATE	STD	WEEKDAY
COTH	MEDIAN	PURESTDS	WORKDAY
CSCH	MIRR	PUREVAR	YIELD

CONVENTIONS USED IN THIS FUNCTION REFERENCE

The remaining sections in this chapter list the Improv functions alphabetically within each function category. Each function is described in detail, and a complete description of the function's syntax and arguments is provided. Function descriptions use the following conventions:

- Function names appear in uppercase (SUM, for example).

- Arguments that are optional are enclosed in brackets ([ ]).

- Argument placeholders in the function syntax statements appear in lowercase italic. (When you enter the function, you must enter the type of information—number, date, and so on—specified by the argument placeholder.) Placeholders used in this reference are listed in the table below.

Placeholder	What You Need to Enter
number, n	A number, or the name of a cell that contains a number, or an expression or function that returns a number.
string	Text (any sequence of letters, numbers, and symbols) enclosed in quotation marks, or the name of a cell that contains text, or an expression or function that returns text.
logical	An expression that evaluates to true or false.
location, group, range	The name of a cell, group, or range, or an expression or function that returns the name of an item, group, or range.

CALENDAR FUNCTIONS

Calendar functions provide a simple method for manipulating dates within Improv. The calendar functions are described below.

D360

D360 returns the number of days between two dates, based on a 360-day year. The syntax for this function is

D360 *(start-date-number,end-date-number)*

The arguments *start-date-number* and *end-date-number* are date numbers, which are usually calculated by another date function.

Related Functions   DATEDIF, WORKDAY

DATE

DATE gives you the number of a day for a specified year, month, and day, using December 31, 1899, as the starting point. Thus, December 31, 1899, is date number 1; January 1, 1900, is date number 2; and so forth. The syntax for this function is

> DATE*(year,month,day)*

where *year* is a number from 0 (the year 1900) to 199 (the year 2099); *month* is a number from 1 to 12; and *day* is a number from 1 to 31.

Related Functions   DATEVALUE, NOW

DATEDIF

DATEDIF gives you the number of years, months, or days between two dates. The syntax for this function is

> DATEDIF *(start-date-number,end-date-number,format)*

The arguments *start-date-number* and *end-date-number* are date numbers, which are usually calculated by another function. The *format* argument determines the format of the resulting output; *format* is expressed as a code from the following table:

format Value	Number Returned by DATEDIF
y	Years
m	Months
d	Days
md	Days, ignoring months and years
ym	Months, ignoring years
yd	Days, ignoring years

Related Function D360

DATEINFO

DATEINFO returns information about a date number. The syntax for this functions is

DATEINFO*(date,attribute)*

where *date* is a date number, which is usually supplied by another date function; and *attribute* is a number from the following table:

attribute Value	Information Returned by DATEINFO
1	Name of a week day, abbreviated (e.g. Mon)
2	Name of a week day (e.g. Monday)
3	A week day, expressed as a number (e.g. 0 is Monday; 6 is Sunday)
4	A week of the year, expressed as a number from 1 to 53
5	Name of a month, abbreviated (e.g. Jan)
6	Name of a month (e.g. January)
7	Number of days in the month specified by *date*
8	Number of days left in the month specified by *date*
9	Last day of the month specified by *date*
10	The quarter the *date* is in, as a number from 1 (Q1) to 4 (Q4)
11	The value 1 if the year specified in *date* is a leap year; 0 if the year is not a leap year
12	A day of the year, expressed as a number from 1 to 366
13	Days left in the year, expressed as a number

DATEVALUE

DATEVALUE returns the date number for a date, which can then be used in calculations. The syntax for this function is

DATEVALUE*("date-string")*

where *date-string* is the relevant date, entered as text and enclosed in quotation marks.

Related Functions   DATE, TIMEVALUE

DAY

DAY returns the day of the month (1 to 31) of the date specified in *date-number*. The syntax for this function is

DAY*(date-number)*

The argument *date-number* is a number from 1 (January 1, 1900) to 73050 (December 31, 2099), which is usually supplied by another date function.

Related Functions   MONTH, YEAR

HOUR

HOUR returns the hour of *time-number*, expressed as a number from 0 (midnight) to 23 (11:00 P.M.). The syntax for this function is

HOUR*(time-number)*

The argument *time-number* is a number from .000000 (midnight) through .999988 (11:59:59 P.M.). Usually another time function supplies *time-number*.

Related Functions   MINUTE, SECOND

MINUTE

MINUTE returns the minutes in a *time-number*, expressed as a number 0 to 59. The syntax for this function is

MINUTE*(time-number)*

The argument *time-number* can be any value from .000000 (midnight) to .999988 (11:59:59 P.M.). Usually another time function supplies *time-number*.

Related Functions   HOUR, SECOND

MONTH

MONTH gives you the month in a specified *date-number*, expressed as a number from 1 to 12. The syntax for this function is

MONTH*(date-number)*

The argument *date-number* can be any number from 1 (January 1, 1900) to 73050 (December 31, 2099). Usually another date function supplies *date-number*.

Related Functions   DAY, YEAR, WEEKDAY

NOW

NOW gives you the current date and time from your computer, expressed as a date and time number. NOW has both a date number, expressed as a whole number, and a time number, expressed as a decimal. The syntax is

@NOW

SECOND

SECOND gives you the seconds, expressed as a number from 0 to 59, in a *time-number*. The syntax for this function is

SECOND*(time-number)*

The argument *time-number* is any decimal value from .000000 (midnight) to .999988 (11:59:59 P.M.).

Related Functions   HOUR, MINUTE

TIME

TIME gives you the time number for the specified hour, minutes, and seconds. The syntax for this function is

TIME*(hour,minutes,seconds)*

where *hour* is a number from 0 (midnight) to 23 (11:00 P.M.); *minutes* is a number from 0 to 59; and *seconds* is a number from 0 to 59.

Related Function   TIMEVALUE

TIMEVALUE

TIMEVALUE gives you the time, entered as text, as a number. The syntax for this number is

TIMEVALUE*(string)*

The argument *string* is the text equivalent of HH:MM:SS A.M./P.M. or HH:MM A.M./P.M., enclosed in quotation marks.

Related Function   TIME

WEEKDAY

WEEKDAY gives you the day of the week as an integer from 0 (Monday) to 6 (Sunday). The syntax for this function is

WEEKDAY*(date-number)*

The argument *date-number* is usually supplied by another function.

Related Functions   MONTH, YEAR

WORKDAY

WORKDAY gives you the date number that is a specified number of days before or after a date, excluding weekends and holidays. The syntax for this function is

WORKDAY*(start-date-number,days,[holidays-list],[weekends-string])*

The argument *start-date-number* can be any integer from 1 (January 1, 1900) to 73050 (December 31, 2099). The argument *days* is a number; a positive number specifies a number of days after *start-date*; a negative number specifies a number of days before *start-date*.

The optional argument *holidays-list* specifies the holidays to exclude from the calculation. The optional argument *weekends-string* indicates which days of the week to consider as weekends.

Related Function   D360

YEAR

YEAR gives you the year from a date number, expressed as a number from 0 (1900) to 199 (2099). The syntax for this function is

YEAR*(date-number)*

The argument *date-number* is any number from 1 (January 1, 1900) to 73050 (December 31, 2099).

Related Functions   DAY, MONTH, WEEKDAY

FINANCIAL FUNCTIONS

These functions provide a powerful means for performing special financial calculations on your date, as described below.

ACCRUED

ACCRUED gives you the accumulated interest for securities with periodic interest payments. The syntax for this function is

ACCRUED *(settlement, maturity, coupon, [par], [frequency], [basis])*

The argument *settlement* is the security's settlement date, expressed as a date number; *maturity* is the security's maturity date, also expressed as a date number. Another function usually supplies the both of these values.

The argument *coupon* is the security's annual coupon rate, and *par* is an optional argument giving the security's par value.

The optional argument *frequency* gives the interval for coupon payments. The value 2 is used if this argument is omitted. The *frequency* value is a code from the following table:

frequency Value	Interval of Coupon Payments
1	Annual
2	Semiannual
4	Quarterly
12	Monthly

The optional argument *basis* is a value from the following table, relating to the method of interest accrual performed:

basis Value	Day-Count Basis
0	30/360
1	Actual/actual
2	Actual/360
3	Actual/365

Related Functions   PRICE, YIELD

CTERM

CTERM gives you the number of compounding periods necessary for an investment to grow to a specified future value. The syntax for this function is

CTERM *(interest, future-value, present-value)*

The argument *interest* is a number, indicating the interest rate per period. You may enter *interest* either as a percentage (with the % symbol) or a decimal value. The *future-value* and *present-value* arguments are both numbers.

Related Functions   TERM, NPER

DDB, VDB

DDB and VDB return the depreciation allowance of an asset for a specified period of time. DDB uses the double-declining balance method of depreciation for its calculations, while VDB uses a variable rate declining balance method. The syntax for these functions are

DDB *(cost,salvage,life,period)*
VDB *(cost,salvage,life,start-period,end-period[,depreciation][,switch])*

The argument *cost* is the amount paid for the asset, and *salvage* is the value of the asset at the end of its life. The value of *cost* must be greater than or equal to *salvage*.

The argument *life* is the number of periods the asset takes to depreciate to its salvage value; the value of *life* must be a number greater than *period*. The *period* argument is the time period for which you want to find the depreciation allowance.

Start-period and *end-period* specify the bounds of the life of the asset. *Depreciation* optionally specifies the straight-line depreciation rate to use. *Switch*, if 0, causes VDB to use straight-line depreciation, if it is greater than the declining-balance depreciation. This is the default. Using a switch of 1 removes this extra processing.

Related Functions   SLN, SYD

FV

FV gives you the future value of an investment earning a specified interest rate per period, at the end of the number of payment periods in *term*. FV assumes the investment you are calculating is an ordinary annuity. The syntax for this function is

FV *(payment,interest,term)*

The arguments *payment* and *term* can be any numbers. The argument *interest*, expressed either as a percentage (with the % symbol) or as a decimal, is the interest rate for the period of time expressed in *term*.

Related Functions   FVAL, PV, PVAL

FVAL

FVAL gives you the future value of an investment of a specified present value, assuming a series of equal payments, earning a periodic interest rate, over the number of payment periods in *term*. FVAL calculates the value for either an ordinary annuity or an annuity due. The syntax for this function is

FVAL*(payments,interest,term,[type],[present-value])*

The arguments *payments* and *term* can be any number. The argument *interest* is the interest rate per period entered either as a percentage (with the % symbol) or as a decimal value.

The optional argument *type* describes whether the investment is an ordinary annuity or an annuity due, and is expressed as a code from the following table:

type Value	What FVAL Calculates
0	Ordinary annuity: payment due at the end of the period
1	Annuity due: payment due at the beginning of the period

The optional argument *present-value* can be any number. It represents the value of the investment at the beginning of the calculation (i.e., original amount of investment, cost of home, etc.)

Related Functions   PV, PVAL

IPAYMT

IPAYMT gives you the cumulative interest portion of the periodic payment on a loan, assuming a specified interest rate and a specified number of payment periods. IPAYMT calculates the interest for a loan using either an ordinary annuity or an annuity due. The syntax for this function is

IPAYMT*(principal,interest,term,start-period,[end-period],[type],[future-value])*

The argument *principal* is the value of the loan; *interest* is the interest rate per period; and *term* is the number of payment periods.

The argument *start-period* is the point in the loan's term at which you begin calculating interest; *end-period* is the point in the loan's term when you want to stop calculating interest.

The optional argument *type* describes whether this is an ordinary annuity or an annuity due, and is expressed as a code from the following table:

type Value	What IPAYMT Calculates
0	Ordinary annuity: payment due at the end of the period
1	Annuity due: payment due at the beginning of the period

The optional argument *future-value* is the future value of the series of payments, and can be any number.

Related Functions PMT, PAYMT, PPAYMT

IRATE

IRATE gives you the periodic interest rate that would be required for an investment to grow to a specified value during a specified time period. IRATE calculates the rate for either an ordinary annuity or an annuity due. The syntax for this function is

IRATE*(term,payment,present-value,[type],[future-value],[guess]*

The arguments *term*, *payment*, and *present-value* are numbers. The optional argument *type* describes whether the investment is an ordinary annuity or an annuity due, and is expressed as a code from the following table:

type Value	What IRATE Calculates
0	Ordinary annuity: payment due at the end of the period
1	Annuity due: payment due at the beginning of the period

The optional argument *future-value* specifies the future value of the series of payments, and can be any number. The *guess* argument is also optional and represents your estimate of the interest rate.

Related Functions NPV, PV, PVAL, FV, FVAL

IRR

IRR gives you the internal rate of return for a series of cash flows generated by an investment. The syntax for this function is

IRR*(guess,group* or *range)*

The argument *guess* represents your estimate of the internal rate of return, and *group* or *range* is the name of a group or range in your worksheet that contains the cash flows.

Related Functions   MIRR, NPV, PV, PVAL, FV, FVAL, RATE

MIRR

MIRR calculates the modified internal rate of return for a series of cash flows generated by an investment. MIRR assumes the cash flows are received at regular, equal intervals. The syntax for this function is

MIRR*(group* or *range,finance-rate,reinvest-rate)*

The argument *group* or *range* represents the group or range in your worksheet that contains the cash flows. The argument *finance-rate* is the interest rate paid on money used in cash flows, and *reinvest-rate* is the interest you receive on cash flows as you reinvest them.

Related Functions   IRR, NPV, PV, PVAL, FV, FVAL, RATE

NPER

NPER gives you the number of periods, at a specified interest rate per period, required for a series of equal payments to accumulate a future value. NPER calculates the number of periods for either an ordinary annuity or an annuity due. The syntax for this function is

NPER*(payments,interest,future-value,[type],[present-value])*

The argument *payments* is the value of the investments; *interest* is the interest rate per period; and *future-value* is the amount you want to accumulate. The optional argument *type* describes whether the investment is an ordinary annuity or an annuity due, and is expressed as a code from the following table:

type Value	What NPER Calculates
0	Ordinary annuity: payment due at the end of the period
1	Annuity due: payment due at the beginning of the period

The optional argument *present-value* specifies the present value of a series of future payments, and can be any number.

Related Function   CTERM

NPV

NPV gives you the net present value of a series of future cash flows, discounted at a fixed interest rate per period. The syntax of this function is

NPV *(interest, group* or *range)*

The argument *interest* is the interest rate per period. The *group* or *range* argument represents the group or range in your worksheet that contains the cash flows.

Related Functions   PV, PVAL, FV, FVAL

PAYMT

PAYMT gives you the payment on a loan at a given interest rate for a specified number of payment periods. PAYMT calculates the payment for either an ordinary annuity or an annuity due. The syntax for this function is

PAYMT *(principal, interest, term, [type], [future-value])*

The argument *principal* is the amount of the loan; *interest* is the interest rate per period; and *term* is the number of payment periods.

The optional argument *type* describes whether the investment is an ordinary annuity or an annuity due, and is expressed as a code from the following table:

type Value	What PAYMT Calculates
0	Ordinary annuity: payment due at the end of the period
1	Annuity due: payment due at the beginning of the period

The optional argument *future-value* is the future value of the series of payments, and can be any number.

Related Functions   IPAYMT, PPAYMT, TERM

PMT

PMT gives you the payment on a loan, at a given interest rate, for a specified number of payment periods. PMT calculates the payment for an ordinary annuity. The syntax for this function is

PMT *(principal,interest,term)*

The argument *principal* is the value of the loan; *interest* is the interest rate per period; and *term* is the number of payment periods.

PPAYMT

PPAYMT gives you the principal portion of the periodic payment on a loan, given a specified interest rate and a specified number of payment periods. The syntax for this function is

PPAYMT *(principal,interest,term,start-period,[end-period],[type],[future-value])*

The argument *principal* is the amount of the loan; *interest* is the interest rate per period; and *term* is the number of payment periods.

The argument *start-period* is the point in the loan's term when you begin calculating principal; *end-period* is the point in the loan's term when you stop calculating principal.

The optional argument *type* describes whether the investment or loan is calculated using an ordinary annuity or an annuity due, and is expressed as a code from the following table:

type Value	What PPAYMT Calculates
0	Ordinary annuity: payment due at the end of the period
1	Annuity due: payment due at the beginning of the period

The optional argument *future-value* is the future value of the series of payments, and can be any number.

Related Functions   PMT, IPAYMT

PRICE

PRICE gives you the price per $100 face value for securities that pay periodic interest. The syntax for this function is

PRICE *(settlement, maturity, coupon, yield, [redemption], [frequency], [basis])*

The argument *settlement* is a date number, and is the security's settlement date; *maturity*, also a date number, is the maturity date.

The argument *coupon* is the security's annual coupon rate, and *yield* is the security's annual yield.

The optional argument *redemption* is the security's redemption value per $100 face value. The *frequency* argument is also optional and gives the interval for coupon payments; the value 2 is used if this argument is omitted. The *frequency* number is a code from the following table:

frequency Value	Frequency of Coupon Payments
1	Annual
2	Semiannual
4	Quarterly
12	Monthly

The optional argument *basis* uses these codes:

basis Value	Day-Count Basis
0	30/360 (0 is the default if you omit *basis*)
1	Actual/actual
2	Actual/360
3	Actual/365

Related Functions   ACCRUED, YIELD

PV

PV gives you the present value of an investment, based on a series of equal payments, discounted at a specified interest rate per period, for a specified number of periods. The syntax for this function is

PV *(payment,interest,term)*

The argument *payment* can be any value; *interest* is the interest rate; *term* is the number of payment periods.

Related Functions   FV, FVAL

PVAL

PVAL gives you the present value of an investment, with a specified future value, based on a series of equal payments, discounted at a periodic interest rate, for a specified number of periods. The syntax for this function is

PVAL *(payments,interest,term,[type],[future-value])*

The argument *payments* is any number; *interest* is the interest rate per period; and *term* is the number of payment periods.

The optional argument *type* describes whether the investment is an ordinary annuity or an annuity due, and is expressed as a code from the following table:

type Value	What PVAL Calculates
0	Ordinary annuity: payment due at the end of the period
1	Annuity due: payment due at the beginning of the period

The optional argument *future-value* is the future value of the series of payments, and can be any number.

Related Functions   FV, FVAL, NPV, PMT, PAYMT

RATE

RATE gives you the interest rate per period necessary for an investment to grow to a future value in the specified number of compounding periods. The syntax for this function is

RATE *(future-value,present-value,term)*

The arguments *future-value*, *present-value*, and *term* are numbers.

SLN

SLN gives you the straight-line depreciation allowance of an asset. The syntax of this function is

   SLN *(cost,salvage,life)*

   The argument *cost* is the amount paid for the asset; *salvage* is the value of the asset at the end of its life; and *life* is the number of periods (typically years) the asset takes to depreciate to its salvage value.

Related Functions   DDB, VDB, SYD

SYD

SYD gives you the sum-of-the-years'-digits depreciation allowance of an asset for a specific period. The syntax of this function is

   SYD *(cost,salvage,life,period)*

   The argument *cost* is the amount paid for the asset; *salvage* is the value of the asset at the end of its life; *life* is the number of periods (typically years) the asset takes to depreciate to its salvage value; and *period* is the time period for which you want to find the depreciation allowance.

Related Functions   DDB, VDB, SLN

TERM

TERM gives you the number of payments necessary for an investment to grow to a specified future value, given a specified interest rate. The syntax for this function is

   TERM *(payments,interest,future-value)*

   The argument *payments* is the number of equal investments; *interest* is the interest rate per period; and *future-value* is the amount you want to accumulate.

Related Function   CTERM

YIELD

YIELD gives you the yield for securities that pay periodic interest. The syntax of this functions is

YIELD *(settlement, maturity, coupon, price, [redemption], [frequency], [basis])*

The argument *settlement* is the security's settlement date; *maturity* is the security's maturity date; *coupon* is the security's annual coupon rate; and *price* is the security's price per $100 face value.

The optional argument *redemption* specifies the security's redemption value per $100 face value, and is any positive value or 0. If you omit the *redemption* argument, YIELD uses 100.

The optional argument *frequency* gives the interval for coupon payments; the value 2 is used if this argument is omitted. The *frequency* number is a code from the following table:

frequency Value	Frequency of Coupon Payments
1	Annual
2	Semiannual
4	Quarterly
12	Monthly

The optional argument *basis* is a code from the following table, relating to the method of interest accrual performed:

basis Value	Day-Count Basis
0	30/360 (0 is the default if you omit *basis*)
1	Actual/actual
2	Actual/360
3	Actual/365

Related Functions   ACCRUED, PRICE

GROUP FUNCTIONS

Group functions perform their calculations on an item group, or on a range of values. The numbers may occur on one or on more than one worksheet in your model.

GROUPAVG

GROUPAVG gives you the average of the numbers in a group or range. The syntax for this functions is

GROUPAVG *(group* or *range)*

Related Functions   AVG, PUREAVG, SELECTAVG

GROUPCOUNT

GROUPCOUNT gives you the number of cells included in a specified group or range. The syntax for this function is

GROUPCOUNT *(group* or *range)*

Related Functions   COUNT, PURECOUNT, SELECTCOUNT

GROUPMAX, GROUPMIN

GROUPMAX gives you the largest number in a group or range. The syntax for this function is

GROUPMAX *(group* or *range)*

GROUPMIN gives you the smallest number in a group or range. The syntax for this function is

GROUPMIN *(group* or *range)*

Related Functions   MAX, PUREMAX, MIN, PUREMIN

GROUPSTD, GROUPSTDS

GROUPSTD gives you the population standard deviation of the numbers in a group or range. GROUPSTD assumes that the numbers in group or range are the entire population. The syntax of this function is

GROUPSTD *(group* or *range)*

GROUPSTDS gives you the sample standard deviation of the numbers in a group or range. GROUPSTDS uses the n–1, or sample method to calculate standard deviation. The syntax of this function is

GROUPSTDS *(group* or *range)*

Related Functions   STD, PURESTD, STDS, PURESTDS, SELECTSTD, SELECTSTDS, GROUPVAR, GROUPVARS

GROUPSUM

GROUPSUM adds the numbers in a specified group or range. The syntax for this function is

GROUPSUM *(group* or *range)*

Related Functions   SUM, SELECTSUM

GROUPVAR, GROUPVARS

GROUPVAR gives you the population variance of the numbers in a group or range. The syntax for this function is

GROUPVAR *(group* or *range)*

GROUPVARS gives you the sample population variance of the numbers in a group or range. The syntax for this function is

GROUPVARS *(group* or *range)*

Related Functions   VAR, VARS, SELECTVAR, SELECTVARS

LOGICAL FUNCTIONS

Logical functions are used in formulas when determining if a specific condition has been met. All logical functions return either a TRUE or FALSE result.

FALSE

FALSE is the logical value 0. Using FALSE rather than the value 0 makes a formula easier to read.

Related Function   TRUE

IF

IF evaluates the argument *condition*. If *condition* is true, IF returns the value x; if *condition* is false, IF returns the value y. The syntax for this function is

IF *(condition,x,y)*

The argument *condition* can be any logical expression; *x* and *y* can be any data value or location containing a data value. The data can be textual or numeric.

Related Function   CHOOSE

ISEMPTY

ISEMPTY determines whether a cell in your worksheet is blank. If the cell is blank, ISEMPTY returns 1 (true); if the cell is not blank, ISEMPTY returns 0 (false). ISEMPTY is frequently used in conjunction with the IF function to alert you to the presence of empty cells in the worksheet. The syntax for this function is

ISEMPTY(*cell*)

where *cell* is the location which is to be checked.

ISERR

ISERR determines whether the argument x is the special value *Error*. If x is the value Error, ISERR returns 1 (true); if x is not the value Error, ISERR returns 0 (false). ISERR is frequently used with the IF function in formulas to stop the effect of *Error* from cascading through your worksheet. The syntax for this function is

ISERR*(x)*

The argument x can be any logical expression.

Related Function   ISNA

ISNA

ISNA determines whether the argument x has the special value NA. If x is the value NA, ISNA returns 1 (true); if x is not the value NA, ISNA returns 0 (false). ISNA is frequently used in formulas to stop the effect of NA from cascading through your worksheet. The syntax for this function is

ISNA*(x)*

The argument x can be any logical expression.

Related Function   ISERR

ISNUMBER

ISNUMBER determines whether the argument x is a number. If x is a number, NA, *Error*, or blank, ISNUMBER returns 1 (true); if x is a string, a range, a group, or the name of a cell that contains text, ISNUMBER returns 0 (false). The syntax for this function is

ISNUMBER(x)

The argument x can be any number, string, cell, group, or condition.

Related Function   ISSTRING

ISSTRING

ISSTRING determines whether to see if x contains a character string. If it contains a string or is the name of a cell that contains a string, ISSTRING returns 1 (true). If x is a number, NA, *Error*, or blank, ISSTRING returns 0 (false). The syntax for this function is

ISSTRING*(x)*

The argument x can be any number, string, cell, or condition.

Related Function   ISNUMBER

TRUE

TRUE is the logical value 1. Use TRUE in conjunction with functions such as IF and CHOOSE to better document your formulas.

Related Function   FALSE

MATHEMATICAL FUNCTIONS

Mathematical formulas are used to perform the more common functions expected in a spreadsheet, including trigonometric, statistical, and numeric conversion functions.

ABS

ABS gives you the absolute value of x. The syntax for this function is

ABS*(x)*

where the argument x can be any number.

ACOS

ACOS gives you the arc cosine of x. The syntax for this function is

ACOS(x)

where the argument x is the cosine of an angle.

Related Functions   COS, ACOSH

ACOSH

ACOSH gives you the arc hyperbolic cosine of x. The syntax of this function is

ACOSH(x)

where the argument x is the hyperbolic cosine of an angle.

Related Functions   ACOS, COSH

ACOTH

ACOTH gives you the arc hyperbolic cotangent of x. The syntax of the function is

ACOTH(x)

where the argument x is the hyperbolic cotangent of an angle.

Related Function   COTH

ACSCH

ACSCH calculates the arc hyperbolic cosecant of x. The syntax of this function is

ACSCH(x)

where the argument x is the hyperbolic cosecant of an angle.

Related Function CSCH

ASECH

ASECH gives you the arc hyperbolic secant of *x*. The syntax of this function is

ASECH*(x)*

where the argument *x* is the hyperbolic secant of an angle.

Related Function SECH

ASIN

ASIN gives you the arc sine of *x*. The syntax of this function is

ASIN*(x)*

where the argument *x* is the sine of an angle.

Related Function SIN

ASINH

ASINH gives you the arc hyperbolic sine of *x*. The syntax of this functions is

ASINH*(x)*

where the argument *x* is the hyperbolic sine of an angle.

Related Functions SINH, ASIN

ATAN

ATAN gives you the arc tangent of *x*. The syntax of this function is

ATAN *(x)*

where the argument *x* is the tangent of an angle.

Related Functions   ATAN2, TAN

ATANH

ATANH gives you the arc hyperbolic tangent of *x*. The syntax of this function is

ATANH *(x)*

where the argument *x* is the hyperbolic tangent of an angle.

Related Functions   ATAN, ATAN2,

ATAN2

ATAN2 gives you the arc tangent using the tangent y/x of an angle. The syntax of this function is

ATAN2 *(x,y)*

where the arguments *x* and *y* can be any values. If *y* is 0, ATAN2 returns 0; if both *x* and *y* are 0, ATAN2 returns *Error*.

These are the value ranges for ATAN2:

x Value	*y* Value	ATAN2(*x,y*) Results (Quadrant)
Positive	Positive	Between 0 and pi/2, inclusive (I)
Negative	Positive	Between pi/2 and pi, inclusive (II)
Negative	Negative	Between –pi and –pi/2, inclusive (III)
Positive	Negative	Between –pi/2 and 0, inclusive (IV)

Related Functions   ATAN, TAN

BETA

BETA calculates the beta function. In order to use this function, the ADDINS20.ISS script must be loaded. The syntax for this function is

BETA(z,w)

where the arguments z and w can be any numbers.

Related Function   GAMMA

COS

COS gives you the cosine of an angle x. The syntax of this function is

COS(x)

where the argument x can be any value from -1.35×10^{10} to 1.35×10^{10}.

Related Function   ACOS

COSH

COSH(x) calculates the hyperbolic cosine of angle x. The syntax of this function is

COSH(x)

where the argument x is an angle measured in radians.

Related Functions   ACOS, COS

COTH

COTH gives you the hyperbolic cotangent of angle x. The syntax of this function is

COTH(x)

where the argument x is any number except 0.

Related Function   ACOTH

CSCH

CSCH gives you the hyperbolic cosecant of angle x. The syntax of this function is

CSCH (x)

where the argument x is any value except 0, measured in radians.

DECIMAL

DECIMAL converts a hexadecimal value to its signed decimal equivalent. The syntax of this function is

DECIMAL *(hexadecimal)*

where the argument *hexadecimal* is a value from 00000000 through FFFFFFFF, entered in quotation marks.

Related Function   HEX

ERF

ERF gives you the error functions integrated between *lower-limit* and *upper-limit*. The syntax of this function is

ERF *(lower-limit, [upper-limit])*

The argument *lower-limit*, the lower bound, can be any number. The optional argument *upper-limit* must be greater than or equal to *lower-limit*. If *upper-limit* is omitted, then ERL will use the range 0 to *lower-limit*.

EXP

EXP gives you the value of the constant e (approximately 2.718282) raised to the power *x*. The syntax of this function is

EXP*(x)*

where the argument *x* can be any value that is less than or equal to 709.

FACT

FACT gives you the factorial of *n*. The syntax of this function is

FACT*(n)*

where the argument *n* can be 0 or any positive number.

GAMMA

GAMMA calculates the gamma distribution function. The syntax of this function is

GAMMA*(x)*

where the argument *x* is any number greater than 0.

Related Function   BETA

INT

INT gives you the integer portion of *x*, without rounding the value. The syntax of this function is

INT*(x)*

where the argument *x* can be any number.

Related Functions   ROUND, ROUNDDOWN, ROUNDUP

LN

LN gives you the natural logarithm of x. The syntax of this function is

LN(x)

where the argument x can be any value greater than 0.

Related Functions   EXP, LOG

LOG

LOG gives you the common logarithm (base 10) of x. The syntax of this function is

LOG(x)

where the argument x can be any value greater than 0.

Related Function   LN

MOD

MOD gives you the remainder (modulus) of x divided by y. The syntax for this function is

MOD(x,y)

where the arguments x and y can be any numbers. If x is 0, MOD returns 0; if y is 0, MOD returns *Error*. The sign (+ or −) of x determines the sign of the result.

RAND

RAND generates a random value from 0 to 1, calculated to 15 decimal places. The syntax is

@RAND

ROUND, ROUNDDOWN, ROUNDUP

ROUND rounds the value *x* to the nearest decimal place specified by *n*. The syntax for this function is

ROUND *(x, n)*

ROUNDDOWN rounds the value *x* down to the nearest decimal place specified by *n*. The syntax for this function is

ROUNDDOWN *(x, n, [type])*

ROUNDUP rounds the value *x* up to the nearest decimal place specified by *n*. The syntax for this function is

ROUNDDOWN *(x, n, [type])*

In all three of the ROUND functions, the argument *x* can be any number. The argument *n* can be any number from −100 to 100. The following table shows how the sign of *x* changes the outcome.

n Value	Action of ROUND, ROUNDDOWN, or ROUNDUP
Positive	Rounds the decimal portion of the number
Negative	Rounds the integer portion of the number
0	Rounds to the nearest integer

The optional argument *type* is used when the number you're rounding is negative. The following table shows how this value changes the action of ROUNDDOWN and ROUNDUP.

type Value	Action of ROUNDDOWN or ROUNDUP
0	ROUNDDOWN rounds away from 0. ROUNDUP rounds toward 0 (0 is the default if you omit *type*)
1	ROUNDDOWN rounds toward 0; ROUNDUP rounds away from 0

Related Function   INT

SECH

SECH calculates the hyperbolic secant of x. The syntax of this function is

SECH(x)

where the argument x can be any number.

Related Function   ASECH

SIN

SIN gives you the sine of the angle x. The syntax of this function is

SIN(x)

where the argument x is an angle measured in radians, and can be any number from -1.35×10^{10} to 1.35×10^{10}.

Related Function   ASIN

SQRT

SQRT gives you the square root of x. The syntax of this function is

SQRT(x)

where the argument x can be 0 or any positive number.

TAN

TAN gives you the tangent of angle x measured in radians. The syntax of this function is

TAN(x)

where the argument x can be any number.

Related Function   ATAN

SELECT FUNCTIONS

These are used to perform specific functions on a set of items based on some selection criteria.

SELECT

SELECT retrieves a number or character string that meets specified criteria. The syntax for this function is

SELECT *(value-range, search-range, key-value1 [key-value2,...])*

The arguments *key-value1, key-value2,* and so on, are a list of numbers, text enclosed in quotation marks, or cell names, separated by commas or semicolons. These are possible values that can be met by SELECT.

The argument *search-range* is the range that SELECT searches to find a match for a *key-value,* and *value-range* is the range containing the values that SELECT selects based on a *key-value* match in the *search-range.*

Related Function   LOOKUP

SELECTAVG, SELECTSUM

SELECTAVG gives you the average of the values that meet specified criteria. SELECTSUM totals these same values meeting the criteria. The syntax for this function is

SELECTAVG *(value-range, search-range, key-value1, [key-value2,...])*
SELECTSUM *(value-range, search-range, key-value1, [key-value2,...])*

The arguments *key-value1, key-value2,* and so on are a list containing any combination of numeric values, text enclosed in quotation marks, or names of cells containing numbers or text, separated by commas or semicolons.

The argument *search-range* is the range that SELECTAVG searches to find a match for a *key-value,* and *value-range* is the range containing the values that SELECTAVG selects based on a *key-value* match in the *search-range.*

Related Functions   AVG, PUREAVG, GROUPAVG

SELECTCOUNT

SELECTCOUNT gives you the number of nonblank cells that meet specific criteria. The syntax for this function is

SELECTCOUNT *(value-range, search-range, key-value1 [key-value2,...])*

The arguments *key-value1*, *key-value2*, and so on, are a list containing any combination of numbers, text enclosed in quotation marks, and names of cells containing numbers or text, separated by commas or semicolons.

The argument *search-range* is the range that SELECTCOUNT searches to find a match for a *key-value*, and *value-range* is the range containing the values that SELECTCOUNT selects based on a *key-value* match in the *search-range*.

Related Functions   COUNT, PURECOUNT

SELECTMAX, SELECTMIN

SELECTMAX gives you the largest number that meets specified criteria within a search range. The syntax for this function is

SELECTMAX *(value-range, search-range, key-value1, [key-value2,...])*

SELECTMIN gives you the smallest number that meets specified criteria within a search range. The syntax for this function is

SELECTMIN *(value-range, search-range, key-value1, [key-value2,...])*

For both the above functions, the arguments *key-value1*, *key-value2*, and so on, are a list containing any combination of numbers, text enclosed in quotation marks, and names of cells containing numbers or text, separated by commas or semicolons.

The argument *search-range* is the range that SELECTMAX or SELECTMIN searches to find a match for a *key-value* ; and *value-range* is the range containing the values that SELECTMAX or SELECTMIN selects based on a *key-value* match in the *search-range*.

Related Functions   MAX, MIN, GROUPMAX, GROUPMIN

SELECTSTD, SELECTSTDS

SELECTSTD gives you the population standard deviation of numbers that meet specified criteria. The syntax for this function is

SELECTSTD *(value-range, search-range, key-value1 [key-value2,...])*

SELECTSTDS gives you the sample standard deviation of numbers that meet specified criteria. The syntax for this function is

SELECTSTDS *(value-range, search-range, key-value1 [key-value2,...])*

For both the above functions, the arguments *key-value1*, *key-value2*, and so on, are a list containing any combination of numbers, text enclosed in quotation marks, and names of cells containing numbers or text, separated by commas or semicolons.

The argument *search-range* is the range that SELECTSTD or SELECTSTDS searches to find a match for a *key-value*, and *value-range* is the range containing the values that SELECTSTD (or SELECTSTDS) selects based on a *key-value* match in the *search-range*.

Related Functions STD, STDS, GROUPSTD, GROUPSTDS

SPECIAL FUNCTIONS

The following special purposes functions do not fit into the groups given thus far, and are therefore grouped here together.

CELLNAME

CELLNAME gives you the name of the current cell in the specified category, as text. The syntax of this function is

CELLNAME *(category name 1, category name 2, ...)*

The argument *category name* is any category name; it must be enclosed in quotation marks.

Related Function GETCELL

CHOOSE

CHOOSE gives you the *x*th value or string from *list*. The syntax of this function is

CHOOSE *(x, list)*

The argument *x* can be 0 or any positive number that is less than or equal to the number of entries in *list* minus 1; *list* is any collection of numbers, strings, or the names of cells containing numbers or strings, separated by commas or semicolons.

Related Function   LOOKUP

ERR

ERR returns the special value *Error*. ERR is usually used as an argument with IF to produce the value *Error* when certain conditions exist. The syntax for ERR is

@ERR

Related Functions   NA, ISERR

GETCELL

GETCELL gives you the contents of a specified cell in a specified worksheet. The syntax of this function is

GETCELL *(worksheet name, cellname)*

The argument *worksheet name* is text, enclosed in quotation marks, that names a worksheet; if you want to refer to the current worksheet, use an empty string (""). The argument *cellname* is text enclosed in quotation marks, or the name of a cell that contains a reference to another cell.

Related Functions   LOOKUP, CELLNAME

INFO

INFO gives you information about your computer hardware. The syntax of this function is

INFO *(attribute)*

where *attribute* is one of the following attribute names:

attribute	Information Returned by INFO
"directory"	Current path
"numfile"	Number of open worksheets in the current model
"osversion"	Operating system version
"recalc"	Current recalculation mode (either automatic or manual)
"release"	Release number of Improv
"system"	Name of the operating system
"totmem"	Total memory in use by Improv

ITEMCOUNT

ITEMCOUNT counts the number of items in the specified category or group. The syntax of this function is

ITEMCOUNT *(name string)*

where *name string* is the name of a category or group enclosed in quotation marks.

Related Function COUNT

ITEMNAME

ITEMNAME gives you the name of the item at a specified position within a group or range. The syntax of this function is

ITEMNAME *(name string, position)*

The argument *name string* is the name of a group or category, enclosed in quotation marks; *position* specifies a position within the named category or group.

LOOKUP

LOOKUP searches a range for a particular value. When it finds a match, it returns the contents of a cell located in the same position in another range. The syntax of this function is

LOOKUP *(key-value,search-range,value-range)*

The argument *key-value* can be any value that is equal to or greater than the first value in the *search-range* ; *search-range* is the range that LOOKUP searches to find a match for the *key-value* ; and *value-range* is the range containing the values that Improv returns after finding a *key-value* match in the *search-range*.

Do not confuse LOOKUP and SELECT. Use LOOKUP when a *key-value* match is a value and does not have to be exact. Use SELECT when the *key-value* match is either a number or text and has to be exact.

Related Function   SELECT

NA

NA returns the special value NA (not available). The syntax is

@NA

Related Functions   ERR, ISNA

STATISTICAL FUNCTIONS

These functions are used to gather specific statistic information on the specified data.

AVG

AVG returns the average of a list of numbers. The syntax of this function is

　　AVG *(list)*

where *list* is any combination of numbers, the names of cells or ranges containing numbers, or expressions that return numbers.

Related Functions   GROUPAVG, SELECTAVG

BINOMIAL

BINOMIAL gives you the cumulative binomial distribution. The syntax of this function is

　　BINOMIAL *(trials, successes, probability, [type])*

The argument *trials* is the number of independent trials; *successes* is the number of successes in *trials*; and *probability* is the probability of success on each trial.

The optional argument *type* is a number from the following table:

type Value	Information Returned by BINOMIAL
0	The probability of exactly *successes* number of successful trials (0 is the default if you omit *type*)
1	The probability of at most *successes* number of successful trials
2	The probability of at least *successes* number of successful trials

Related Functions   COMBIN, PERMUT

CHIDIST

CHIDIST gives you the chi-square distribution. The syntax of this function is

　　CHIDIST *(x, degrees-freedom, [type])*

The argument x is the value at which to evaluate the chi-square distribution. If you use the type parameter, the value you receive depends on this *type* value, as shown in the following table:

If *type* Value Is	Then x Value Is
0	Upper bound for value of the chi-square cumulative distribution random variable; a value greater than or equal to 0 (0 is the default if you omit *type*)
1	A probability; a value from 0 to 1
2	Value of chi-distribution random variable; a value greater than or equal to 0

The argument *degrees-freedom* is the number of degrees of freedom for the sample. The optional argument *type* is a number from the following table:

type Value	Information Returned by CHIDIST
0	Significance level corresponding to x (0 is the default if you omit *type*)
1	Critical value that corresponds to significance level of x
2	Value of probability density level at x

Related Functions   FDIST, TDIST

COMBIN

COMBIN calculates the binomial coefficient for n and r. The syntax of this function is

COMBIN(n,r)

The argument n is the number of values. The argument r is the number of values in each combination, and must be less than or equal to n.

Related Functions   BINOMIAL, PERMUT

COUNT, PURECOUNT

COUNT counts the number of nonblank cells in *list*. PURECOUNT counts the number of cells in a list, counting only cells that contain values. The syntax of these functions is as follows:

COUNT *(list)*

PURECOUNT *(list)*

where *list* is any combination of cells, ranges, or groups.

Related Functions   SELECTCOUNT, ITEMCOUNT, GROUPCOUNT

MAX, PUREMAX

MAX gives you the largest number in a list. PUREMAX gives you the largest number in a list, ignoring blank cells and cells that do not contain numbers. The syntax of these two functions is

MAX *(list)*

PUREMAX *(list)*

where *list* is any combination of numbers, the names of cells containing numbers, or expressions that return numbers, separated by commas or semicolons.

Related Functions   GROUPMAX, SELECTMAX

MEDIAN

MEDIAN gives you the median value in a list. The syntax of this function is

MEDIAN *(list)*

where *list* is any combination of numbers, the names of cells containing numbers, or expressions that return numbers, separated by commas or semicolons.

Related Functions   AVG, PUREAVG

MIN, PUREMIN

MIN gives you the smallest number in a list. PUREMIN returns the smallest number in a list, ignoring blank cells and cells that do not contain numbers. The syntax of these two functions is

MIN *(list)*

PUREMIN *(list)*

where *list* is any combination of numbers, the names of cells containing numbers, or expressions that return numbers, separated by commas or semicolons.

Related Functions   GROUPMIN, SELECTMIN

NORMAL

NORMAL gives you the normal distribution function for x. The syntax of this function is

NORMAL *(x, [mean], [std], [type], [region])*

The argument x is the upper bound for the value of the normal random variable; x can be any value. The optional argument *mean* is the mean of the distribution; *std*, also optional, is the standard deviation of the distribution.

The optional argument *type* uses a code from the following table:

type Value	Information Returned by NORMAL
0	Cumulative distribution function (0 is the default if you omit *type*)
1	Inverse cumulative distribution
2	Probability density function

The optional argument *region* uses a code from the following table:

region Value	What NORMAL Integrates
0	From negative infinity to x (0 is the default if you omit *region*)
1	From x to infinity
2	From $-x$ to x
3	From 0 to x

Related Functions   FDIST, TDIST

PERMUT

PERMUT gives you the number of permutations of r objects that can be selected from a total of n objects. The syntax for this function is

PERMUT *(n,r)*

The arguments n and r can be any positive number or 0.

Related Function   COMBIN

SKEWNESS

SKEWNESS gives you the skewness of the values in a range. The syntax for this function is

SKEWNESS *(range,[type])*

The argument *range* is a range that contains numbers. The optional argument *type* is a number from the following table:

type Value	SKEWNESS Calculates
0	Population skewness (0 is the default if you omit *type*)
1	Sample skewness

Related Functions   STD, PURESTD, SELECTSTD, and GROUPSTD; STDS, PURESTDS, SELECTSTDS, and GROUPSTDS; VAR, PUREVAR, SELECTVAR, and GROUPVAR; VARS, PUREVARS, SELECTVARS, and GROUPVARS

STD and PURESTD, STDS and PURESTDS

STD gives you the population standard deviation of the numbers in a list. PURESTD gives you the population standard deviation of the numbers in a list, ignoring cells that do not contain numbers. The syntax for these two function is

STD *(list)*

PURESTD *(list)*

The argument *list* is any numbers, names of cells containing numbers, or expressions that return numbers, separated by commas or semicolons; *list* can also be a range or the name of a group.

STDS gives you the sample standard deviation of the numbers in a list. PURESTDS gives you the sample population standard deviation of the numbers in a list, ignoring cells that do not contain numbers. The syntax for these two functions is

STDS *(list)*

PURESTDS *(list)*

The argument *list* is any numbers, names of cells containing numbers, or expressions that return numbers, separated by commas or semicolons; *list* can also be a range or the name of a group.

Related Functions   GROUPSTD, GROUPSTDS, SELECTSTD, SELECTSTDS

SUM

SUM adds the numbers in list. The syntax for this function is

SUM *(list)*

where *list* can be any combination of numbers, names of cells that contain numbers, or expressions that return numbers, separated by commas or semicolons.

Related Functions   GROUPSUM, SELECTSUM

SUMPRODUCT

SUMPRODUCT multiplies the numbers in multiple ranges and sums the product. The syntax for this function is

SUMPRODUCT *(list)*

where *list* is any combination of ranges or groups, separated by commas or semicolons.

VAR and PUREVAR, VARS and PUREVARS

VAR gives you the population variance of the numbers in a list. PUREVAR gives you the population variance in a list of numbers, ignoring cells that do not contain values. The syntax for these two functions is

VAR *(list)*

PUREVAR *(list)*

where *list* can be any combination of numbers, the names of cells containing numbers, or expressions that return numbers, separated by commas or semicolons.

VARS gives you the sample population variance of the numbers in a list. PURE-VARS gives you the sample population variance in a list of numbers, ignoring cells that do not contain values. The syntax for these two functions is

VARS *(list)*

PUREVARS *(list)*

where *list* can be any combination of numbers, the names of cells containing numbers, or expressions that return numbers, separated by commas or semicolons.

Related Functions   GROUPVAR, GROUPVARS, SELECTVAR, SELECT-VARS

STRING FUNCTIONS

These functions, unlike others covered here, are specifically provided to manipulate text values, not numeric data.

CHAR

CHAR gives you the character that corresponds to x. The syntax of this function is

CHAR(x)

where x can be any integer from 0 to 255.

Related Function   CODE

CODE

CODE returns the code number that corresponds to the first character in the string. The syntax of this function is

CODE$(string)$

where *string* is text enclosed in quotation marks, or the name of a cell containing text.

Related Function   CHAR

EXACT

EXACT compares two text strings, and determines whether they are identical. The syntax of this function is

EXACT$(string1,string2)$

where *string1* and *string2* are text enclosed in quotation marks.

FIND

FIND gives you the position in *lookup-string* at which the first occurrence of *search-string* appears. The syntax of this function is

FIND *(search-string,lookup-string,start-number)*

The arguments *search-string* and *lookup-string* are text strings enclosed in quotation marks, or the name of a cell containing text. The argument *start-number* can be 0 or any positive number. The leftmost character in *lookup-string* is at *start-number* 0 (in the text string "APPLE", the letter *A* is in position 0).

LEFT

LEFT gives you *n* characters from the beginning of *string*. The syntax of this function is

LEFT *(string,n)*

The argument *string* is any text enclosed in quotation marks; *n* is 0 or any positive number.

Related Functions   MID, RIGHT

LENGTH

LENGTH gives you the number of characters in *string*. The syntax of this function is

LENGTH *(string)*

where *string* is any text enclosed in quotation marks.

LOWER

LOWER converts all the letters in *string* to lowercase. The syntax of this function is

LOWER *(string)*

where *string* is any text enclosed in quotation marks.

Related Functions   UPPER, PROPER

MID

MID copies characters from a text string, beginning with the character at *start-number*. The syntax of this function is

MID *(string,start-number,n)*

The argument *string* is any text enclosed in quotation marks. The argument *start-number* can be 0 or any positive integer; the first character in *string* has a *start-number* of 0. The argument *n* can be 0 or any positive number.

Related Functions   LEFT, RIGHT

N

N gives you, as a value, the entry in the first cell of a group or range. If the cell contains a string, N returns the value 0. The syntax for this function is

N *(group* or *range)*

where the *group* or *range* argument specifies a group or range of cells in your worksheet.

Related Functions   S, ISNUMBER

PROPER

PROPER capitalizes the first letter of each word in the given string and converts the remaining letters to lowercase. The syntax for this function is

PROPER *(string)*

where *string* is any text enclosed in quotation marks.

Related Functions   LOWER, UPPER

REPEAT

REPEAT duplicates *string* the number of times specified in *n*. The syntax for this function is

REPEAT *(string, n)*

where *string* is the string that should be replicated, and *n* is the number of times *string* should be repeated.

REPLACE

REPLACE replaces or appends characters in the original character string with new characters. The syntax for this function is

REPLACE *(original-string, start-number, n, new-string)*

The arguments *original-string* and *new-string* are text enclosed in quotation marks. The argument *start-number* is 0 or any positive number, indicating the position of a character in *original-string*. The argument *n*, which can be 0 or any positive number, indicates the number of characters to remove. If *n* is 0, REPLACE appends *new-string* to *original-string*; if *n* equals the number of characters in *original-string*, REPLACE will replace the entire *original-string* with *new-string*.

Related Function FIND

RIGHT

RIGHT gives you the last characters in *string*. The syntax for this function is

RIGHT *(string, n)*

The argument *string* is any text enclosed in quotation marks; *n* is 0 or any positive number.

Related Functions LEFT, MID

S

S returns the entry in the first cell of a group or range. The syntax for this function is

S(*group* or *range*)

where *group* or *range* specifies a group or range in your worksheet.

Related Functions   N, ISSTRING

STRING

STRING changes the value of a number into text with n decimal places. The syntax for this function is

STRING(*x,n*)

The argument *x* can be any number; *n* can be any number from 0 to 15.

Related Function   VALUE

TRIM

TRIM removes leading, trailing, and consecutive spaces from a character string. The syntax for this function is

TRIM(*string*)

where *string* is any text.

UPPER

UPPER changes all the letters in a character string to uppercase. The syntax for this function is

UPPER(*string*)

where *string* is the text that is to be converted.

Related Functions   LOWER, PROPER

VALUE

VALUE changes a number entered as text to its corresponding numeric value. The syntax for this function is

VALUE*(string)*

where *string* is any text enclosed in quotation marks.

Related Function   STRING

Improv 2

- Core LotusScript Commands

- Improv-Specific Functions

- C-Language Functions

Handbook

APPENDIX B

LotusScript

LotusScript is a programming language that allows you to automate tasks you perform routinely.

The LotusScript language can be divided into three sections:

- ◢ Core LotusScript: a core set of commands and functions used to describe your objects and actions, the order in which you want actions performed, how to handle errors, built-in functions that perform common computations, and commands to build your own specialized functions.

- ◢ Improv-specific functions: functions that reproduce the effects of Improv actions, such as displaying a dialog box for your input.

- ◢ C-language functions: functions that can be used within C programs you write, which must include certain C-language conventions and link to a library file.

These topics are described further in this Appendix. For more information on using LotusScript in your own models, you may wish to refer to Chapter 17.

CORE LOTUSSCRIPT COMMANDS

Most of the core LotusScript commands and functions are similar to the BASIC programming language.

Data Types

LotusScript has 13 different data types for variables and named constants.

Some data types describe the contents of the element: the STRING type is for character strings, the NUMBER type is for numeric values. If you describe an element as a STRING, you are not able to perform arithmetic operations on it.

Some data types refine the precision of the element: DOUBLE contains double-precision floating-point values. Use the more precise data types only when you need that level of precision.

The LotusScript data types are shown below.

Data Type	Description
ANY	Contains values of any LotusScript data type; the data type doesn't need to be specified
ARRAY	Contains an organized group of data, referred to by position within the array
BOOLEAN	Contains only TRUE and FALSE values
CURRENCY	Contains numeric values representing amounts of money
DATE	Contains numeric values representing dates and times
DOUBLE	Contains double-precision floating point numeric values

Data Type	Description
ERROR	Contains an error value
FLOAT	Contains any floating point numeric value
INTEGER	Contains an integer value
LIST	Contains an organized group of data, referred to by name within the list
LONG	Contains a long integer value; use this data type only when you need a number greater than 32,767 or less than –32,768
NUMBER	Contains any numeric value (either integer or floating point)
SINGLE	Contains single-precision, floating point numeric values
STRING	Contains character strings

Operators and Order of Precedence

LotusScript operators consist of characters and keywords that perform an action on data values, such as "+", the addition operator; "*", the multiplication operator; or ">", the greater than operator. The order in which the operators perform their action, called the order of precedence, will affect the resulting value, much the same as the use of parentheses in algebra.

Order of Precedence	Operator	Operation Performed
1	FUNCTION( )	Functions evaluation
2	(expression)	Parenthetical sub-expression evaluation. Up to 30 levels of nested parentheses are allowed
3	^	Exponentiation
4	–	Negation
5	*, /	Multiplication and division
6	\	Integer division
7	MOD	Modulo division (remainder)
8	–,+	Subtraction and addition
9	=, <>, <, <=, >, >=	Comparison of magnitude of LotusScript values
10	NOT	Logical NOT
11	AND	Logical AND
12	OR	Logical OR
13	XOR	Logical exclusive OR
14	EQV	Logical equivalence
15	IMP	Implication (first operand false or second operand true)
16	=	Assignment

Punctuation

In addition to the operators, LotusScript uses several punctuation marks as special characters. Punctuation separates arguments in a list (a comma or semicolon), or defines the beginning of a character string ("Jane").

Character	Meaning
<newline>	Terminates a statement
, (comma)	Separates the parts of a script statement
; (semicolon)	Separates fields in the PRINT statement
: (colon)	Separates more than one statement on a single line
%, &, !, #, @, $, ?,~	Serve as suffix characters to declare data types
( ) (parenthesis)	Separates components in script statements; causes the enclosed expression to be calculated before other operators in the statement
" " (quotation marks)	Surrounds literal text strings on a single line
' (single quotation mark)	Marks the beginning of a comment
{ } (curly braces)	Surrounds multi-line literal text strings
_ (underscore)	Marks a line continuation character

Variable and Array Handling Functions

Several functions perform various actions on variables, arrays, and lists. LEN returns the length of a text string; you could use it determine whether a text string is empty. DIM allocates computer memory storage for variables; use it to specify the dimension (length) of the variable.

Remember that all functions return a value.

Function	Action
DATATYPE	Gives the data type of a variable
DEFtype	Sets the default data type for variables
DELETE	Deletes individual elements of lists, or entire arrays or lists
DIM (Function)	Gives the number of dimensions for a variable, array, or list
DIM Statement	Initializes storage for variables, arrays, or lists
ERASE	Erases arrays or lists
INDEXOF	Gives the index of an array element or the name of a list element
LBOUND	Gives the value of the lowest index value for an array dimension
LEN	Gives the length of a text string in characters or the size of a variable in bytes
NAMEOF	Gives the name of a variable, array, or list
OPTION BASE	Sets the default minimum index for array elements
OPTION DECLARE	Suppresses automatic declaration of unknown variables

Function	Action
REDIM	Changes the size of a previously declared array
TYPEOF	Gives the declared data type of a variable
UBOUND	Gives the highest index value for an array dimension

Loops

A loop repeats a series of steps a specified number of times, or until a condition is satisfied. A DO WHILE loop could be used to step through all the rows of cells of a worksheet, without specifying the number of rows. A DO UNTIL loop could be used to repeat a series of steps until a specified condition is met; for instance, until the accumulated interest reaches $1,000.

Loop Syntax	Description
DO WHILE/UNTIL - LOOP	Tests a condition, then performs the steps enclosed in the loop UNTIL the condition becomes true, or WHILE the condition remains true
DO - LOOP WHILE/UNTIL	Performs the steps in the loop, then tests a condition and repeats UNTIL the condition becomes true, or WHILE the condition remains true
FOR - NEXT	Repeats the enclosed steps for a specified number of times
FOR - NEXT (array iterator)	Steps through the elements of an array or list
WHILE - WEND	Tests a condition, then repeats WHILE the condition remains true

Conditionals

A conditional checks whether a condition is true or false. The IF-THEN-ELSE construct makes a decision based on whether the IF condition is valid. The SELECT CASE construct allows you to outline several possible cases; the program stops at the first case that is valid and performs the actions listed after the CASE statement.

Syntax	Description
IF-THEN-ELSE	Conditional that enumerates an IF/THEN condition
IF-THEN-ELSEIF	Conditional that enumerates multiple IF/THEN conditions
SELECT CASE	Selects one of several cases as valid, depending on the value of a variable

Branches

A branch command redirects the flow of the action to a specific location in the script. You can use it to interrupt the flow of a DO WHILE loop, or to redirect flow if a condition is fulfilled.

Syntax	Description
GOTO	Branches to a specified label

Error Handling

LotusScript handles errors through user-defined structures that tell the script what to do when an error occurs. You can use error handling when you are debugging, or include error routines to direct your script when an unforeseen event occurs.

Function	Description
ERROR	Changes a string or number into an ERROR data type
ERROR HANDLER ... END HANDLER	Defines a named error-handler routine
ON ERROR	Defines an anonymous error-handler routine
PASS	Passes control to an error handler for this error
RESUME	Resumes execution after an error is processed by an error-handling routine
SIGNAL ERROR	Emits an error condition from an object and sends an error message
STOP	Halts script execution and then opens the debug window

Mathematical Functions

LotusScript includes several functions that compute numeric values using common mathematical formulas, such as pi or square root. Use these functions when you want to make a computation.

Function	Action
ABS	Computes the value of a number without respect to its sign (negative or positive)
ACOS	Computes the arc cosine (in radians) of a value
ASIN	Computes the arc sine (in radians) of a value
ATAN2	Computes the arc tangent (in radians) of the ratio of two values
ATN	Computes the arc tangent (in radians) of a value

Function	Action
COS	Computes the cosine of an angle expressed in radians
EXP	Computes the value e raised to the power supplied as an argument
LOG	Computes the natural logarithm of a value
LOG10	Computes the base 10 logarithm of a value
PI	Gives the value of PI
RANDOMIZE	Re-initializes the random number generator
RND	Returns a random number between 0 and 1
SIN	Computes the sine of an angle expressed in radians
SQR	Computes the square root of a value
TAN	Computes the tangent of an angle expressed in radians

Input, Output, and Printing

These statements control input and output to the computer. For example, including BEEP causes the computer to make a noise. The PRINT statement sends text to the computer screen.

Function	Action
BEEP	Generates a tone on the computer's speaker
INPUT	Allows user input
OPTION TAB	Sets the number of spaces in a tab
OUTPUT	Displays an alert box with a message, then waits for the user to hit a key
PRINT	Prints text to the computer (screen)
SPC	Prints a specified number of spaces
TAB	Moves the print cursor to a specified character position in the computer (screen)

User-Defined Functions and Subroutines

In addition to the built-in functions LotusScript provides, you can create your own functions and subroutines for actions you frequently perform. A user-defined function must begin with FUNCTION and end with END FUNCTION. Remember that a function performs its prescribed action and then returns a value; a subroutine performs its action but does not return a value.

Keyword	Action
CALL	Calls a LotusScript subroutine

Keyword	Action
END FUNCTION/SUB	Ends the function or subroutine
EXIT	Exits a function or subroutine before reaching the END statement
FUNCTION	Begins the definition of a function
SUB	Begins the definition of a subroutine

String-Handling Functions

LotusScript offers several built-in functions that manipulate character strings. UCASE$ converts all alphabetical characters in a string to uppercase. You can use these functions for formatting.

Function	Action
ASC	Gives the numeric code (ASCII value) for the first character in astring
CHR$	Gives the character associated with a numeric character code (ASCII value)
DELETE$	Deletes a specified number of characters from a string
ENVIRON$	Gives information on the computer operating environment
FORMAT$	Converts a number to a character string and formats it
INSERT$	Inserts one character string into another
INSTR	Searches for one text string in another
LCASE$	Converts all alphabetic characters in a string to lowercase
LEFT$	Retrieves the leftmost n (number of) characters of a string
LTRIM$	Deletes leading spaces from a string
MID$	Gives a specified number of characters from the middle of a string
REPLACE$	Replaces characters in the middle of a string
RIGHT$	Gives the rightmost n (number of) characters of a string
RTRIM$	Deletes trailing spaces from a string
SPACE$	Gives a string containing the specified number of blank spaces
STR$	Converts a number to an unformatted character string
STRING	Converts any numeric value to a string
STRING$	Gives a string of characters, all of which are the same
TRIM$	Truncates or pads (with spaces) a string to a given length
UCASE$	Converts alphabetic characters in a string to uppercase

Numeric Value-Handling Functions

Some built-in functions manipulate numeric values. You can use ROUND to round a value to the nearest integer. You can use CURRENCY to convert numbers to monetary values.

Function	Action
BIN$	Converts numbers to binary strings
BOOLEAN	Converts numbers to boolean (true or false) values
CONST	Creates a named constant
CURRENCY	Converts a number to CURRENCY
DOUBLE	Converts a number to DOUBLE
FIX	Truncates a decimal value to an integer
FLOAT	Converts an integer to a floating point value
FRACTION	Returns the fractional part of a floating point value
HEX$	Converts a number to a hexadecimal string
INT	Returns the next lower integer value to a floating point argument
INTEGER	Converts a number to INTEGER
LONG	Converts a number to LONG
NUMBER	Converts other types to numbers
OCT$	Converts a number to an octal string
ROUND	Rounds a number to the nearest integer value
SGN	Returns the sign of a numeric value
SINGLE	Converts a number to SINGLE
VAL	Converts a string value to a numeric value

Date and Time Functions

The built-in date and time functions manipulate date and time values. Use TODAY to give you the computer system's date. Many of these functions can be used to change arguments to date values so that you can perform date calculations on them.

Function	Action
DATE	Converts a number to a date value
DATE$	Converts a date value to a string, or gives the system date as a string
DATESERIAL	Converts day, month, and year arguments to a date value
DATEVALUE	Converts a string to a date value
DAY	Gives the day of the month from a date value
HOUR	Gives the hour of the day from a time value
MINUTE	Gives the minute of the hour from a time value
MONTH	Gives the month of the year from a date value
NOW	Gives the current date/time
SECOND	Gives the second of the minute from a time value
TIME$	Converts a time value to a character string
TIMER	Gives elapsed seconds since midnight
TIMESERIAL	Gives a time as a decimal value
TIMEVALUE	Changes a time string into a time serial number
TODAY	Gives the current date without the time

Function	Action
WEEKDAY	Gives the weekday from a date value
YEAR	Gives the year from a date value

IMPROV-SPECIFIC FUNCTIONS

There are approximately 200 Improv-specific LotusScript functions that reproduce the effects of Improv actions, such as the commands on the Improv menu.

Handle, Selection, and Iterator Functions

The handle, selection, and iterator functions create and change the Improv objects, such as a group or a formula. Is Valid Selection checks whether a selection handle is valid.

Selection Functions

Function	Action
Get Selection	Creates a handle to the current selection
Set Selection	Moves the current selection using a selection handle
Set Selection By Name	Moves the current selection to a named selection and creates a selection handle
Is Valid Selection	Checks whether a handle refers to a valid selection

Handle Functions

Function	Action
Create Selection Handle	Creates a handle to any selection you specify
Free Selection Handle	Frees the memory used to store a selection handle
Modify Selection Handle	Changes the selection referred to by a handle
Is Valid Selection Handle	Checks whether a handle exists

Iterator Functions

Function   Action

Create Iterator   Creates an iterator to proceed through parts of an object
Free Iterator   Frees the memory used to store an iterator
Get Next Element   Retrieves a handle to the next object in the iterator
Is Valid Iterator   Checks whether an iterator exists

Lotus Dialog Editor and Dialog Box Access Functions

Improv includes the Lotus Dialog Editor, which lets you create custom dialog boxes for use in your applications. You can use a custom dialog box to retrieve information for your script. The function Dialog Box displays a custom dialog box.

Function   Custom Dialog Access

Alert Box   Display alert boxes
Dialog Box   Display dialog boxes
Fill functions   Set dialog box defaults and text
Retrieving Information   Get user selections and entries from dialog boxes

Script Performance Functions

Improv includes two functions that improve script performance. Update Model allows you to update the model on the screen only when needed, and thus improves performance.

Function   Description

Enable Refresh   Enables or disables screen refresh (disabling improves performance)
Update Model   Updates/Refreshes a model

Information Functions

Information functions retrieve information about objects (cells or formulas) in an Improv model. They do not allow you to change the resulting information, but you can use it to determine what action to take. Get Cell Calc Type determines whether a cell value is calculated by a formula or was entered by the user.

Function	Information Retrieved
Get Cell Calc Type	Determines whether a cell's value was calculated by a formula or entered by the user
Get Cells for Formula	The cell(s) calculated by a formula
Get Formulas for Cell	The formula(s) that calculate a given cell
Get Formula Intersection	The cells that the left sides of two formulas have in common
Get Formula Overlaps	A list of formulas that overlap other formulas
Get Formula Inline Errors	Inline errors for a formula
Get Formula Status	Gives the status of a formula
Get Error Text	Gives the text for an error code
Get Item Information	Gives an item's parent and children (in a hierarchy) in the current view
Get Model Info	Gives model's status and filename
Get Selection Info	Gives type, name, status, and location
Get Summary Item	Gives the name of a group's summary item
Get Undo State	Gives the current state of the Undo command
Get Improv Version/Get System Properties	Gives environment and system information

File Menu Functions

Improv includes a complete set of functions that perform the same action as the commands on all the Improv menus. There are functions for the File, Edit, Create, Worksheet, Presentation, Script, Tools, and Window menus. New creates a new Improv model, just as on the File menu; Copy copies the current selection to the clipboard, just as on the Edit menu.

Improv File Menu Functions

Function	Action
New	Creates a new Improv model
Open Import	Opens an Improv model or imports a file into Improv
Close	Closes an open Improv model
Save/Save As Export	Saves an Improv model or exports a file from Improv
Revert to Saved	Closes the current model and reopens the last saved version of the model
Page Setup	Sets the page layout for printing
Print	Prints a view or presentation
Print Setup	Changes the printer settings
Exit	Closes all models and exits the application

Improv Edit Menu Functions

Function	Action
Undo	Backs out the last action performed by the user
Cut	Moves a selection to the clipboard
Copy	Copies a selection to the clipboard
Paste	Moves the clipboard contents to an Improv selection
Paste Special	Performs operations on values or graphics pasted into a worksheet or presentation
Add	Adds an Improv element of the selected type to the worksheet
Delete	Deletes a selection
Select All	Selects all of the cells or items in the current worksheet
Select Item Names	Selects only the item names in the current item selection
Select Cells Only	Selects only the cells in the current item selection

Improv Create Menu Functions

Function	Action
Worksheet	Creates a new worksheet
Formula	Creates a new formula
Category	Creates a new category
Item Group	Groups Items together
Items	Adds items to a category
View	Creates a new view
Presentation	Creates an empty Presentation window
Chart	Creates a chart
Hotview	Creates a hotview
Draw	Draws in a presentation
Object	Creates an OLE (object linking and embedding) object
Script	Creates a script, either through recording a series of keystrokes and mouse events, or by directly entering one or more LotusScript commands in a script window.
Stop Recording	Turns off the Script recorder

Improv Worksheet Menu Functions

Function	Action
Settings/Style	Opens the InfoBox
Get Settings/Style	Retrieves InfoBox settings
Change Settings/ Style	Changes InfoBox settings

Function	Action
Mark Cells/Formulas	Marks cells calculated by a formula or the formula that calculates selected cells
Add Group Summary	Adds a summary to an item group
Collapse Group	Collapses an item group to show only the summary
Expand Group	Expands a collapsed item group
Ungroup Items	Breaks an item group into its component items
Data Fill	Fills cells or item names with values
Sort Items	Sorts items by key or by item name
Hide Items	Hides selected items
Show Items	Reveals hidden items in a selection
Show All	Reveals all hidden items
Add/Clear Page Break	Adds or removes a page break in the current selection

Improv Presentation Menu Functions

Function	Action
Settings/Style	Opens the InfoBox
Get Settings/Style Settings	Retrieves InfoBox settings
Change Settings/Style	Changes InfoBox settings
Bring to Front/Send to Back	Moves a presentation object to the front or back
Group	Groups presentation objects
Ungroup	Breaks up groups of presentation objects

Improv Script Menu Functions

Function	Action
Record into Script	Begins the recording of a script.
Stop Recording	Turns off the script recorder
Run Script	Runs a script
Attach Script	Attaches a script to an object or action

Improv Tools Menu Functions

Function	Action
SmartIcons	Sets or retrieves the SmartIcons location or displays a named set of icons
Get User Setup	Retrieves the current User Setup dialog settings
Set User Setup	Changes the current User Setup dialog settings

Function	Action
Run Script	Runs a script
Attach Script	Attaches a script to an object or action

Improv Window Menu Functions

Function	Action
Browser	Opens/Closes the Browser
SmartIcons	Displays/Hides the SmartIcons
Status Bar	Displays/Hides the status bar
Console	Opens/Closes the console
Tile	Places the Improv windows into a tiled layout
Cascade	Places the Improv windows into a cascaded layout

Direct Manipulation Functions

These functions emulate direct manipulations of objects on the screen; that is, any action you would take without the use of a menu command. Entering Cell Values enters values into cells.

> Categories
> Window Manipulation
> Category Manipulation
> Cell and Formula Manipulation
> Column and Row Manipulation
> Text Manipulation
> Presentation Object Manipulation

C-LANGUAGE FUNCTIONS

Using the C programming language, you can extend Improv by creating your own @ functions (for use in Improv formulas), accessing information in dialog boxes, and customizing the Improv menu. You can also write trigger functions, which respond to specific events that occur within Improv.

Using these functions requires that you use a dynamic link library (DLL) file to connect the C program to Improv. Specifics of C programming, and the use of DLLs, is beyond the scope of this book.

Improv

- Default Worksheet

- Default SmartIcon Sets

- Default Chart

- User Pro Setup Defaults

Handbook

APPENDIX C

Quick Reference to Improv Defaults

This appendix is an overview of Improv's default settings. Throughout this book, you will see references to these defaults, particularly in Chapter 16, "Customizing Improv." Where appropriate, this appendix contains cross-references to the information in these chapters.

DEFAULT WORKSHEET

When you start Improv or choose File New, Improv's default worksheet, UNTI-TLED.IMP, will appear on your screen, as shown in Figure C-1. Notice that the title box of the default worksheet says "Worksheet1 View1 Untitled1."

You may want to change the default worksheet to include particular items, formatting, and so forth. To do this, create a new worksheet with the features you want, name the file (for example, WORKSHEET.IMP), and designate that file as your startup model, as follows:

1.   Choose User Setup on the Tools menu.

2.   Choose Paths.

3.   In the Default Paths dialog box, enter the name of the new default worksheet in the Startup Model text box, shown just below. (Notice that the Startup Model text box is empty in its default state.)

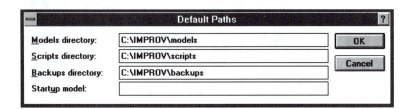

FIGURE C-1

Default worksheet,
UNTITLED.IMP

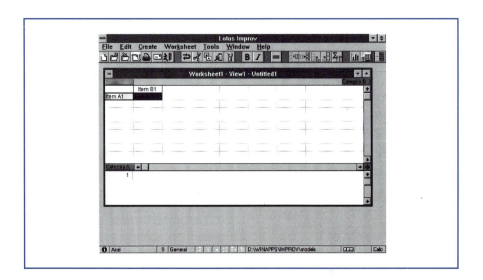

Note

See Chapter 16 for more information on techniques for adding custom worksheets, including the use of Improv's templates.

Default Worksheet Header/Footer

The default worksheet header is the worksheet name, centered in the header. The default worksheet footer is the word "Page," followed by the page number, centered in the footer.

To change the default header and footer, choose File Page Setup, and open the Header/Footer dialog box. Here you can change the placement of the headers and footers, the type font, style, and size, and the information displayed in the text marker.

DEFAULT SMARTICON SETS

Improv provides three sets of SmartIcons for your use. The icons in these sets—Worksheet, Presentation, and Script—are listed in the table just below.

To change the default icons in any set, choose Tools SmartIcons. In the list box at the top-center of the SmartIcons dialog box, select the icon set you want to change. Then drag in or out the icons you want to add or remove; the icons available to you are in the list on the left, and the selected SmartIcon set is in the list in the center. In Figure C-2, the arrow is dragging the Page Setup SmartIcon to the default Worksheet SmartIcon set. The table below shows the default set of icons available at different times in Improv.

FIGURE C-2

SmartIcons dialog box

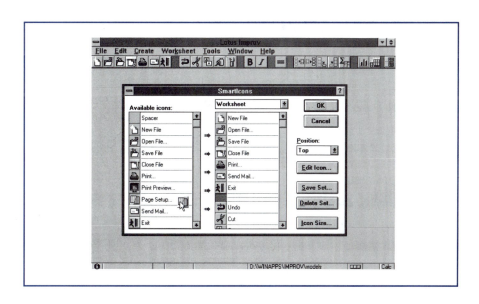

Note

See the inside front and back covers of this book for a list of all the Improv SmartIcons.

SmartIcon Set	Default Icons Included
Worksheet SmartIcons	New File, Open File, Save File, Close File, Print, Send Mail, Exit Undo, Cut, Copy, Paste, Delete Bold, Italic Create Formula Create Item Group, Ungroup Items, Collapse Group, Expand Group, Add Group Summary Create Chart, Create Hotview Show Browser
Presentation SmartIcons	New File, Open File, Save File, Close File, Print, Send Mail, Exit Undo, Cut, Copy, Paste, Delete Bold, Italic Create Rectangle, Create Line, Create Oval, Create Text Block, Create Button Send to Back, Bring to Front, Group, Ungroup Show Browser
Script SmartIcons	New File, Open File, Save File, Close File, Print, Send Mail, Exit Undo, Cut, Copy, Paste, Delete Run Script, Record Into Script Show Browser

DEFAULT CHART

The default chart in Improv is a bar chart, with one x-axis and one y-axis. The chart includes a legend, x- and y-axis tick-mark labels, and a frame. Figure C-3 shows an example of a default chart created from the Summary/Comparison table in Improv's LOAN.IMP model (see Chapter 20 for a discussion of LOAN.IMP).

To change the default chart settings, choose Presentation Settings, or click the InfoBox icon (see Chapter 4 for a discussion of the InfoBox).

USER SETUP DEFAULTS

The following paragraphs describe the default settings in the Tools User Setup dialog box (Figure C-4), as discussed in Chapter 16. Most of Improv's default settings can be controlled from this dialog box.

FIGURE C-3

Default chart of
Summary Comparison
Table from LOAN.IMP

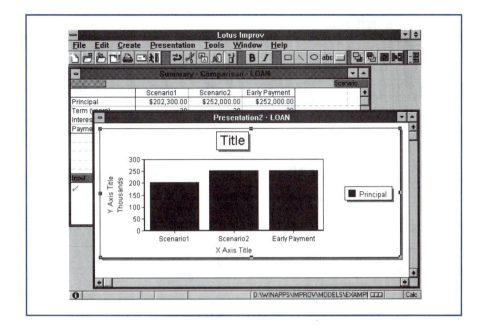

FIGURE C-4

User Setup
dialog box

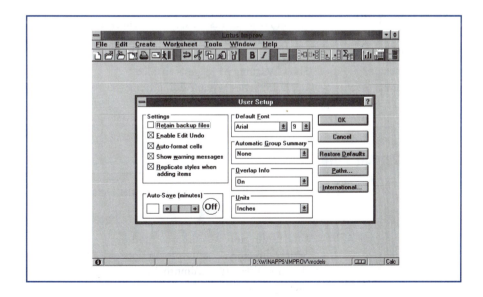

Default Font

Caution

Changing the default font will affect all worksheets!

Improv's default font is Arial 9 point. Note that Improv uses this font for text in data and formula panes, as well as in text blocks within presentations.

To choose a new default font and size, open the User Setup dialog box, and open the Default Font list boxes.

Be careful: When you select a new default font, Improv will change the font in some, but not all areas of *existing* worksheets, as shown in the following table:

Areas Affected	Areas Not Affected
Formula panes	Data panes
Browsers	Text blocks
Script windows	
Console windows	

The changed default font will *not* be reflected in data panes and text blocks within existing worksheets, but it *will* show up in the data panes and text blocks in worksheets you create *after* you change the default font.

Default Settings

Tip

Disabling Edit Undo will improve memory use and system performance (speed).

Here are the default conditions for the check box settings in the User Setup dialog box:

Retain Backup Files - disabled (unchecked)
Enable Edit Undo - enabled (checked)
Auto-Format Cells - enabled
Show Warning Messages - enabled
Replicate Styles When Adding Items - enabled

Default Paths

Here are the default path designations in the Default Paths dialog box, accessed through the Paths command button:

Models directory: c:\improv\models
Scripts directory: c:\improv\scripts
Backups directory: c:\improv\backup
Startup model: (undesignated)

International

Here are the default International settings, accessed through the International command button:

Collate Options: International; Numbers first
File Import Character Set for 1-2-3 (.wk1) files: LICS
File Import Character Set for Text files: ANSI

Improv 2

Handbook

APPENDIX D

Improv Character Set

Improv has a character set that allows you to enter, display, and print a character that does not appear on your keyboard.

To bring up a character in the character set, use the following compose sequence:

1.   Double-click the cell or item in which you wish to enter the character.

2.   Press ALT+F1.

3.   Type the compose sequence from the Improv character set.

4.   Press ENTER.

For example, to bring up the Copyright symbol © in Cell B1, you would:

1.   Double-click Cell B1.

2.   Press ALT+F1.

3.   Type **CO** (or co, Co, cO).

4.   Press ENTER.

Note

Characters in the compose sequence may be either upper- or lowercase, or any combination.

The complete Improv character set is shown in Table D-1.

TABLE D-1

Compose Sequences
for Improv

Description	Character	Compose Sequence
Cent sign	¢	c l c / C l or C /
British pound sterling symbol	£	L = l = L– or l–
Guilder	ƒ	f f
International currency sign	¤	XO xo X0 or x0
Yen sign	¥	Y = y = Y - or y -
Left angle quotes	«	< <
Right angle quotes	»	> >
Low double quotes, closing	„	"v
High double quotes, opening	"	" ^
Open bracket	[	((
Close bracket	]	))
Open brace	{	(–
Close brace	}	) –
Backslash	\	/ /
Bar	|	^ /
Tilde	~	- -
Pound sign	#	+ +
Vertical line, broken	¦	/ <space>
Copyright symbol	©	CO co C0 or c0
End of line symbol/ Logical NOT		-]
Registered trademark symbol	®	RO ro R0 or r0
Degree symbol	°	^ 0
Greek mu, lowercase	μ	/ u
Center dot	.	^ .
At sign	@	a a or A A
Paragraph symbol	¶	!p or !P
Section symbol	§	SO so S0 or s0
Trademark symbol	™	T M T m or t m

Continued

TABLE D-1

Compose Sequences
for Improv (continued)

Description	Character	Compose Sequence
OE ligature, uppercase	Œ	O E
oe ligature, lowercase	œ	o e
Overline character	‾	^ -
Caret	^	v v
Grave accent	`	<space> `
Cedilla accent	¸	, ,
Question mark, inverted	¿	? ?
Exclamation point, inverted	¡	! !
Plus or minus sign	±	+ -
Multiplication sign	×	x x or X X
Division sign	÷	: -
One superscript	^{1}	^ 1
Two superscript	^{2}	^ 2
Three superscript	^{3}	^ 3
One quarter	$\frac{1}{4}$	1 4
One half	$\frac{1}{2}$	1 2
Three quarters	$\frac{3}{4}$	3 4
Feminine ordinal indicator	^{a}	a _ or A _
Masculine ordinal indicator	^{o}	O _ or o _
A grave, uppercase	À	A `
A acute, uppercase	Á	A '
A circumflex, uppercase	Â	A ^
A tilde, uppercase	Ã	A ~
A umlaut, uppercase	Ä	A "
A ring, uppercase	Å	A *
AE diphthong, uppercase	Æ	A E
C cedilla, uppercase	Ç	C ,
E grave, uppercase	È	E `
E acute, uppercase	É	E '
E circumflex, uppercase	Ê	E ^
E umlaut, uppercase	Ë	E "

Description	Character	Compose Sequence
I grave, uppercase	Ì	I `
I acute, uppercase	Í	I '
I circumflex, uppercase	Î	I ^
I umlaut, uppercase	Ï	I "
Icelandic eth, uppercase	Ð	D -
N tilde, uppercase	Ñ	N ~
O grave, uppercase	Ò	O `
O acute, uppercase	Ó	O '
O circumflex, uppercase	Ô	O ^
O tilde, uppercase	Õ	O ~
O umlaut, uppercase	Ö	O "
O slash, uppercase	Ø	O /
U grave, uppercase	Ù	U `
U acute, uppercase	Ú	U '
U circumflex, uppercase	Û	U ^
U umlaut, uppercase	Ü	U "
Y acute, uppercase	Ý	Y '
Y umlaut, uppercase	Ÿ	Y "
Icelandic thorn, uppercase	Þ	P -
German sharp, lowercase	ß	s s
a grave, lowercase	à	a `
a acute, lowercase	á	a '
a circumflex, lowercase	â	a ^
a tilde, lowercase	ã	a ~
a umlaut, lowercase	ä	a "
a ring, lowercase	å	a *
ae diphthong, lowercase	æ	a e
c cedilla, lowercase	ç	c ,
e grave, lowercase	è	e `
e acute, lowercase	é	e '
e circumflex, lowercase	ê	e ^

TABLE D-1

Compose Sequences
for Improv (continued)

Description	Character	Compose Sequence
e umlaut, lowercase	ë	e "
i grave, lowercase	ì	i `
i acute, lowercase	í	i '
i circumflex, lowercase	î	i ^
i umlaut, lowercase	ï	i "
Icelandic eth, lowercase	ð	d -
n tilde, lowercase	ñ	n ~
o grave, lowercase	ò	o `
o acute, lowercase	ó	o '
o circumflex, lowercase	ô	o ^
o tilde, lowercase	õ	o ~
o umlaut, lowercase	ö	o "
o slash, lowercase	ø	o /
u grave, lowercase	ù	u `
u acute, lowercase	ú	u '
u circumflex, lowercase	û	u ^
u umlaut, lowercase	ü	u "
y acute, lowercase	ý	y '
Icelandic thorn, lowercase	þ	p -
y umlaut, lowercase	ÿ	y "

Index

About the Author...

Denise Martineau is a technical writer and an award-winning researcher. She has documented several major business applications for Fortune 500 companies, and specializes in spreadsheets, DBMS systems, and client-server architecture.

Patricia Quinn is a freelance technical writer with over six years experience producing user-reference manuals for a variety of accounting and business software applications. She attended the University of Oregon and lives in Alameda, California.

L. John Ribar is a programmer and author of several acclaimed books on C Programming, including Osborne/McGraw-Hill's **C DiskTutor**. Ribar is the President of Picasso Software Group, a software development firm in York, Pennsylvania, specializing in the creation of Windows-based applications and tools.

Covers Improv 2.0 and 2.1 for Windows

EXCEL → IMPROV

EXCEL	IMPROV
Enter value cell 1, Data Series	Worksheet Data Fill
Data Find	Select Functions
Data Sort	Worksheet Sort Items
File Open, Edit Copy or Cut, Edit Paste Special	File Open, Edit Copy or Cut, Edit Paste
File Open, select file in box; Text.. select delimiter	File Open, Identify file to import
File Open, elect wildcard filename	Window Browser
File Save	File Save
Activate chart, choose Type from Gallery menu, select variety of chart in dialog box	Create Chart
File Print	File Print
File Exit	File Exit
Formula Special, Constants and Text	Worksheet Style
Formula Define	Name item or category

EXCEL → IMPROV

EXCEL	IMPROV
	Rearrange categories
Edit Copy, Edit Paste Special, check Transpose box	DEL key Click and drag column line Window Browser
Edit Clear, Formulas	
Format Column Width	
Edit Delete, Entire Row or Column	
Format Style, Style Name, Define, Number, select format	Tools User Setup
Format Column Width Hide	Worksheet Hide Items
Edit Insert; Entire Row or Column (Dialog boxes)	Edit Add Item; Create Worksheet Tools User Setup
Format Font	Font button on status bar or Worksheet Style
File Page Setup, Printer Setup	File Print Setup
File Close	File Close
Edit Copy, Paste Options Add-ins Add... open ADDINFNS.XLA	Edit Copy, Paste File Open, open ADDINS20.DLL

Commands / Accelerators / Function Keys

Command	Action
Edit Add	
Edit Delete	
Create Formula	

Accelerator	Action
ENTER key	
DEL key	
= (equal sign)	

Function Key	Action
F1	Help
F2	Edit current selection
ALT+F3	Displays Run script dialog box
CTRL+F4	Close document
ALT+F4	Exit Improv
F6	Switch between data and formula panes
CTRL+F6	Display next document
ALT+F6	Zoom data or formula pane
F9	Recalculate

IMPROV KEYBOARD SHORTCUTS

Control	Command
CTRL+A	Edit Select All
CTRL+C	Edit Copy
CTRL+G	Create Item Group
CTRL+H	Worksheet Hide Items
CTRL+K	Manually check formulas
CTRL+M	Worksheet Mark Formulas
CTRL+N	File New
CTRL+O	File Open
CTRL+P	File Print
CTRL+S	File Save
CTRL+V	Edit Paste
CTRL+W	Create Worksheet
CTRL+X	Edit Cut
CTRL+Z	Edit Undo

QUATTRO PRO → IMPROV

QUATTRO PRO	IMPROV
/Edit | Fill	Worksheet Data Fill
/Database | Sort	Worksheet Sort Items
/File | Open; /Tools | Combine	Edit Cut, Edit Paste, File Open
/Tools | Import	File Open, identify file to import; F6; highlight filename; SHIFT+F7 or plus (+)
/Options | File List	Window Browser
/File | Save	File Save
/Tools | Xtract	Edit Cut, File Close
/Graph | Overall	Create Chart
/Print	File Print
/File | Exit	File Exit
/Style | Define Style | Create	Worksheet Style
/Edit | Name | Labels	Worksheet Style
/Edit | Name | Create	Name item or category

QUATTRO PRO → IMPROV

QUATTRO PRO	IMPROV
/Edit | Transpose	Rearrange categories
/Edit | Erase Block	DEL key
/Style | Block Size | Setup	Click and drag column line
	Window Browser
/Options | Format	Tools User Setup
/Style | Hide Column | Hide	Worksheet Hide Items
/Edit | Insert	Edit Add Item, Create Worksheet
/Style | Font	Font button on status bar or Worksheet Style
/Options | Hardware | Printers	File Print Setup
/File | Erase	File Close
/Edit | Copy Special	Edit Copy, Paste
/Edit | Duplicate	n/a
/Tools | Library | Load (.OLL file)	File Open; open ADDINS20.DLL

IMPROV KEYBOARD SHORTCUTS

Control	Command
CTRL+A	Edit Select All
CTRL+C	Edit Copy
CTRL+G	Create Item Group
CTRL+H	Worksheet Hide Items
CTRL+K	Manually check formulas
CTRL+M	Worksheet Mark Formulas
CTRL+N	File New
CTRL+O	File Open
CTRL+P	File Print
CTRL+S	File Save
CTRL+V	Edit Paste
CTRL+W	Create Worksheet
CTRL+X	Edit Cut
CTRL+Z	Edit Undo

Accelerator	Command
ENTER key	Edit Add
DEL key	Edit Delete
= (equal sign)	Create Formula

Function Key	Action
F1	Help
F2	Edit current selection
ALT+F3	Displays Run script dialog box
CTRL+F4	Close document
ALT+F4	Exit Improv
F6	Switch between data and formula panes
CTRL+F6	Display next document
ALT+F6	Zoom data or formula pane
F9	Recalculate

LOTUS 1-2-3 / IMPROV

LOTUS 1-2-3	IMPROV
/DATA FILL	Worksheet Data Fill
/DATA QUERY	Select functions
/DATA SORT	Worksheet Sort Items
/FILE COMBINE	Edit Cut, Edit Paste, File Open
/FILE IMPORT	File Open, Identify file to import
/FILE LIST	Window Browser
/FILE SAVE	File Save
/FILE XTRACT	Edit Cut, File Close
/GRAPH	Create Chart
/PRINT	File Print
/QUIT	File Exit
/RANGE FORMAT	Worksheet Style

LOTUS 1-2-3	IMPROV
/RANGE LABEL	Worksheet Style
/RANGE NAME	Name item or category
/RANGE TRANSPOSE	Rearrange categories
/RANGE ERASE	DEL key
/WORKSHEET COLUMN	Click and drag column line
/WORKSHEET DELETE	Window Browser
/WORKSHEET GLOBAL	Tools User Setup
/WORKSHEET HIDE	Worksheet Hide Items
/WORKSHEET INSERT	Edit Add Item, Create Worksheet
/WORKSHEET STATUS	Tools User Setup
/PRINT PRINTER OPTIONS SETUP	File Print Setup
/FILE ERASE	File Close, No

Accelerator	Command
ENTER key	Edit Add
DEL key	Edit Delete
= (equal sign)	Create Formula

Function Key	Action
F1	Help
F2	Edit current selection
ALT+F3	Displays Run script dialog box
CTRL+F4	Close document
ALT+F4	Exit Improv
F6	Switch between data and formula panes
CTRL+F6	Display next document
ALT+F6	Zoom data or formula pane
F9	Recalculate

IMPROV KEYBOARD SHORTCUTS

Control	Command
CTRL+A	Edit Select All
CTRL+C	Edit Copy
CTRL+G	Create Item Group
CTRL+H	Worksheet Hide Items
CTRL+K	Manually check formulas
CTRL+M	Worksheet Mark Formulas
CTRL+N	File New
CTRL+O	File Open
CTRL+P	File Print
CTRL+S	File Save
CTRL+V	Edit Paste
CTRL+W	Create Worksheet
CTRL+X	Edit Cut
CTRL+Z	Edit Undo